The
Reference Shelf®

Russia

Edited by Richard Joseph Stein

The Reference Shelf
Volume 82 • Number 4
The H.W. Wilson Company
New York • Dublin
2010

The Reference Shelf

The books in this series contain reprints of articles, excerpts from books, addresses on current issues, and studies of social trends in the United States and other countries. There are six separately bound numbers in each volume, all of which are usually published in the same calendar year. Numbers one through five are each devoted to a single subject, providing background information and discussion from various points of view and concluding with a subject index and comprehensive bibliography that lists books, pamphlets, and abstracts of additional articles on the subject. The final number of each volume is a collection of recent speeches, and it contains a cumulative speaker index. Books in the series may be purchased individually or on subscription.

Library of Congress has cataloged this serial title as follows:

Russia / edited by Richard Joseph Stein.
    p. cm. — (The reference shelf ; v. 82, no. 4)
    Includes bibliographical references and index.
    ISBN 978-0-8242-1099-1 (alk. paper)
1. Russia—History. 2. Soviet Union—History. 3. Russia (Federation)—History. 4. Post-communism—Russia (Federation) I. Stein, Richard Joseph.
    DK42.R77 2010
    947—dc22

                                        2010024983

Visit H.W. Wilson's Web site: www.hwwilson.com

Printed in the United States of America

Contents

Preface

Russia is a complex nation with a rich and colorful history. It is a land that spans two continents, 14 countries, and nine time zones. It stretches from Europe in the west to China in the east, and its more than 145 million inhabitants represent some 160 ethnicities. Western Russia holds the bulk of the populace and boasts a very European culture. Eastern Russia, composed mostly of Siberia, meanwhile, is home to Lapps and Eskimos, two of the groups that make up the region's large indigenous population.

Russia's history is as varied as its land. From the medieval kingdom of Kievan Rus' to the expansive Soviet Union, Russia has reinvented itself numerous times. In the middle of the 20th century, it emerged from World War II as one of two global superpowers. For decades, the Union of Soviet Socialist Republics, or USSR, rivaled the United States, building a vast communist empire that would last until 1991.

In the two decades since the collapse of the Soviet Union, Russia has struggled to maintain its stability and influence. Today the country faces major challenges, among them poverty, government corruption, regional tensions, and the threat of terrorist attacks. On the other hand, the economy has largely recovered from its post-Soviet swoon, and Russia has taken its place alongside Brazil, India, and China as one of the world's four rising economic powers. In foreign relations, Russia has reasserted itself, waging a controversial war on the neighboring country of Georgia. Many western observers saw in this conflict the re-emergence of an imperial Russia, one not afraid to pursue its interests—with military might, if need be—in its historic sphere of influence. President Dimitry Medvedev and Prime Minister Vladimir Putin lead a country uncertain of its future and acutely aware of its past.

The articles collected in this volume of The Reference Shelf paint a broad picture of Russia. The book opens with four historical chapters and ends with one dedicated to the issues facing contemporary Russia. Articles in the first chapter, "Early History: From Medieval to Imperial Russia," center on the establishment of Kievan Rus', the kingdom that later became Russia, and the emergence of the Russian Empire. Kievan Rus' was founded by Varangians, adventurous Scandinavian traders and warriors who traveled east from their native lands. The Varangians captured the city of Kiev, which is in present-day Ukraine, and laid the foundation for a large empire. In time, Moscow replaced Kiev as the kingdom's center, and under the leadership of two men named Ivan—Ivan the Great and Ivan the Terrible—the Rus' defeated Mongol invaders and expanded their territory. Over the next 400 years, a succession of rulers, called czars, added still more land, transforming Russia into a major power. Along the way, the country waged numerous wars with its Western European neighbors, culminating in World War I. From the ashes of that devastating conflict rose a new government, one that would forever change the course of Russian history.

From 1905 to 1917, a series of events led to the overthrow of the monarchy and the establishment of a new form of government—a communist system shaped by the philosophies of Karl Marx. Through revolution and civil conflict, a group of radicals known as Bolsheviks seized power from the post-monarchy Russian Provisional Government, laying the groundwork for the Soviet Union. Articles in the second chapter examine the period from the unsuccessful 1905 Russian Revolution, through the revolt of 1917, and into the first decades of the newly formed Soviet Union.

Selections in the third chapter follow the Soviet Union through its 1991 collapse. The USSR emerged from World War II a superpower, with forces deployed throughout Eastern Europe, and the only nation capable of challenging the United States for global dominance. This rivalry, known as the Cold War, lasted nearly 50 years. Although the two countries never formally engaged in combat, they fought a series of proxy wars and stockpiled arms, stoking fears of nuclear war. By the 1980s, amid unrest at home and a disastrous war in Afghanistan, the Soviet Union had begun to falter. The fall of the Berlin Wall, in 1989, spelled the end for the USSR, which finally dissolved two years later, after a failed *coup d'etat*.

In the tumultuous period that followed, Russia's economy lay in tatters. People were jobless and destitute, and many elderly citizens lost their homes and savings. Eventually a middle-class emerged, spurred by new businesses and entrepreneurship, and the nation again reinvented itself. Entries in the fourth chapter examine this post-Soviet era.

Selections in the fifth and final chapter focus on present-day Russia, touching on recent subway bombings—byproducts of a centuries-old conflict with Chechnya—relations with China, civil unrest in the west, life in the nation's capital, salmon poaching in the east, and a host of other issues.

Russia is, was, and probably always will be an extremely complex country. It is no easy feat to produce a small, introductory volume on such a large subject. Therefore, I would like to acknowledge those at the H.W. Wilson Company who have helped me in this endeavor—my colleagues Joseph Miller, Paul McCaffrey, Kenneth Partridge, and Carolyn Ellis.

Richard Joseph Stein
July 2010

1

Early History:
From Medieval to Imperial Russia

Courtesy of the State Russian Museum

Medieval Russian icon of Saints Boris and Gleb, from the 14th century.

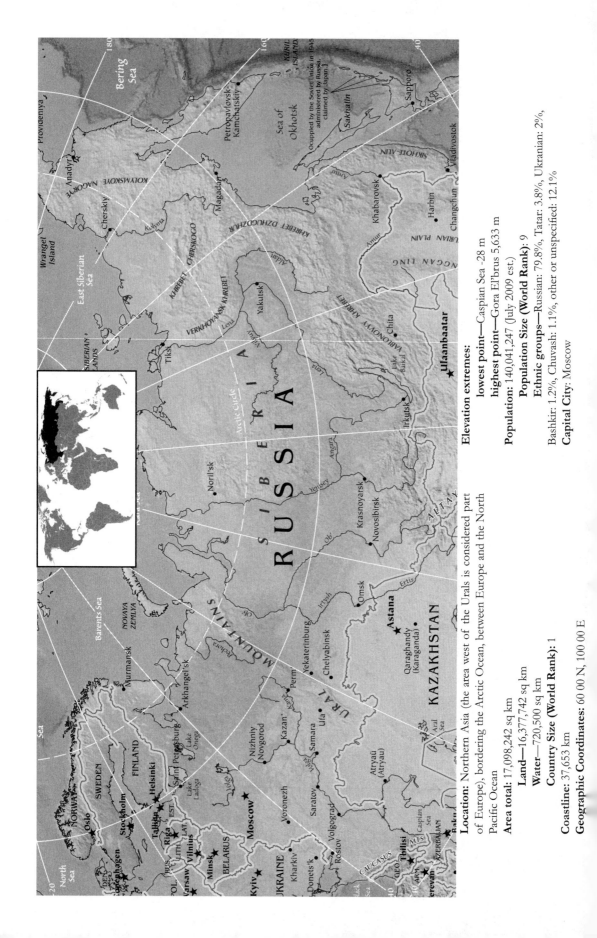

Location: Northern Asia (the area west of the Urals is considered part of Europe), bordering the Arctic Ocean, between Europe and the North Pacific Ocean

Area total: 17,098,242 sq km

    Land—16,377,742 sq km

    Water—720,500 sq km

    Country Size (World Rank): 1

Coastline: 37,653 km

Geographic Coordinates: 60 00 N, 100 00 E

Elevation extremes:

    lowest point—Caspian Sea -28 m

    highest point—Gora El'brus 5,633 m

Population: 140,041,247 (July 2009 est.)

    Population Size (World Rank): 9

    Ethnic groups—Russian: 79.8%, Tatar: 3.8%, Ukranian: 2%, Bashkir: 1.2%, Chuvash: 1.1%, other or unspecified: 12.1%

Capital City: Moscow

Editor's Introduction

Russia began as an outpost founded by a mix of Scandinavian traders, known as "Rus'," and the indigenous Slavic population during the ninth and tenth centuries A.D. Novgorod, a city in modern western Russia, was its center. Eventually the Rus' captured the important Slavic city of Kiev, which lies in present-day Ukraine. The Rus' created trade routes to the south, exchanging goods with the Byzantine Empire, their powerful neighbor, and the countries of the Middle East, and they expanded both their influence and land. Their kingdom was known as Kievan Rus', and it eventually extended from the Baltic to Black Seas, and as far west as Poland.

In the early 13th century, following a long stretch of internal fighting, a fragmented Kievan Rus' fell to Mongol occupation. The center of the kingdom eventually shifted from Kiev to a formerly insignificant trading town called Moscow, thus creating the more powerful Grand Duchy of Muscovy. Under the rule of Ivan III, or Ivan the Great, the Rus' regained independence from the Mongols after a century of rule and tripled the size of their kingdom. His grandson, Ivan IV, or Ivan the Terrible, became the first czar, further expanding Russia's influence and territory. Russia became an empire under Peter I, known as Peter the Great, and by the 19th century, it had become the largest country in the world in terms of land mass.

Given the complex nature of Russian history, the articles collected in this first chapter offer but a brief overview, sketching the country's growth from outpost to empire. In the first selection, "The Era of Vladimir I," excerpted from the book *Medieval Russia, 980–1584*, Janet Martin focuses on Russia's early history, explaining how Prince Vladimir I, a descendant of the Scandinavian family that founded the Riurik Dynasty, united fractious Slavic tribes under the banner of Kievan Rus'. The excerpt describes Vladimir's accession to the throne, his ancestors, and the heritage of the peoples that made up Kievan Rus'.

In the next selection, "The Foundations of Russian Culture and Art," Souren Melikian reviews what he calls "the most remarkable show of art from Russia ever staged anywhere." Held at the Louvre in Paris, France, the exhibition features medieval works of art—among them manuscripts and sculptures—drawn from various Russian museums. In addition to describing the art, Melikian gives a brief history of the ethnic groups that formed Kievan Rus': Scandinavian Vikings,

Finns, and Slavs. The writer also examines the eventual Christianization of Kievan Rus', a mass conversion that enabled Vladimir I to marry Princess Anne, the sister of the powerful Byzantine emperor. Melikian goes on to discuss another key influence on early Russian art, Islam, highlighting the country's mix of Eastern and Western cultures.

The subsequent piece, "Peter I, Czar of Russia," comes from the *Columbia Electronic Encyclopedia*. It centers on Peter I, known as Peter the Great, founder of St. Petersburg, a western city that served as the capital of the Russian Empire for more than 200 years. The article describes his upbringing, ascension to the throne in 1696, and efforts to reform Russia. Peter the Great traveled throughout Europe and returned home with many ideas, attempting to modernize Russia. Although Russia officially became an empire during his rule, many opposed his reforms, and he remains a controversial figure in the nation's history.

In the following article Jennifer Siegel reviews the book *Russia Against Napoleon*, by Dominic Lieven. Lieven chronicles the French invasion of Russia in 1812 and dispels long-accepted myths that downplay Russia's influence in the defeat of Napoleon's Grande Armée, among them that the harsh Russian winter—not Russian arms—dealt the fatal blow to the French emperor's war machine and his dreams of continental mastery. Chronicled in Leo Tolstoy's famous novel *War and Peace*, the defeat of Napoleon played a pivotal role in the development of Russian power and influence across the continent and stands as a vital and defining chapter in Russian history.

In 1861, Alexander II put an end to serfdom, a practice that had been in place for more than 200 years, ushering in Russia's industrial age. Serfs were peasants who had few rights and were legally bound to their landowners. Though not quite analogous, the institution of serfdom bore many similarities to the system of slavery practiced at the time in the United States. Many Russian intellectuals and elites felt that serfdom had become an outdated model, and that by doing away with it, Russia would become more like its European neighbors. In this chapter's final entry, "The Emancipation of the Russian Serfs, 1861," Michael Lynch explains how serfdom's demise was structured to benefit landowners more than the freed serfs, who received legal autonomy but were burdened with hefty financial debts to their former masters. The author calls Emancipation "an outstanding example of tsarist ineptitude."

THE ERA OF VLADIMIR I[*]

By Janet Martin

Excerpted from *Medieval Russia, 980–1584*

In the year 980, an obscure prince landed on the northern shores of a land that became known as Rus and, later, Russia. Almost a decade earlier his father, the ruler of this land, had placed him in charge of the area surrounding one of its towns, the recently founded Novgorod. But after his father died (972) and one of his elder brothers killed the other (977), this prince, Vladimir (Volodimer) Sviatoslavich, fled abroad. After several years of exile he now led a band of Varangians (Norsemen) across the Baltic from Scandinavia. His intention was to depose his half-brother Iaropolk and assume the throne of Kiev.

VLADIMIR'S SEIZURE OF THE KIEVAN THRONE

Upon landing in Rus', Prince Vladimir immediately sought allies to join him against Iaropolk. He turned to the prince of Polotsk (Polatsk), Rogvolod, a fellow Varangian but unrelated to Vladimir and his family, and requested the hand of his daughter Rogneda in marriage. But she haughtily refused him, calling him the "son of a slave" and indicating a preference for Iaropolk. Vladimir responded by leading his Varangian force, along with Slovenes, Chud', and Krivichi from his former domain of Novgorod, against Polotsk. He defeated and killed Rogvolod and his sons, captured Rogneda, and forced her to become his bride. Polotsk was attached to the realm of Vladimir's family, the Riurikid dynasty.

Vladimir then marched toward his brother's capital, the city of Kiev. Growing out of settlements established in the sixth and seventh centuries, Kiev was located far to the south of Novgorod on hills overlooking the west or right bank of the Dnieper River. By 980 it had become the political center of a domain, known as Kievan Rus', that extended from Novgorod on the Volkhov River southward across the divide where the Volga, the West Dvina, and the Dnieper Rivers all had their origins, and down the Dnieper just past Kiev. It also included the lower reaches of the main tributaries of the Dnieper. Arriving at the city, Vladimir entered into negotiations with his brother. But in the midst of their talks two of Vladimir's Varangians murdered Iaropolk. Vladimir Sviatoslavich became the sole prince of Kievan Rus'.

Prince Vladimir's claim to the Kievan throne rested only in part on the military force he used to secure it. It was also based on heritage. Vladimir was one of the sons of Sviatoslav, prince of Kiev from 962 to 972. The Russian Primary Chronicle traces Sviatoslav's lineage back through his father Igor' and mother Olga to a Norseman named Riurik. The legend of Riurik claims that in the ninth century a group of quarreling eastern Slav and Finnic tribes that had dwelled in what is now northwestern Russia invited Riurik and his brothers to come to their lands, rule over them, and bring peace and order to their peoples.

While the chronicle account incorporates myth and cannot be taken literally, it does reflect the fact that Scandinavian Vikings, called Rus', were present in the territories of the eastern Slav and Finnic tribes by the ninth century and that they eventually became rulers or princes over the native population. Vladimir's ancestors, founders of the dynasty that was later named after Riurik, led one of those Viking bands. Vladimir's victory over Rogvolod signaled the completion of the process pursued by Igor and Sviatoslav to eliminate rival bands and establish exclusive ascendancy over enough of the native tribes to fashion a cohesive principality out of their territories. Although the Slav tribes shared a common language and there is some evidence of a federation among them prior to the establishment of Scandinavian rule, it was their common recognition of the Riurikid dynasty that bound them into the state that became known as Kievan Rus'.

The Foundations of Russian Culture and Art[*]

By Souren Melikian
The New York Times, March 5, 2010

Politicians who sometimes wonder about the deeper motivations of Russian diplomacy should pay a long visit to the most remarkable show of art from Russia ever staged anywhere.

On view at the Louvre, "Holy Russia" offers much more than a fascinating display of works of art from far-flung institutions inside and outside Russia.

The exhibition book, edited by Jannic Durand of the Louvre and Tamara Igumnova of the Moscow Historic State Museum, effectively puts together the material evidence illustrating the conflicting components that went into the making of Russian culture from its inception. The Kingdom of Rus, as it was originally known, came about as a synthesis of human groups and cultural characteristics that seemed as fit to go together as fire and water. It was founded in the ninth century by marauding Scandinavians pouring from present-day Sweden into lands largely populated by Finns mixing with Slavs who were slowly arriving from territories west of present-day Russia.

The earliest surviving Russian chronicle, "An Account of Ancient Times," tells of the alliance forged by the Slavs and the Finns against the "Variagi," as Russians call the ancient invaders. Their feats extended as far as France where the "Varègues" or "Varenges" left their name to the town of Varengeville in Normandy—a detail ignored in the exhibition book. A chieftain called Rurik became the ruler of the new kingdom. Thus came into existence the Rurikid dynasty, the first in Russia that owes its name to the land of the Rus, known alike to the Latin chroniclers of medieval Europe and to Iranian geographers using Arabic, the international language of the Muslim East.

How deep the Scandinavian imprint was can be gauged from the weapons and jewels recovered from tombs on territories stretching from the north of modern Russia to the south of present-day Ukraine. The 10th-century fibulae excavated from a funerary chamber in the northern town of Pskov and another discovered in Kiev, now the capital of Ukraine, are no different from costume jewels of this type found in Scandinavia.

The rise of Christianity was the unifying factor that laid the foundation of Russian culture. As early as 959 a Princess Olga sent an embassy to the Germanic emperor Otto requesting the dispatch of a bishop, partly in the hope of raising the status of the kingdom of the Rus. To no avail. It was only in 987 that her grandson Vladimir, keen to obtain the hand of the Byzantine emperor's sister, Princess Anne, agreed in exchange to adhere to Christianity. Byzantium, shaken by uprisings in its non-Greek possessions, desperately needed to recruit Variagi mercenaries. The deal was concluded. As good as his word, Vladimir ordered in 988 the conversion of the entire population of Kiev, which became the historical birthplace of Russian culture.

Acceptance of the new religion was not immediate. In the struggle for the throne of Kiev that followed Vladimir's death, his younger sons Boris and Gleb, who had converted to Christianity, were slain by their brother Sviatopolk. Their memory as saintly martyrs was henceforth perpetuated in icons, the Russian word borrowed from Byzantine Greek for holy "images."

A 14th-century icon from the monastery of Zverin in Novgorod shows the two brothers wearing an attire that reveals a third component in the complex mix of Russian art—the Middle Eastern element. While their swords reproduce the Western model, the pearl-studded leather strips hanging from their belts and their armlets are royal costume fittings worn by the emperors of Sasanian Iran and their early Islamic successors.

The multiple strands, North European, Byzantine and Middle Eastern, kept recurring through much of Russian history, occasionally interweaving in astonishing fashion.

A magnificent limestone capital from the Church of Nativity erected between 1192 and 1196 in the town of Vladimir has the shape of a Romanesque capital, but its formal ornament is carved in a style reminiscent of the repertoire of Islamic Iran with its distant Hellenistic legacy. A pillar from the same church associates five-lobed palmettes common in 10th- and 11th-century Iran with knotted motifs reminiscent of Viking ornament.

The fascination with Northern Europe, more particularly Germanic lands, was lasting. An armilla, or shoulder application, depicting the resurrection of Jesus in champlevé enamels on gilt copper, made in the late 12th century somewhere between the Rhine and the Meuse, was listed in the Cathedral of the Dormition treasury in Vladimir by the 17th century. The head of a man from the town of Old Riazan would not surprise in Romanesque sculpture from Burgundy.

By then a profoundly original figural art was blossoming, most of it known mainly from fragments. The head of a man painted in the late 12th century on the walls of the now vanished first cathedral in Smolensk is remarkable for its expressiveness.

An apex was reached in the first third of the 13th century. The twin influences of Ottonian Germany and Byzantine Greece blend in its ultimate masterpiece, the golden doors of the Cathedral of the Nativity in the town of Suzdal. The scenes painted in gold on the dark metallic ground are Byzantine in inspiration without really resembling Greek medieval art, while the lion masks are based on German prototypes. These too have a distinctive expressiveness.

Somehow, the mid-13th-century Mongol invasion followed by devastation and 200 years of occupation did not stop artistic creation.

Russian manuscript painting, unknown outside its homeland, produced stunning masterpieces. On a vellum leaf from "Simon's Psalter" illuminated in Novgorod, Jesus stands in a stylized landscape, giving the viewer the searching look of a man intentionally alive.

Drastically opposite trends thrived simultaneously. The icon of Saints George, Climachus and Blaise, painted in Novgorod around the same time, is stylized in a rigid manner based on early Byzantine tradition. The elongated Climachus, about three times the size of George and Blaise, stands against an erstwhile emerald green and intense red ground, revealing a taste for contrasted colors that would be revived in avant-garde painting of the 20th century.

Western influence continued to creep in. Admirable frescoes have been revealed by fragments excavated in Pskov, where the Church of the Nativity and other ecclesiastical constructions demolished by Peter the Great stood until the 18th century. Two female figures in long veils, presumed to be saints, owe as much to awareness of Gothic art from 14th-century Germany in the handling of their smiling faces, as they do to the Byzantine Renaissance for the folds of their drapes.

The attraction to West European art persisted well into the 15th century. The silver-gilt and gilt copper panaghiarion signed in 1435 by Master Ivan Arip offers spectacular evidence of the admiration felt for German goldsmiths. The polylobed base and the raised stand with elaborate fleur-de-lis are in the best tradition of flamboyant Gothic monstrances. Curiously, the four lions and the kneeling angels supporting the paten and cover used in the Orthodox ritual send back echoes to much earlier German art.

The multiplicity of strands from East and West never dried up in Russia. When a steel helmet with gold overlay was commissioned for Ivan the Terrible who ruled from 1533 to 1547, the work was entrusted to a Muslim armorer, apparently called in from the lands of the Mongol-Turkic Golden Horde in southern Ukraine, if not from further south. This is shown by the characteristic Turkish shape of the helmet as well as the Iranian-derived arabesques associated with a large border of stylized Arabic script.

To the Russians themselves, the twin attraction to East and West never felt contradictory. Sergei Shchukin, one of the greatest collectors of French Impressionism, also had an outstanding collection of Iranian manuscript painting. In ballet, that supreme Russian achievement in Western-type performing arts, the Eastern touch is evident—as shown by Leon Bakst's designs.

Nothing has changed. Early art and its ancient roots tell you why.

Peter I, Czar of Russia[*]

Peter I or Peter the Great, 1672–1725, Czar of Russia (1682–1725), Major
Figure in the Development of Imperial Russia

Excerpted from *Columbia Electronic Encyclopedia*, 2007

EARLY LIFE

Peter was the youngest child of Czar Alexis, by Alexis's second wife, Natalya
Naryshkin. From Alexis's first marriage (with Maria Miloslavsky) were born Feodor
III, Sophia Alekseyevna, and the semi-imbecile Ivan. On Feodor III's death (1682),
a struggle broke out for the succession between the Naryshkin and Miloslavsky
factions. The Naryshkins at first succeeded in setting Ivan aside in favor of 10-year-
old Peter. Shortly afterward, however, the Miloslavsky party incited the *streltsi*
(semi-military formations in Moscow) to rebellion. In the bloody disorder that followed, Peter witnessed the murders of many of his supporters. As a result of the
rebellion Ivan, as Ivan V, was made (1682) joint czar with Peter, under the regency
of Sophia Alekseyevna.

A virtual exile, Peter spent most of his childhood in a suburb of Moscow, surrounded by playmates drawn both from the nobility and from the roughest social
elements. His talent for leadership soon became apparent when he organized military games that became regular maneuvers in siegecraft. In addition, Peter began
to experiment with shipbuilding on Lake Pereyaslavl (now Lake Pleshcheyevo).
Peter learned the rudiments of Western military science from the European soldiers and adventurers who lived in a foreign settlement near Moscow. His most
influential foreign friends, Patrick Gordon of Scotland, François Lefort of Geneva, and Franz Timmermann of Holland, came from this colony. In 1689, Sophia
Alekseyevna attempted a coup against Peter; this time, however, aided by the loyal

part of the *streltsi*, he overthrew the regent. For several years, until Peter assumed personal rule, the Naryshkins ran the government. Ivan V, whose death in 1696 left Peter sole czar, took no part in the government.

SOLE RULER

Foreign Policy

Russia was almost continuously at war during Peter's reign. In the 16th and early 17th cent. the country had fought periodically in the northwest against Sweden, in an attempt to gain access to the Baltic Sea, and in the south against the Ottoman Empire.

While continuing the policy of his predecessors, Peter drew Russia into European affairs and helped to make it a great power. His earliest venture was the conquest of Azov from the Ottomans in 1696, after an unsuccessful attempt in 1695. Peter then embarked on a European tour (1697–98), traveling partly incognito, to form a grand alliance against the Ottoman Empire and to acquire the Western techniques necessary to modernize Russia's armed forces. He failed to form an anti-Ottoman alliance, but his conversations with the Polish king and others led eventually (1699) to a coalition against Sweden.

Peter also gained considerable knowledge of European industrial techniques (he even spent some time working as a ship's carpenter in Holland) and hired many European artisans for service in Russia. In 1698 he returned to Russia, began to modernize the armed forces, and launched domestic reforms. After concluding (1700) peace with the Ottomans, Peter, in alliance with Denmark and the combined Saxony-Poland, began the Northern War (1700–1721) against Charles XII of Sweden. Although disastrously defeated at first, he routed Charles at Poltava in 1709 and by the Treaty of Nystad (1721) retained his conquests of Ingermanland, Karelia, and Livonia.

Peter's conquests in the south were less permanent. Azov was restored to the Ottoman Empire in 1711; Derbent, Baku, and the southern coast of the Caspian Sea, conquered in a war (1722–23) with Persia, were soon lost again. In the east, Russia extended its control over part of Siberia but failed to subjugate either Khiva or Bokhara. Peter's first diplomatic missions to China were unsuccessful but his efforts led to the Treaty of Kyakhta (1727), which fixed the Russo-Chinese border and established commercial relations. Peter's interest in imperial expansion led to the financing of the first voyage of Vitus Bering.

Domestic Policy

Peter had returned to Russia in 1698 at the news of a military revolt allegedly instigated by Sophia Alekseyevna. He took drastic vengeance on his opponents and forced Sophia into a convent. On the day after his return, Peter personally cut off the beards of his nobles and shortly thereafter ordered them to replace their long robes and conical hats with Western dress. This attack on the symbols of old Muscovy marked the beginning of Peter's attempt to force Russia to adopt European appearance and other features of Western culture. Most of Peter's reforms followed his predecessors' tentative steps, but his demonic pace and brutal methods created an impression of revolutionary change.

The reforms were sporadic and uncoordinated; many of them grew out of the needs of Peter's almost continuous warfare. He introduced conscription on a territorial basis, enlarged and modernized the army, founded and expanded the navy, and established technical schools to train men for military service. To finance this huge military establishment, he created state monopolies, introduced the first poll tax, and placed levies on every conceivable item. Peter encouraged and subsidized private industry and established state mines and factories to provide adequate supplies of war materials. Peter reformed the administrative machinery of the state. He introduced a supervisory senate and a new system of central administration and tried to reform provincial and local government.

Peter also attempted to subordinate all classes of Russian society to the needs of the state. He enlarged the service nobility (the body of nobles who owed service to the state), imposed further duties on it, and forced the sons of nobles to attend technical schools. To control the nobles he introduced the Table of Ranks, which established a bureaucratic hierarchy in which promotion was based on merit rather than on birth. The nobility's economic position was strengthened by changes in the laws of land tenure. The serfs (who paid the bulk of taxes and made up most of the soldiery) were bound more securely to their masters and to the land. Peter subordinated the church to the state by replacing the patriarchate with a holy synod, headed by a lay procurator appointed by the czar.

Peter introduced changes in manners and mores. The ban on beards and Muscovite dress was extended to the entire male population, women were released from their servile position, and attempts were made to improve the manners of the court and administration. Peter sent many Russians to be schooled in the West and was responsible for the foundation (1725) of the Academy of Sciences. He reformed the calendar and simplified the alphabet. The transfer of the capital from Moscow to St. Petersburg, built on the swamps of Ingermanland at tremendous human cost, was a dramatic symbol of Peter's reforms. Although Peter sought to enforce all his reforms with equal severity, he was unable to eradicate the traditional corruption of officials or to impose Western ways on the peasantry.

His reforms were often considered whimsical and sacrilegious and met widespread opposition. The conservatives among the clergy accused him of being the antichrist. The discontented looked to Peter's son, Alexis, who was eventually tried for treason on flimsy evidence and was tortured to death (1718). In 1721, Peter had himself proclaimed "emperor of all Russia." In 1722 he declared the choice of a successor to be dependent on the sovereign's will; this decree (valid until the reign of Paul I) preceded the coronation (1724) of his second wife as Empress Catherine I. She was a Livonian peasant girl whom Peter had made his mistress, then his wife (1712) after repudiating his first consort. Her accession on Peter's death was largely engineered by Peter's chief lieutenant and favorite, A. D. Menshikov. Although many of Peter's innovations were too hasty and arbitrary to be successful, his reign was decisive in the long process of transforming medieval Muscovy into modern Russia.

PERSONALITY AND ACHIEVEMENTS

Peter's personal traits ranged from bestial cruelty and vice to the most selfless devotion to Russia; his order to his troops at Poltava read, "Remember that you are fighting not for Peter but for the state."

Despite the convulsive fits that plagued him, he had a bearlike constitution, was of gigantic stature, and possessed herculean physical prowess. He drank himself into stupors and indulged in all conceivable vices but could rouse himself at a moment's notice, and he was willing to undergo all the physical exertions and privations that he exacted from his subjects.

Peter subordinated the lives and liberties of his subjects to his own conception of the welfare of the state. Like many of his successors, he concluded that ruthless reform was necessary to overcome Russia's backwardness. Peter remains one of the most controversial figures in Russian history. Those who regard Russia as essentially European praise him for his policy of Westernization, and others who consider Russia a unique civilization attack him for turning Russia from its special path of development. Those impressed by imperial expansion and state and social reforms tend to regard Peter's arbitrary and brutal methods as necessary, while others appalled by his disregard of human life conclude that the cost outweighed any gains.

BIBLIOGRAPHY

The first biographer of Peter the Great was Voltaire. See later biographies by R.K. Massie (1980) and H. Troyat (1987); study by N. V. Riasanovsky (1985); L. Hughes, *Russia in the Age of Peter the Great* 1998).

Moscow on the Seine[*]

By Jennifer Siegel
The Wall Street Journal, April 20, 2010

Early in the evening of March 29, 1814, the Russian army glimpsed the spires of Napoleon's capital for the first time. An officer, Alexander MikhailovskyDanilevsky, later recalled a general cry of " 'Paris! Paris!' . . . Forgotten in a moment were the fatigues of the campaign, wounds, fallen friends and brothers: overwhelmed with joy, we stood on the hill from which Paris was barely visible in the distance." The soldiers' enthusiasm was not unwarranted. After two years of nearly continuous fighting against Napoleon in the longest campaign in European history—a campaign that had marched the Russian army from Vilna in the west, eastward to Moscow, then all the way to Paris—the end to the conflict seemed for the first time to be as close at hand as the city rising on the horizon.

Dominic Lieven relates the tale of this campaign with masterly skill in "Russia Against Napoleon." It is a story that students of European history and admirers of Russian literary classics think they know well: Napoleon invaded Russia in 1812 and stayed too long; was trapped by the Russian winter and stymied by the nationalistic heroism of the Russian people; destroyed his Grande Armée in an ill-timed retreat across the snow-covered, war-ravaged fields; and was slowly pushed back to Paris by the reformed and newly invigorated coalition of Great Powers (Britain, Austria, Prussia and Russia). In 1814, as every schoolchild once knew, Napoleon was dispatched to Elba, leaving open the possibility that Russia would dominate the recently liberated Continent.

Mr. Lieven, a professor of Russian history at the London School of Economics, paints a far more textured picture of Russia's crucial role in halting Napoleon's advance and containing France within its historic borders. "Russia Against Napoleon" is informed by Russian sources and focuses not only on Russia's oft-praised people but also on the country's oft-underappreciated leadership in the early 19th century.

Along the way, Mr. Lieven debunks various myths that play down the achievements of Russia's military. As he notes, France itself—but also Russia's allies and even Russia's great nationalist writer, Leo Tolstoy—preferred to portray Russia's victory as the triumph of a hardy, resistant people and the vagaries of circumstance. Mr. Lieven insists on restoring credit to Russia's military forces, as well as to its leaders. Among the book's many virtues, it explains in engaging detail how Russia managed to mount first a defense against the greatest military mind of the day and then a successful offensive, culminating with the Cossack Life Guard "in their scarlet tunics and darkblue baggy trousers" parading down the Champs Elysées.

In Mr. Lieven's eyes, this story has two great heroes, and neither is Mikhail Kutuzov, the Russian general lionized by Tolstoy and, later, Stalin. Mr. Lieven praises Kutuzov, the commander in chief of the Russian forces, for his courage, skillful soldiering and mastery of public relations, but the author does not consider him the military genius that tradition has trained us to see. Rather it is the czar, Alexander I, and the historically undervalued Mikhail Barclay de Tolly, minister of war and the commander of the Russian forces before and after Kutuzov, who inspire Mr. Lieven's admiration.

Barclay de Tolly was responsible for Russia's successful strategy of "deep retreat," which he had recommended as early as 1810. The idea was to lure the French far into Russia's heartland, stretching out their supply lines and making a potential French retreat crippling and costly. He was under constant criticism in his day for abandoning Russian ground to the French in 1812 without any real resistance, and he was under perpetual suspicion from the "Old Russian" camp at court and in the army because of his "foreign origins"—even though his family, of Scottish descent, had lived in the Russian Empire since the mid-17th century. In Mr. Lieven's hands, Barclay de Tolly comes across as tireless, dedicated, brave and strategically sound.

And Czar Alexander, often portrayed as unpredictable and ungrounded, frequently shows good leadership and diplomatic finesse in Mr. Lieven's telling. The seemingly all-powerful monarch struggled against the constraints imposed by his empire's enormous size, scattered population, inefficient communications, brutal weather and inept bureaucracy. Those challenges were magnified by a landowning aristocracy that effectively had the power of the purse; Alexander had to rely on the nobility for raising manpower and tax revenues.

Despite these constraints, Alexander proved an effective wartime leader, particularly after 1812, when the conflict moved out of Russia and diplomacy became paramount. He recognized that only a peace signed in Paris could guarantee the restoration of order in Europe and the security of Russia; but he also saw that Russia alone could never defeat the French forces. A victory over Napoleon was possible only because Alexander managed to form a grand alliance and keep it intact. This coalition-building, Mr. Lieven argues, was the czar's greatest achievement.

Russia's triumph is also a story of logistics, supplies and, above all, the horse. The country's leaders mobilized what Mr. Lieven calls "the sinews of Russian power": its vast population (although much smaller than the combined numbers at Napoleon's disposal); its outstanding and plentiful horse stock; its arms manufacturing; and even the sometimes unstable Russian economy. Of these, it is the horse, and Russia's ability to mobilize its light cavalry to harass Napoleon's rearguard as it retreated across the great European plain, that receives the greatest attention in "Russia Against Napoleon." Coming in a close second to the horse in significance were the victuallers who managed to feed and supply more than a half-million troops during the two-year campaign.

Mr. Lieven ends by arguing that in 1814, as in the present day, the security of Russia and the security of Europe were interdependent. True enough, but he also shows in this absorbing book that the defeat of Napoleon hinged on the resources, leadership and sacrifice of the Russian empire.

The Emancipation of the Russian Serfs, 1861*

A Charter of Freedom or an Act of Betrayal?

By Michael Lynch
History Review, December 2003

In 1861 serfdom, the system which tied the Russian peasants irrevocably to their landlords, was abolished at the Tsar's imperial command. Four years later, slavery in the USA was similarly declared unlawful by presidential order. Tsar Alexander II (1855–81) shared with his father, Nicholas I, a conviction that American slavery was inhumane. This is not as hypocritical as it might first appear. The serfdom that had operated in Russia since the middle of the seventeenth century was technically not slavery. The landowner did not own the serf. This contrasted with the system in the USA where the negro slaves were chattels; that is, they were regarded in law as the disposable property of their masters. In Russia the traditional relationship between lord and serf was based on land. It was because he lived on his land that the serf was bound to the lord.

The Russian system dated back to 1649 and the introduction of a legal code which had granted total authority to the landowner to control the life and work of the peasant serfs who lived on his land. Since this included the power to deny the serf the right to move elsewhere, the difference between slavery and serfdom in practice was so fine as to be indistinguishable. The purpose behind the granting of such powers to the Russian *dvoriane* (nobility of landowners) in 1649 had been to make the nobles dependent on, and therefore loyal to, the tsar. They were to express that loyalty in practical form by serving the tsar as military officers or public officials. In this way the Romanov emperors built up Russia's civil bureaucracy and the armed services as bodies of public servants who had a vested interest in maintaining the tsarist state.

As the table shows, the serfs made up just over a third of the population and formed half of the peasantry. They were most heavily concentrated in the central and western provinces of Russia.

WHY WAS IT NECESSARY TO END SERFDOM?

In a number of respects serfdom was not dissimilar to the feudalism that had operated in many parts of pre-modern Europe. However, long before the 19th century, the feudal system had been abandoned in western Europe as it moved into the commercial and industrial age. Imperial Russia underwent no such transition. It remained economically and socially backward. Nearly all Russians acknowledged this. Some, known as slavophiles, rejoiced, claiming that holy Russia was a unique God-inspired nation that had nothing to learn from the corrupt nations to the west. But many Russians, of all ranks and classes, had come to accept that reform of some kind was unavoidable if their nation was to progress.

Russian Population in 1859	
Free men (e.g., *dvoriane*, clergy, merchants)	12 million
States Peasants not bound to a land-owner	25 million
Serfs (peasants living on land bound to a lord)	23 million
Total	**60 million**

It became convenient to use serfdom to explain all Russia's current weaknesses: it was responsible for military incompetence, food shortages, over population, civil disorder, industrial backwardness. These were oversimplified explanations but there [is] some truth in all of them: serfdom was symptomatic of the underlying difficulties that held Russia back from progress. It was, therefore, a particularly easy target for the intelligentsia, those intellectuals who in their writings argued for the liberalising of Russian society, beginning with the emancipation of the exploited peasants.

As often happened in Russian history, it was war that forced the issue. The Russian state had entered the Crimean War in 1854 with high hopes of victory. Two years later it suffered a heavy defeat at the hands of the Allied armies of France, Britain and Turkey. The shock to Russia was profound. The nation had always prided itself on its martial strength. Now it had been humiliated.

ALEXANDER II'S ROLE

By an odd twist of fate, defeat in the war proved of value to the new Tsar. Although he had been trained for government from an early age, foreign observers had remarked on how diffident and unsure he appeared. The war changed all that. Coming to the throne in 1855 in the middle of the conflict, Alexander II was unable to save Russia from military failure, but the humiliation convinced him that, if his nation was to have stability and peace at home and be honoured abroad, military and domestic reforms were vitally necessary. The first step on that path would be the removal of serfdom, whose manifest inefficiency benefited neither lord, peasant, nor nation. Alexander declared that, despite Russia's defeat, the end of the war marked a golden moment in the nation's history. Now was the hour when every Russian, under the protection of the law, could begin to enjoy 'the fruits of his own labours'.

Alexander was right in thinking the time was propitious. It had long been appreciated that some land

---

> ### Main Terms of Emancipation, 1861
> **Serfs** made legally free of their landlords
> **Ex-serfs** were then allowed
>
> - **to own property**
> - **to buy land assigned them from their previous owner's estates**
> - **to marry according to their choice**
> - **to trade freely**
> - **to sue in courts**
> - **to vote in local elections**

---

reform was necessary. To the social and economic arguments were now added powerful military ones. The army was the great symbol of Russia's worth. As long as its army remained strong Russia could afford to ignore its backwardness as a nation. But the Crimean defeat had undermined this notion of Russia's invincibility. Few now had reasoned objections to reform. Serfdom was manifestly not working. It had failed to provide the calibre of soldier Russia needed.

So it was that in 1856, the second year of his reign, Alexander II (1855–81) announced to the nobles of Russia that 'the existing condition of owning souls cannot remained unchanged. It is better to begin to destroy serfdom from above than to wait until that time when it begins to destroy itself from below'. These words have often been quoted. What is less often cited is his following sentence: 'I ask you, gentlemen, to figure out how all this can be carried out to completion.' Alexander was determined on emancipation, but he shrewdly judged that—by [giving] over to the landowners the responsibility for detailing how this was to be done—he had made it very difficult for them either to resist his command or to blame him if their plans were subsequently shown to be faulty. This was evidence of the remarkable power and influence that the tsar exercised as absolute ruler.

Over the next five years, thousands of officials sitting in a range of committees drafted plans for the abolition of serfdom. When their work was done they presented their proposals to Alexander who then formally issued them in an Imperial Proclamation. When it was finally presented, in 1861, the Emancipation statute, which accompanied the Proclamation, contained 22 separate measures whose details filled 360 closely printed pages of a very large volume. Alexander declared that the basic aim of emancipation was to satisfy all those involved in serfdom, serfs and landowners alike:

Called by Divine Providence We vowed in our hearts to fulfil the mission which is entrusted to Us and to surround with Our affection and Our Imperial solicitude all Our faithful subjects of every rank and condition.

BETRAYAL OF THE PEASANTS?

Impressive though these freedoms first looked, it soon became apparent that they had come at a heavy price for the peasants. It was not they, but the landlords, who were the beneficiaries. This should not surprise us: after all, it had been the *dvoriane* who had drafted the emancipation proposals. The compensation that the landowners received was far in advance of the market value of their property. They were also entitled to decide which part of their holdings they would give up. Unsurprisingly, they kept the best land for themselves. The serfs got the left-overs. The data shows that the landlords retained two-thirds of the land while the peasants received only one-third. So limited was the supply of affordable quality land to the peasants that they were reduced to buying narrow strips that proved difficult to maintain and which yielded little food or profit.

Moreover, while the landowners were granted financial compensation for what they gave up, the peasants had to pay for their new property. Since they had no savings, they were advanced 100 per cent mortgages, 80 per cent provided by the State bank and the remaining 20 by the landlords. This appeared a generous offer, but as in any loan transaction the catch was in the repayments. The peasants found themselves saddled with redemption payments that became a lifelong burden that then had to be handed on to their children.

The restrictions on the peasants did not end there. To prevent emancipation creating too much disruption, the government urged the peasants to remain in their localities. This was easy to achieve since, for obvious reasons, the great majority of the ex-serfs bought their allotments of land from the estates where they were already living. It was also the case that the land available for purchase came from a stock of land granted to the village and was then sold on to individual peasants.

A further aid to the authorities in maintaining control was the reorganisation of local government, which was one of the key reforms that followed in the wake of emancipation. The government, through its land 'commandants' (officials appointed to oversee emancipation) insisted that the *mir* (the village commune) become the focus of life in the countryside. The motive was not cultural but administrative. The *mir* would provide an effective organisation for the collection of taxes to which the freed serfs were now liable; it would also be a controlling mechanism for keeping order in the countryside. Arguably, after 1861, the freed Russian peasant was as restricted as he had been when a serf: Instead of being tied to the lord, the peasant was now tied to the village.

What all this denoted was the mixture of fear and deep distaste that the Russian establishment traditionally felt towards the peasantry. Often contemptuously referred to as the 'dark masses', the peasants were seen as a dangerous force that had to be kept down. Beneath the generous words in which Emancipation had been couched was a belief that the common people of Russia, unless controlled and directed, were a very real threat to the existing order of things. Whatever emancipation may have offered to the peasants, it was not genuine liberty.

THE SIGNIFICANCE OF EMANCIPATION

Emancipation proved the first in a series of measures that Alexander produced as a part of a programme that included legal and administrative reform and the extension of press and university freedoms. But behind all these reforms lay an ulterior motive. Alexander II was not being liberal for its own sake. According to official records kept by the Ministry of the Interior (equivalent to the Home Office in Britain) there had been 712 peasant uprisings in Russia between 1826 and 1854. By granting some of the measures that the intelligentsia had called for, while in fact tightening control over the peasants, Alexander intended to lessen the social and political threat to the established system that those figures frighteningly represented. Above all, he hoped that an emancipated peasantry, thankful for the gifts that a bountiful tsar had given them, would provide physically fitter and morally worthier recruits for Russia's armies, the symbol and guarantee of Russia's greatness as a nation.

There is a sense in which the details of Emancipation were less significant than the fact of the reform itself. Whatever its shortcomings, emancipation was the prelude to the most sustained programme of reform that imperial Russia had yet experienced (see the Timeline). There is also the irony that such a sweeping move could not have been introduced except by a ruler with absolute powers; it could not have been done in a democracy. The only comparable social change of such magnitude was President Lincoln's freeing of the negro slaves in 1865. But, as a modern Russian historian (Alexander Chubarov, *The Fragile Empire*, New York, 1999, p.75) has provocatively pointed out: 'the [Russian] emancipation was carried out on an infinitely larger scale, and was achieved without civil war and without devastation or armed coercion'.

Yet when that achievement has been duly noted and credited, hindsight suggests that emancipation was essentially a failure. It raised expectations and dashed them. Russia gave promise of entering a new dawn but then retreated into darkness. This tends to suggest that Alexander II and his government deliberately set out to betray the peasants. This was certainly the argument used by radical critics of the regime. It is important to consider, however, that land reform always takes time to work. It can never be a quick fix. Alexander's prime motive in introducing emancipation was undoubtedly the desire to produce results that were beneficial to his regime. But this is not to suggest that he was insincere in his wish to elevate the condition of the peasants.

Where he can be faulted is in his failure to push reform far enough. The fact is that Alexander II suffered from the besetting dilemma that afflicted all the reforming tsars from Peter the Great onwards—how to achieve reform without damaging the interests of the privileged classes that made up imperial Russia. It was a question that was never satisfactorily answered because it was never properly faced. Whenever their plans did not work out or became difficult to achieve, the Romanovs abandoned reform and resorted to coercion and repression. Emancipation was intended to give Russia economic and social stability and thus prepare the way for its industrial and commercial growth. But it ended in failure. It both frightened the privileged classes and disappointed the progressives. It went too far for those slavophiles in the court who wanted Russia to cling to its old ways and avoid the corruption that came with western modernity. It did not go far enough for those progressives who believed that a major social transformation was needed in Russia.

There is a larger historical perspective. It is suggested by many historians that, for at least a century before its collapse in the Revolution of 1917, imperial Russia had been in institutional crisis; the tsarist system had been unable to find workable solutions to the problems that faced it. If it was to modernise itself, that is to say if it was to develop its agriculture and industry to the point where it could sustain its growing population and compete on equal terms with its European and Asian neighbours and international competitors, it would need to modify its existing institutions. This it proved unable or unwilling to do.

Therein lies the tragedy of Emancipation. It is an outstanding example of tsarist ineptitude. Its introduction held out the possibility that Russia could build on this fundamentally progressive measure and modify its agricultural economy in such a manner as to cater for its vast population, which doubled to 125 million during the second half of the 19th century. But the chance was lost. So reduced was the peasant as an agricultural worker by 1900 that only half of his meagre income came from farming. He had to sustain himself by labouring. So much for Alexander II's claim that he viewed the task of improving the condition of the peasants as 'a sacred inheritance' to which he was honour bound.

ISSUES TO DEBATE

• To what extent did defeat in the Crimean War provide Alexander II with an ideal opportunity to introduce major reforms?

• In what ways were the Russian peasants better off because of Emancipation, in what ways worse off?

• Do you accept the view that the Emancipation of the Serfs was symptomatic of the unwillingness of the tsarist system to embrace much needed root and branch reform?

FURTHER READING

Russell Sherman and Robert Pearce, *Russia 1815–1881* (Hodder & Stoughton, 2nd edition, 2002)

Olga Crisp, *Studies in the Russian Economy Before 1914* (Macmillan, 1976)

Lionel Kochan, *The Making of Modern Russia* (Penguin, 1983)

Alexander Chubarov, *The Fragile Empire* (Continuum, 1999)

Richard Pipes, *Russia under the Old Regime* (Penguin, 1966)

Alfred J. Rieber, *The Politics of Autocracy* (Paris, 1966)

David Saunders, *Russia in the Age of Reaction and Reform 1801–1881* (Longman, 1992)

Peter Waldron, *The End Imperial Russia, 1855–1917* (Macmillan, 1997)

W.E. Mosse, *An Economic History of Russia 1856–1914* (Tauris, 1992)

Maureen Perrie, *Alexander II, Emancipation and Reform* (Historical Association, 1993)

Peter Gattrell, *The Tsarist Economy 1850–1917* (Batsford, 1982)

Jerome Blum, *Lord and Peasant in Russia* (Princeton UP, 1972)

TIMELINE

1855	Death of Nicholas I, accession of Alexander II, while Russian position in Crimean war is hopeless
1856	Treaty of Paris ends the war
1857	Alexander instructs each province to consider reform
1859	Drafting Commissions appointed to consider proposals
1861	Emancipation decree; riots by peasants; beginning of expansion of schools
1862	Public budget set and published; regional military commands established
1863	Universities given significant autonomy
1864	Zemstva established
1865	Press given greater freedom
1866	Assassination attempt on Alexander II
1867	Second assassination attempt
1872	First women admitted to Moscow University
1881	Alexander II assassinated by Narodnya Volya

2

Revolutionary Russia and the
Early Soviet Era

Courtesy of Alan Cordova (http://www.flickr.com/photos/acordova)

Grand Kremlin Palace, the Ivan the Great Bell Tower, the Vodovzvodnaya Tower, and Archangel Cathedral in the Kremlin, the longtime seat of Russian and Soviet government in Moscow.

Vladimir Ilyich Ulyanov (1870–1924), also known as V. I. Lenin, the leader of the Bolsheviks and the Soviet Union's first head of state.

Editor's Introduction

Although Russia began the 20th century as an established world power, it had only recently emerged from a feudal system of government. As a result, it did not yet have the economic might of its Western neighbors. The country's wealth expanded through industrialization, but it was unevenly distributed, and the lower classes failed to benefit directly from this growth. Soon inflation caused a substantial rise in prices, and wages did not keep pace. Fed up with deplorable working conditions and widespread poverty, the people demanded change.

By early 1905, thousands of workers had taken to the streets in protest. On January 22, a group of roughly 150,000 marched to the Winter Palace in St. Petersburg to deliver their demands to Czar Nicholas II. Palace guards shot at the protesters, killing hundreds. Known as "Bloody Sunday," the violent episode sparked the Revolution of 1905. In an attempt to appease the workers, Nicholas II created a legislative assembly known as the Duma and instituted many other reforms, none of which were enough to save the monarchy.

Over the next decade, the situation went from bad to worse. Russia paid a heavy price for its involvement in World War I, and the industrialization that preceded the fighting resulted in appalling conditions for factory workers. At the same time, the country was suffering famines, and the people blamed the royal family for failing to address these problems. After more than 300 years of rule, the Romanovs were about to lose their grip on Russia.

The Revolution of 1917 occurred in two stages: the February and October Revolutions. During the February Revolution, Czar Nicholas II—the last Romanov ruler of Russia—was overthrown and eventually executed along with his family. The October Revolution, lead by Vladimir Lenin and the Bolsheviks, laid the groundwork for the Soviet Union, which was formally established in 1922. The articles in this chapter focus on the lead-up to the revolutions, the rise of the Bolsheviks, the subsequent civil war, and the early years of the Union of Soviet Socialist Republics (USSR).

In "Witnessing a Revolution," the first article in this chapter, Charlotte Alston looks back at journalist Harold Williams' accounts of the beginning of the 1905 revolution. Reporting for the *Manchester Guardian* in December 1904 and January 1905, Williams witnessed and documented the events leading to the revolution. As Alston points out, Williams believed the October Manifesto, a reform package Nicholas II implemented following the Bloody Sunday massacre, would save the country from revolution—a supposition that proved incorrect. In the short sidebar "'Bloody Sunday' In St. Petersburg," the next piece in this chapter, Richard Cavendish sheds additional light on the Winter Palace incident, summarizing the key facts.

In the following selection, "The World According to Marx," Rupert J. Taylor provides a brief explanation of communism, tracing its origins to *The Communist Manifesto*, published in 1848 by German thinkers Karl Marx and Friedrich Engels. Taylor's piece covers the implementation of Russian communism and summarizes the next 70 years of history, touching on why the Soviet Union eventually collapsed.

With "Russia and World War One," the subsequent entry, Chris Trueman focuses on the various circumstances that contributed to the fall of the monarchy in 1917. Among them was the exceedingly costly war with Germany and the Central Powers, which had started three years earlier, in 1914. After seizing power, the Bolsheviks ended Russia's involvement in the conflict, signing the Treaty of Brest-Litovsk in March 1918.

In the following selection, "Lenin in Power," Russell Tarr describes the transition that occurred when Lenin and the Bolsheviks took over the reins of government. It was anything but a smooth transfer of power, and Lenin had many opponents even before the establishment of the Soviet Union. Civil war broke out after the fall of the Provisional Government, and Tarr explains how the Bolsheviks managed to defeat their rivals and emerge the dominant party.

In the final article, "Reinventing Stalin," Rebecca Reich reviews *Stalin: A Biography* by Robert Service, which considers the violent nature of Lenin's successor, Joseph Stalin. Stalin used terror and intimidation to solidify his hold over the nation, sending millions of Russians to gulags, or working camps, and ordering the executions of hundreds of thousands. His tactics were ruthless and brutal, and Service acknowledges that the leader "had tendencies in the direction of a paranoid and sociopathic personality disorder." Stalin famously mistrusted others and would stop at nothing to liquidate those he perceived as threats. His proclivity for violence has earned him comparisons to Adolf Hitler—a man he greatly admired.

Witnessing a Revolution*

By Charlotte Alston
History Today, January 2005

In December 1904, on the eve of the 1905 Russian Revolution, Harold Williams arrived in St Petersburg as the first permanent correspondent of the *Manchester Guardian* in a foreign capital. His appointment reflected the commitment of the newspaper's editor, C.P. Scott, to expanding the *Manchester Guardian*'s news service, but also Scott's interest in the cause of Russian constitutional reform. In Britain, as in much of Western Europe, the Russian government was widely regarded as autocratic, repressive and outdated. Williams joined a growing group of Western correspondents and observers who had come to Russia in the hope of witnessing a revolution.

In the winter of 1904–05, the situation in Russia appeared to be critical. The Russo-Japanese war, hugely unpopular and publicly mismanaged, was at its height; Port Arthur, which had been under siege by the Japanese since the summer of 1904, fell at the beginning of 1905. Members of the liberal intelligentsia and zemstvo (county council) representatives were agitating for reform of the system of government. The Minister of the Interior, Prince Sviatopolk-Mirskii, who had been appointed after the assassination of V. K. Plehve in July, had attempted to push through a series of reforms, but it had become clear by December that the Tsar had no intention of implementing them. In the major cities, demands grew for a constituent assembly. On January 3rd/16th (throughout this article, dates are given first according to the Julian calendar, still used in Russia at this time) the workers in the Putilov ironworks in St Petersburg came out on strike. Within days, 120,000 workers across the city had joined them.

Williams was a New Zealander with a doctorate in philology and a remarkable aptitude for learning languages (by the end of his life he knew as many as fifty). His brief from Scott was to chart the progress of the movement for reform, or, if it turned out as such, revolution. He was 'to continue in the work at least until something like a constitutional government was established in Russia'. Williams's first journalistic appointment had been for *The Times* in Stuttgart, where he worked closely with a group of Russian emigres. They provided him with connections with members of the Russian constitutional movement who helped him to find his feet in St Petersburg. His articles, which appeared in the *Manchester Guardian* under the headlines 'Reform in Russia', 'Russia's Troubles', and 'The Russian Upheaval', laid emphasis on demands for constitutional reform, on preparations for fresh demonstrations, and on disappointment at the Tsar's response in the imperial ukas of December 1st/13th; although this promised some administrative reforms, it made no mention of popular representation.

During the strikes in St Petersburg, plans were made for a procession to the Tsar, to present a petition of the workers' demands. The march would be led by Father Georgii Gapon, a former student of the St Petersburg Theological Academy, now the head of the police-sponsored labour union, the Assembly of Russian Factory and Mill Workers. Gapon was largely ignorant of political theory, and the procession was designed to be peaceful and religious in nature; the workers were marching to the Tsar to ask for his protection, rather than to oppose him. Nevertheless, many of the demands that made up the petition were overtly political. They ranged from the right to establish trade unions and the institution of an eight-hour day, to the termination of the Russo-Japanese war, freedom of speech and of the press, and the convocation of a constituent assembly.

Williams interviewed Gapon on January 6th/19th, and was impressed. 'His manner was simple . . . he was evidently thoroughly sincere.' Gapon's personality was not commanding, but it was easy to imagine in him 'a power to win the affections of the working men to whom he has devoted his life'. Later in the week Williams began to express concern that the workers did not appear to understand some of the demands they were being called on to march for, and that they were being asked to take oaths that they were prepared to die for their cause. He was struck by 'the careless way in which [Gapon] spoke of the possibility of his own death or the butchery of his followers, and the lack of a sense of the grave responsibility he was taking upon himself.'

On the morning of January 9th/22nd, those involved in the march and those determined to watch it rose early. Williams's first telegram was sent at 5.20am—in it he reported that the strikers were keeping perfect order as they prepared for the march. Until 10am the Nevsky Prospect, St Petersburg's main thoroughfare, was 'quieter than an ordinary Sunday morning'. At half past eleven Williams went out with Emile Dillon, the correspondent of the *Daily Telegraph*, and they saw 'scores of people, chiefly working men in black overcoats and black lambskin caps . . . streaming northwards in the direction of the Neva.' He was astonished that the men had been allowed to pass the troops posted on the outskirts of the city:

> But as we passed on further we saw bands of Cossacks riding by, big ruffianly looking fellows, in caps with red bands and beaver overcoats. They sat their horses splendidly, and smiled as though delighting in the prospect of a day's sport.

On hearing that there had been shooting at the Narva Gate, one of the entrances to the city from the Schlusselburg industrial region, Williams and Dillon hired a sleigh—it had snowed heavily overnight—and drove over to the Vyborg side of the city. At the Troitsky Bridge they encountered part of the procession; a 'black mass of people', who 'walked along with a shambling gait, and smiled awkwardly at bystanders, as though their sudden and unaccustomed conspicuousness made them shy.' In a nearby public garden the marchers were confronted by a group of Cossacks, who fired on the crowd, killing and injuring a number of people.

Williams and Dillon returned to the city, approaching the Winter Palace from the east. The surrounding streets were dense with crowds, but the palace square was quiet:

> Cossacks rode about, and lines of Cossacks and gendarmes kept back the people from the palace square, which lay white and clear, a few soldiers who were posted in the centre playing at fisticuffs to warm themselves. The great red front of the palace showed no sign of life, and the balcony on which so many thousands had expected the Tsar would appear to grant his people the gift of freedom was empty; the Tsar seemed very far away.

The petition was due to be presented at 2pm (although the Tsar was still at Tsarskoe Selo, his palace outside St Petersburg), and as this hour approached the crowd that was being kept back from the palace square became restless. Williams was listening to a meeting of the city's intelligentsia in the public library when a man arrived and announced that troops had fired on the procession in front of the palace. The members of the meeting went out into the street, and Williams went with them. By this time, however, the outraged crowd was pouring away from the palace:

> No one could go anywhere near the scene of slaughter. As we drove we were overtaken by a sleigh followed by working men running along bareheaded and shouting out bitterly against the Government. In one of the sleighs was a wounded student, and in another a fearful and sickening sight, the dead body of a student with a big red hole in the left side of his head; his brains had been blown out . . . All doubt was over now. The Tsar had given his answer in blood. And the people, who had been so peaceful and confident all the week, now suddenly broke into a fury. All afternoon the riots went on on the Nevsky.

As many as 200 people were killed, and 800 injured in the march on the Winter Palace on January 9th/22nd. The world press expressed horror at the brutality of the incident, and at the appalling mishandling of the event by the Tsar and his advisors. In the *Manchester Guardian*, Williams wrote: 'The great opportunity came to the Tsar of receiving the unbounded loyalty of his people, and with colossal folly he rejected it. And of those who were supposed to advise him one cannot write fittingly now. We are simply watching from hour to hour the issues of this tremendous wrong.'

Bloody Sunday marked the beginning of a year of disturbances in Russia. The riots in St Petersburg were followed by uprisings in Moscow, Warsaw, Riga and other regional centres. Williams travelled a great deal during 1905; in March he was in Warsaw, writing on the strength of the national movement there, and in the summer he was at Kiev and Odessa, covering the riots and the mutiny of the crew of the battleship *Potemkin*. In October a railway strike brought the Russian transport system to a standstill, and in St Petersburg there was a general strike of 'unheard of dimensions'. There were also steps towards reform. The Tsar's first tentative proposals, issued in February, were badly received by all elements of the opposition. When the strikes and riots escalated throughout the autumn, the Tsar, under severe pressure from his advisors, was forced to issue a manifesto allowing for a constituent assembly with legislative powers, elected on a wide franchise.

The October Manifesto divided opinion among the opposition to the autocracy. While the more radical elements were still unsatisfied, the moderate parties saw it as real progress. Although this would not remain the case in years to come, in October 1905 the manifesto seemed to Williams and to the *Manchester Guardian* to be a clear step in the right direction, and as such it marked the beginning of the end of Williams's work for the newspaper. His articles were now appearing under the headlines 'Russia's Joy', and 'In Liberty's Name'. In an article published immediately after the issue of the manifesto, Williams wrote:

> The difference between St Petersburg today and yesterday is like the difference between night and morning. It is difficult to believe this is the same city . . . the general feeling is one of relief at the opportunity to think, speak, and move in freedom.

'BLOODY SUNDAY' IN ST PETERSBURG[*]

JANUARY 22ND, 1905

BY RICHARD CAVENDISH
HISTORY TODAY, JANUARY 2005

That Sunday Morning in St Petersburg (it was January 9th, Old Style), some 150,000 people gathered at the six designated assembly points to converge on the Winter Palace and present a petition to the Tsar, Nicholas II, who as the 'little father' of his people would surely be bound to sympathise with them. The march was organised by an Orthodox priest, Father George Gapon, head of the Assembly of Russian Factory and Mill Workers, one of several trade unions set up the previous year with the approval of the ministry of the interior to be a safety valve for grievances and to promote loyalty to the regime. Gapon, however, alarmed the authorities by his socialist attitude and took advice from the Union of Liberation, an organisation of middle-class liberal intellectuals campaigning for parliamentary democracy. At the beginning of January, when four of his members were sacked from their jobs, he started a strike which spread rapidly until 120,000 workers were out.

Dressed in their Sunday best, with the women and children at the front, the marchers carried icons, crosses or pictures of the Tsar. They sang hymns as if in a religious procession and the less optimistic of them had prepared themselves for martyrdom. Their petition, inspired by the Union of Liberation, asked for the working day to be cut to eight hours, for the right to strike and for the election of a constituent assembly by secret ballot and universal suffrage. They never reached the Winter Palace, where Nicholas was in any case not in residence. Not thinking the situation was seriously threatening, he had gone off to the country.

His ministers meanwhile had decided to block the march short of the Winter Palace. Thousands of armed troops were stationed at key points, but there was not expected to be any need for force. When the advancing columns appeared, however, while some of the soldiers fired warning shots into the air, some panicked and fired straight into the packed crowds. At the Narva Gate, where Father Gapon himself led the marchers, forty people were shot dead and the horrified Gapon cried out, 'There is no God anymore, there is no Tsar'. At the Troitsky Bridge, marchers were charged and slashed with sabres by Cossack cavalry and on the Nevsky Prospect cannon were used against the crowd.

The day's total death toll is put at about 200 with some 800 more wounded.

If anything was needed to undermine common people's allegiance to the Tsar, this was it. Gapon prudently retreated abroad, while a wave of protests and strikes across the country built up into a full-blown revolution which presently forced Nicholas II to issue the October Manifesto, promising to introduce democracy. Gapon returned and was murdered by a government agent. The manifesto had drawn the revolutionary movement's teeth, for the time being.

The World According to Marx[*]

By Rupert J. Taylor
Canada and the World Backgrounder, 1994

For centuries Russians suffered under the absolute rule of the Tsars (kings). But, the last Tsar, Nicholas II, was overthrown in 1917.

Once the Tsar had fallen, there were many groups eager to pick over the ruins of his empire. The Bolsheviks (communists) under the leadership of V.I. Lenin proved to be the strongest. By early November 1917, Lenin was powerful enough to command forces capable of seizing control of Russia.

On 7 November, Bolshevik forces occupied Petrograd—which was renamed Leningrad—and put in place a Council of People's Commissars under Lenin's leadership.

There followed four years of civil war as other groups tried to wrest control from the Bolsheviks. The Bolsheviks won survival of their regime by withdrawing from the war with Germany. The Treaty of Brest-Litovsk, which brought peace with Germany, also gave freedom to Finland, the Baltic republics, Poland, and Ukraine.

At the end of the civil war, (the Bolsheviks won) the Soviet state was created. Ukraine was reabsorbed into the Soviet Union with Lenin as leader.

The people who seized control of Russia in 1917 represented a small fraction of the population. At the time of the Revolution the Bolshevik Party only had 350,000 members in a land of 150 million people. It was the singleminded leadership of Lenin that raised the Bolsheviks from being an obscure group of intellectuals to governors of the world's largest country. Lenin was a man with a mission, and this was to put into practice the theory of a German philosopher, Karl Marx.

In 1848, Marx and another German intellectual, Friedrich Engels, published *The Communist Manifesto*. In it, they outlined their notions about the proper order for society.

In common with many thinkers of his day, Marx was deeply interested in the ideas of freedom and equality—two commodities in very short supply for the masses in the Europe of the time. He saw that a small group of private individuals—those who owned the factories and land—held all the power. He called this ruling class the bourgeoisie; the workers he called the proletariat.

Marx and Engels predicted that, as capitalism advanced, the ownership of industry would be concentrated into fewer and fewer hands. They said that capitalists would exploit workers and consumers in their drive for ever higher profits. They believed, therefore, that the means of production should be seized by the workers through revolution.

In his writings on revolution, Marx saw two stages. In the socialist stage, the workers would establish a "dictatorship of the proletariat," by overthrowing their former oppressors, the bourgeoisie. The abundance of goods created by capitalism would then, for the first time, be distributed according to socialist ideals: "From each according to his abilities, to each according to his needs," as Marx put it.

When this redistribution of wealth had been perfected the highest and final form of social organization—communism—would be reached. No longer would there be any exploitation, because the means of production would belong to all. Government, which acted in the interests of bourgeoisie during the capitalist era, would be unnecessary during the communist stage and would "wither away."

Marx had believed that the workers would rise up of their own accord and pitch out their masters; Lenin recognized the need for leadership. He set up the "vanguard of the proletariat," a band of dedicated revolutionaries. It was their job to lead the workers before and after the revolution. They did this by organizing "soviets" (councils) of workers on factory floors, in soldiers' barracks, and among peasants in the fields.

One of the first acts of the new Russian government in 1917 was to issue "The Decree on Land." "Landlord property is abolished, immediately and without compensation," said the Decree. All land was declared to be the property of all the people. The big landowners, the royal family, and the church, lost all their land—162 million hectares of it.

This seizure of land paved the way for agricultural reform. Farms were "collectivized," meaning the land belonged to the state and was worked by the peasants who had worked it before as serfs. Now, in theory, the peasants owned the land and were entitled to benefit from their farming of it. After the land had been taken over, the banks, industrial enterprises, transportation system, mines, and all other capitalist ventures were seized.

However, the notion of equality among all people just didn't work out in practice. The ideal of communism was perverted by those who preached it. The workers were liberated from the tyranny of capitalist bosses, but they were then placed firmly under the heel of communist bosses. Communism was used as an instrument of oppression. For anyone who stepped out of line the consequences were severe.

Lenin died in 1924 and he was succeeded by one of the great villains of the 20th century, Josef Stalin. He crushed opposition within the Soviet Union ruthlessly, and is thought to have been responsible for the deaths of 40 million people.

At the start of World War II, Stalin signed a pact with the German Nazi leader Adolf Hitler. The deal was that the two countries would not attack each other and would carve up Central and Eastern Europe between them.

So, when Hitler invaded western Poland in 1939, the Soviet Union seized eastern Poland, and the Baltic states, and tried to take Finland. The Finns fought the vastly bigger Red Army to a standstill, and Stalin had to be content with minor gains.

On 22 June 1941, Hitler's armies caught Stalin's forces completely off guard in a surprise attack. In five months, the Germans overran Ukraine and were threatening Moscow and Leningrad. Then, winter arrived. The German advance was frozen and military aid for the Soviets began to arrive from the West. Slowly, the tide turned and the Germans were pushed back. As the Germans retreated, the Soviets took control of most of Central and Eastern Europe.

By the end of the war, in the famous words of British prime minister Winston Churchill, "From Stettin in the Baltic to Trieste in the Adriatic an Iron Curtain has descended across the Continent."

The Soviet Union now controlled East Germany, Poland, Czechoslovakia, Hungary, Romania, Yugoslavia, Albania, and Bulgaria (Yugoslavia and Albania later broke away from Soviet domination but remained communist). Communist governments, handpicked by Stalin, were installed in each of these countries. Soviet troops occupied most areas, and any dissent was crushed by the secret police. The Cold War had begun.

Forces of the East bloc (the Soviet Union and its allies) now faced those of the West (the United States and its allies). Both sides bristled with weapons, and the likelihood of another all-out world war ebbed and flowed for the next four decades.

Then, along came Mikhail Gorbachev. In 1985, Mr. Gorbachev became leader of the Soviet Union. The country, he said, was in a "Pre-crisis" situation. Unreformed for nearly 70 years, the Soviet economy had become a dinosaur. Based on central planning and control, about 150 government departments ran the entire economy.

As a result, between 1971 and 1985, Soviet economic growth fell sharply. Consumer goods production suffered badly because priority was given to heavy industry and military needs. Shortages were widespread. Soviet citizens had difficulty getting enough soap, shoes, toothpaste, and other products. Most serious were food shortages and rationing became extensive by the early 1980s.

Mr. Gorbachev hoped to avoid disaster through a reform program which he called perestroika (economic restructuring). While perestroika was being unleashed on the economy, Westerners got used to hearing another Russian word—glasnost (openness).

Under the old Soviet system information was strictly controlled. The people were told only what the Communist Party wanted them to be told. Major disasters could be passed off as runaway successes because there was no independent media to tell the truth. For seven decades, Soviet citizens were fed a diet of half-truths and outright lies. Foreign radio signals were jammed so that the people were isolated from news from outside.

Under glasnost Mr. Gorbachev swept away most of the censorship and information control of the Stalinist system. For the first time, government policy was debated openly in the news media and by people on the streets. The jamming of Western broadcasts stopped. By the end of 1990, freedom of the press and religion had been approved. Books, long famous in the West but banned in the Soviet Union, such as *Dr. Zhivago*, could now be bought and read.

Mr. Gorbachev tried to bring about these reforms within the communist system. He failed miserably. Once the people of Central and Eastern Europe got a taste of freedom and democracy they decided they wanted the whole meal. A weakened Soviet government was no longer able to prop up its puppet leaders in other countries. In November and December 1989, the communist governments of Czechoslovakia, East Germany, Hungary, and Romania collapsed. Soon Bulgaria, Poland, and Hungary split with Moscow.

Next, the Soviet Union itself began to fall apart. By the end of 1991, it ceased to exist—split into 15 separate republics. The experiment with communism, at least in Europe, was over.

SUGGESTED ACTIVITIES

1. Discuss the leadership qualities of Lenin. Through your discussion draw up a list of the qualities you think leaders should have. Do you think the qualities needed for leading a revolution are the same as those needed for running a country in peacetime?

2. For an eyewitness account of the Russian Revolution, read "Ten Days That Shook the World," by John Reed.

Russia and World War One[*]

By Chris Trueman
History Learning Site

World War One was to have a devastating impact on Russia. When World War One started in August 1914, Russia responded by patriotically rallying around Nicholas II.

Military disasters at the Masurian Lakes and Tannenburg greatly weakened the Russian Army in the initial phases of the war. The growing influence of Gregory Rasputin over the Romanovs did a great deal to damage the royal family and by the end of the spring of 1917, the Romanovs, who had ruled Russia for just over 300 years, were no longer in charge of a Russia that had been taken over by Kerensky and the Provisional Government. By the end of 1917, the Bolsheviks led by Lenin had taken power in the major cities of Russia and introduced communist rule in those areas it controlled. The transition in Russia over the space of four years was remarkable—the fall of an autocracy and the establishment of the world's first communist government.

Nicholas II had a romantic vision of him leading his army. Therefore, he spent much time at the Eastern Front. This was a disastrous move as it left [the tsarina] Alexandra in control back in the cities. She had become increasingly under the influence of the one man who seemingly had the power to help her son, Alexis, afflicted by haemophilia. Alexandra believed that Rasputin was a man of God and referred to him as "Our Friend". Others, appalled at his influence over the tsarina, called him the "Mad Monk"—though not in public unless they wanted to incur the wrath of Alexandra.

Rasputin brought huge disrepute on the Romanovs. His womanising was well known and he was considered by many to be debauched. How many of the stories are true and how many exaggerated will never be known, because after his death people felt free enough from his power to tell their own stories. However, his simple reputation while he was alive was enough to do immense damage to the Romanovs.

Rasputin was a great believer in the maintenance of autocracy. If it was to be diluted, it would have negatively affected his position within Russia's social hierarchy.

Ironically, with the devastation that World War One was to cause in Russia, it was Rasputin who advised Nicholas not to go to war as he had predicted that Russia would be defeated. As his prophecies seemed to be more and more accurate, his influence within Russia increased. Rasputin had always clashed with the Duma. They saw his position within the monarchy as a direct threat to their position. Alexandra responded to their complaints about Rasputin's power by introducing legislation that further limited their power.

The Duma took their complaints directly to the emperor. In September 1915, their representatives met Nicholas at his military headquarters to express their discontent that there was no government ministry back in the cities that had the confidence of the people. He told them to go back to St Petersburg and carry on working. At the end of September, another group went to see Nicholas to ask for a government that had the people's confidence. Nicholas would not see them. After this, Rasputin's power in St Petersburg was unchallengeable. As long as he had the support of the tsarina, he had power as Alexandra all but dominated her husband. As long as Alexis, the sole male heir to the throne, was ill, Rasputin had power over Alexandra.

When the Duma was dissolved in September 1915, Rasputin took charge of just about all aspects of government in St Petersburg. He held audiences on matters of state and then forwarded the problem discussed on to the relevant minister. Protected by the tsarina, Rasputin also involved himself in the war itself. He insisted that he look at the plans for prospective campaigns and that he know about the timing of the plans so that he could pray for [their] success. This was a gift for the sophisticated German Intelligence Service.

Ministers who criticised Rasputin or who disagreed with his policies were summarily dismissed. Scheratov (Interior), Krivosheim (Agriculture) and Gremykim himself were all dismissed for daring to criticise "Our Friend". Gremykim was replaced by Sturmer who simply agreed with everything Rasputin said. While he had the support of Alexandra because of the position he had adopted towards Rasputin, Sturmer put his energy into embezzling the Treasury. Protopopov was appointed Minister of the Interior—he had spent 10 years in prison for armed robbery.

While chaos ensued at home, the war at the front was going badly. Poland was lost to the Germans in 1916 and they advanced to just 200 miles from Moscow. It became clear that the morale of the ordinary Russian soldier was extremely poor and desertion became a growing problem. Food supplies were poor and erratic. As the front line got closer to the home front, it became obvious to many that both fronts were in total chaos.

In October 1916, rail workers in Petrograd (St Petersburg) went on strike in protest about their working conditions. Soldiers were sent from the front to coerce the strikers back to work. They joined the rail men. Sturmer, having recalled the

Duma, was alarmed by this development but he also seriously misunderstood the implications of what had happened.

The Duma met on November 14th 1916. Milykov, the leader of the Progressives, made an attack on the government, asking at the end of each comment he made about the government "Is this folly or treason?" Far more disturbing for the government was when the conservative Shulgin and the reactionary leader Purishkavitch made attacks on the government. Milykov would have been expected—but not the other two.

Sturmer wanted Milykov arrested. But in a rare example of decisiveness, Nicholas dismissed him on December 23rd 1916. He was replaced as premier by Trepov—a less than competent conservative. Alexandra also remarked that "he is no friend of Our Friend." Trepov lasted only until January 9th 1917, when he was allowed to resign. Government was on the verge of a complete breakdown.

Nicholas was isolated at the war front but was frequently too indecisive to be of any use. Alexandra still tried to dominate the home front with Rasputin. Food was in short supply as was fuel. The people of Petrograd were cold and hungry—a dangerous combination for Nicholas.

On December 30th 1916, Rasputin was assassinated by Prince Yusipov. Alexandra bullied her husband into ordering an imperial funeral—something reserved for members of the royal family or senior members of the aristocracy or church.

Senior members of the royal family [openly discussed] how much support there would be for Alexis to rule with a regent—a clear indication that they recognised the reign of Nicholas could not go on. Grand Duke Paul sent a letter to the army generals at the front to ascertain their views on whether Nicholas should be replaced. However, there was so much intrigue taking place that it is difficult to exactly know who said what to whom.

By January 1917, it was clear that Nicholas had lost control of the situation. Yet in this month, amidst what must have seemed like chaos, a congress of Allied powers met to discuss future policies.

On February 27th, the Duma met for the first time after the Christmas recess. It met against a background of unrest in Petrograd. There was a general strike in the city, which had been called as a result of the arrest of the public representative of the Public Munitions Committee. The city had no transport system. There was food stored in the city, but no way of moving it around. Food shortages and food queues brought even more people out onto the streets.

On March 12th, those in a bread queue, spurred on by the cold and hunger, charged a bakery. The police fired on them in an effort to restore order. It was to prove a very costly error for the government as around the city about 100,000 were on strike and on the streets. They quickly rallied to the support of those who had been fired on. Nicholas ordered that the military governor of the city, General Habalov, should restore order. Habalov ordered the elite Volhynian Regiment to do just this. They joined the strikers and used their might to disarm the police. The city's arsenal was opened and prisoners were freed from prisons that were later burned. What had been a small disturbance at a city baker's, had turned into a full-scale rebellion—such was the anger in Petrograd.

On March 13th, more soldiers were ordered on to the streets to dispel the strikers. They saw the size of the crowds and returned to their barracks, thus disobeying their orders.

The Duma appointed a provisional committee, which was representative of all parties. Rodzyanko was selected to lead it. Alexander Kerensky was appointed to take charge of troop dispositions in an effort to defeat any effort that might be made by the government to dissolve the Duma. Kerensky was an interesting choice as he was a member of the Petrograd Soviet and had links with many factory workers committees within Petrograd.

It is known that Rodzyanko telegraphed Nicholas requesting that he appoint a Prime Minister who had the confidence of the people.

"The last hour has come when the destiny of the country and the dynasty is being decided."

Rodzyanko received no answer to his telegraph.

On March 14th, rumours swept through the city that soldiers from the front were being sent in to put down the uprising. The Duma established a Provisional Government in response to this perceived threat. The important Petrograd Soviet gave its support to the Provisional Government on the condition that it summoned a constituent assembly, universal suffrage was to be guaranteed and that civil rights were to be enjoyed by all.

In reality, the Provisional Government in Petrograd had little to fear from troops at the front. Discipline was already breaking down and thousands of soldiers deserted. The Petrograd Soviet had sent an instruction to the front that soldiers should not obey their officers and that they should not march on the capital.

At this moment in time, Nicholas was caught between the war front and Petrograd. He received news of small disturbances in his capital and gathered together a group of loyal soldiers to put them down. He had no idea of the sheer scale of the 'disturbances'. He also had no idea of the political input into this uprising. Nicholas did not make it to Petrograd because of a heavy snow storm. He was forced to stop at Pskov. It was only here that Nicholas received a copy of Rodzyanko's telegram. It was also at Pskov that Nicholas learned that all his senior army generals believed that he should abdicate. On the night of March 15th, two members of the Provisional Government also arrived to request the same. With as much dignity as he could muster, Nicholas agreed and handed the throne to his brother, Michael. He confirmed the existence of the Provisional Government and asked that all Russians everywhere support it so that Russia would win her fight against Germany.

Michael refused the throne unless it was handed to him after the people had voted for him. This was never going to happen and Romanov rule over Russia came to an end.

The March revolution was not a planned affair. Lenin was in Switzerland, the Bolsheviks did not even have a majority in the Petrograd Soviet and the Duma had not wanted the end of the Romanovs. So why did it happen?

The ruling dynasty must take a great deal of the blame. Nicholas was an ineffective ruler who had let his wife dominate him to such an extent that the royal family became inextricably linked to a disreputable man like Gregory Rasputin. Such an association only brought discredit to the Romanovs.

The ruling elite also failed to realise that the people would only take so much. They took their loyalty for granted. In February/March 1917, lack of food, lack of decisive government and the cold pushed the people of Petrograd onto the streets. The people of Petrograd did not call for the overthrow of Nicholas—it happened as a result of them taking to the streets calling for food. People had to burn their furniture to simply get heat in their homes. Very few would tolerate having to queue in the extreme cold just for food—food that might run out before you got to the head of the queue. The spontaneous reaction to police shooting at protestors in a bread queue showed just how far the people of Petrograd had been pushed. That it ended with the abdication of Nicholas II was a political byproduct of their desire for a reasonably decent lifestyle.

Lenin in Power[*]

By Russell Tarr
History Review, September 2006

INTRODUCTION

Between 1917 and 1924 the Bolshevik party went through a baptism of fire which transformed it from a revolutionary splinter group into a party of government. During that period it faced intense opposition from a bewildering array of political, military, social and national groups. By the time of Lenin's death, in January 1924, the regime was, despite all the odds, still in power—but at what cost was this success achieved and to what extent was it superficial rather than real?

POLITICAL OPPOSITION: CONSTITUENT ASSEMBLY TO 'RED TERROR'

Politically, the Bolshevik party faced massive opposition following its seizure of power in 1917. The Social Revolutionaries (the party of the peasants) had more support in the countryside, whilst the Bolsheviks (the party of the proletariat) did not command the overwhelming support of the Soviets. Nevertheless, having made so much political capital out of the Provisional Government's failure to call a Constituent Assembly throughout 1917, Lenin had no choice but to call elections immediately. For the Bolsheviks, the results were depressingly predictable: they gained barely a quarter of the available seats, whilst the SRs gained almost half.

Given his precarious position, Lenin's response to this setback at first sight appears reckless: he contemptuously dissolved the Assembly, calling his action 'true democracy' because he knew the needs of the proletariat better than they did

---

themselves. He then set up Soviets throughout the country in a desperate attempt to break the power of the SR-dominated Zemstvos. By the end of May 1918 Lenin felt confident enough to expel opposition parties from the Central Executive Committee and to declare that 'our party stands at the head of soviet power. Decrees and measures of soviet power emanate from our party.' Trotsky justified this by saying that 'We have trampled underfoot the principles of democracy for the sake of the loftier principles of a social revolution'. By the time of Lenin's death political opposition parties had been formally banned and the Bolshevik Party (renamed the Communist Party in 1919) reigned supreme.

CAUSES OF BOLSHEVIK SUCCESS

(a) Weaknesses of opponents

The Social Revolutionaries in particular had suffered for years from bitter splits over such issues as the validity of terrorism, participation in the Duma and support for the Provisional Government. So it was no surprise that when the moment came they were deeply divided over whether they should participate in the new Bolshevik government. Ultimately, seven leftist Social Revolutionaries joined the government at the end of 1917 and helped to draft the decree which legitimised the seizure of the land by the peasants. This not only exacerbated the divisions in the party, but consolidated the position of the Bolsheviks in the countryside.

(b) Ruthlessness of Bolsheviks

The weaknesses of their opponents made it much easier for the Bolsheviks to crush them. In summer 1918 a failed rebellion by the SRs in Moscow and an assassination attempt on Lenin persuaded the Bolsheviks to unleash the 'Red Terror'. This was presided over by the CHEKA, formed shortly after the October Revolution under the leadership of Dzerzhinsky ('we stand for organised terror: this should be frankly stated'). Within months, membership of the Menshevik and SR parties had fallen by two-thirds. The following year, Victor Serge felt that the Soviet state had 'reverted to the procedures of the Inquisition' and by the time of Lenin's death an estimated 250,000 opponents had been liquidated.

MILITARY OPPOSITION: BREST-LITOVSK AND CIVIL WAR

Whilst the Constituent Assembly undermined the regime's political opponents, the peace treaty signed with Germany in March 1918 served to unite its military opponents. Upon seizing power, Lenin was determined to secure 'peace at any price': the war had already brought down the Tsar and the Provisional Government, and if the Bolshevik regime was not to go the same way then the war needed to end. Under the punitive Treaty of Brest-Litovsk, Russia ceded Finland, the Baltic states and Poland—a million square kilometres of territory containing 80 per cent of her coal mines and 30 per cent of her population.

Even within the Bolshevik party, the treaty was deeply unpopular: Lenin secured its ratification by the Central Committee only by threatening his resignation, and even then by only a majority of one. Given the unpopularity of the treaty within the party, it is hardly surprising that it united anti-Bolshevik military forces. Three 'White Army' commanders posed a serious threat to the Bolshevik regime based around Moscow: Kolchak attacked from the East, Denikin from the South, and Yudenitch from the West. This movement, which had in total over 250,000 troops, was united by a hatred of the Bolsheviks and a desire to restart the war against Germany. This latter objective won them the support of Russia's former allies, who invaded Russia themselves: Britain and France took control of Murmansk and Archangel in the North, whilst the Americans attacked from the Far East, helping Japan to take control of Vladivostok. At one stage, the Bolsheviks had lost control of almost three-quarters of Russia. However, by spring 1920 all three armies had been defeated and Lenin could finally turn his attention to rebuilding the Russian economy.

CAUSES OF BOLSHEVIK SUCCESS

(a) Personal unity

Although the Whites had a number of able generals, this advantage was off-set by the fact that many of them (for example, Denikin and Kolchak) did not get on with each other and there was no effective overall leader to co-ordinate their efforts. The foreign powers too were divided: Lloyd George criticised both Churchill's 'obsession' with the Civil War and the refusal of the French to commit resources to the campaign. In contrast, whilst the Reds had similar rivalries these were not as damaging because they had a recognised leader in Lenin.

(b) Ideological unity

The contrast between the fragmented Whites and the focused Reds was a result of ideology as much as personality: Red soldiers were not only twice as numerous as Whites, but were also united in a common cause. In contrast, the Whites had divided loyalties. Their patriotic rallying cry of 'Russia: one and indivisible' was both hopelessly vague and utterly unconvincing, given their reliance upon foreign aid, which was a propaganda disaster.

(c) Geographical unity

Personal and ideological factors were compounded by geographical consider-ations. Firstly, the position of the Bolsheviks in the compacted heartland of Russia gave them a strategic advantage. It not only made it easier for them to organise and coordinate their defence but also gave them the largest chunk of the population and most of the war industry. Moscow and Petrograd stayed in Red hands for the entire Civil War. In contrast, the three main White armies were located at opposite ends of Russia—Denikin and Kolchak were 10,500 kilometres apart and had to communicate via Paris! Secondly, the large size of Russia gave the Reds strategic depth. When under attack on one front they could safely give ground until troops were transferred from other fronts to repel the attack.

OPPOSITION FROM NATIONAL MINORITIES

Whilst personal, ideological and geographical factors go some way to explaining the success of the Reds in the Civil War, the handling of national minorities— whose long-repressed national aspirations for independence suddenly re-emerged in the chaos of war—was another important factor.

As Lynch has pointed out, 'The sheer size of Russia meant that local and regional considerations predominated over larger ideological issues'. By 1918, there were 33 sovereign governments in Russia, and both Reds and Whites realised that the battle for the hearts and minds of national minorities was of paramount importance: However, the only way to win this propaganda war was to promise them independence—and neither side was prepared to fulfil this promise. The Whites made their slogan 'Russia, one and indivisible' whilst Joseph Stalin formulated a doctrine of 'proletarian self-determination' which stated that national independence would be recognised only 'upon the demand of the working population', which in practice only included those Bolsheviks subject to control by Moscow.

(a) Successes

The South—The Ukraine

After the Central Powers withdrew from the Ukraine at the end of 1918, this fertile area (Russia's 'bread basket') descended into anarchy as Denikin's White army, supplemented with Ukranian nationalists, competed with the Red Army for control. Baron Peter Wrangel, Denikin's successor and the ablest White general, employed Kadets to institute land reform, enabling him to win peasant support and to occupy considerable areas to the north. His resistance was only smashed in late 1920, when 150,000 Whites fled to Constantinople.

The East—Transcaucasia and Asia

In 1920, the Red Army attacked the three Transcaucasian Republics: in the spring, they conquered Azerbaijan; Armenia surrendered in the winter; and early in 1921 the Mensheviks were driven out of Georgia despite strong resistance. In Central Asia, the Bolsheviks conquered the khanates of Khiva and Bukhara and set up several artificial client national states.

(b) Failures

The North—Finland and the Baltic States

Anti-Communist Finns defeated Bolshevik-supported Red Finns to create an independent Finland in late 1917. The Baltic states of Latvia, Lithuania and Estonia, assisted by German occupiers, declared independence and, despite attacks from Red forces, ultimately retained it until 1940.

The West—Poland

To reconstitute a Greater Poland, Marshal Pilsudski attacked Russia and captured Kiev in May 1920. A Soviet counter-offensive led by General Tukhachevsky almost succeeded in conquering the Poles; they eventually rallied, however, drove out the Red Army, and forced Soviet Russia to accept an armistice and later the unfavourable Treaty of Riga in March 1921.

'WAR COMMUNISM' (1918–21)

The crisis of civil war pushed the Bolsheviks towards a drastic economic policy called 'War Communism' which included the rapid nationalization of all industry and the requisitioning of all surplus grain from the peasants. Whilst this succeeded in meeting the immediate needs of the Communist state, it created deep resentment in both the proletariat and the peasantry which eventually escalated into outright rebellion.

(a) Peasantry

At the outset of the Civil War, the peasantry preferred the Soviet programme of peace, land and worker control to that of the Whites, who wanted to restart the war with Germany and were sceptical both of land reform and of workers' rights. Four out of five peasants conscripted into the White armies promptly deserted.

However, by early 1918 the honeymoon was over. The loss of the Ukraine, disruption of transport routes and the break-up of the most profitable farms produced chronic food shortages in Petrograd and Moscow which pushed the Bolsheviks towards a policy of requisition and collectivisation. Requisitioning was depicted in propaganda as a war of the poor peasants against the Kulaks, but in reality the average peasant resented grain requisitioning by workers and party officials from the towns. In 1918 over 7,000 members of requisition squads were murdered.

(b) Proletariat

The key to solving the problem of the peasantry was to provide the countryside with the industrial goods it needed, which would then give them an incentive to deliver foodstuffs for the towns and the army.

Initially, the proletariat formed the bedrock of Bolshevik support, and, Lenin— arguing that 'any worker will master a ministry within a few days'—used workers' factory committees as a means of controlling management and directing economic policy. However, as with the peasantry, the honeymoon period did not last. Economic crisis convinced Lenin that the workers lacked the self-discipline to supply the Red Army with its essential needs. So in 1918 he introduced compulsory labour for all citizens between the ages of 16 and 50 and limited the influence of the Workers' Councils by setting up a Supreme Council of the National Economy (*Vesenkha*) staffed by former plant owners, managers, and other bourgeois specialists ('knowledgeable, experienced, business-like people').

On the one hand, the nationalisation of industry and the efforts of *Vesenkha* to control and coordinate the economy and labour force gave the Bolsheviks an overall view of available human and material resources which enabled them to organise munitions production and army supplies much better than could their White opponents. On the other hand, this policy was deeply divisive in a political sense. Left Communists and the proletariat in general, whilst in favour of nationalisation in principle, were critical of the use of capitalists and of the withdrawal of support for Workers' Councils.

THE CRISIS YEAR—1921

By 1921, the policy of War Communism had brought the country to the verge of chaos. In the countryside, around 6 million peasants had died of starvation and reports circulated in the foreign press that mothers were tying their children to opposite corners of their huts for fear that they would eat each other. In the towns, riots broke out in Petrograd and Moscow, which had seen their populations fall by 70 per cent and 50 per cent respectively.

However, it was the Kronstadt naval rebellion in March 1921 that gave the regime its greatest scare and destroyed its credibility to the greatest degree. Kronstadt was a naval town on an island off the coast of Petrograd. It had initially been 'the pride and joy of the revolution' (Trotsky), training the guns of the battleship *Aurora* on the Winter Palace and crushing opposition to the dissolution of the Constituent Assembly the following year. Yet by 1921 16,000 soldiers and workers had signed a petition calling for 'Soviets without Bolsheviks': freely elected Soviets, and freedoms of speech, press and association. As in Moscow and Petrograd the Reds reacted brutally, dissolving the Kronstadt Soviet, executing several hundred ringleaders and expelling over 15,000 sailors from the fleet.

'NEW ECONOMIC POLICY' (1921–24)

Though the rebellions were mercilessly crushed, Lenin now compared the communist state to a man 'beaten to within an inch of his life' and, describing Kronstadt as 'the flash which lit up reality better than anything else', promptly replaced War Communism with the New Economic Policy (NEP). This permitted private ownership of small-scale industry and ended grain requisitioning in favour of a tax in kind (eventually settled at 10 per cent of the harvest), with peasants able to sell their surpluses on the open market. By the end of 1922 the crisis began to ease, aided by £20 million of aid from the American Relief Association, and by 1923 grain production had increased by half. As Lenin had predicted, a mixed economy had emerged, with the state controlling industry whilst agriculture and trade were in private hands.

However, whilst agriculture recovered rapidly, industry did not. Therefore, whilst agricultural prices fell, industrial prices continued to rise. This meant that farmers could not afford to buy industrial goods and were tempted back towards subsistence farming. By the time of the Twelfth Party Congress in 1923, industrial prices were running at three times the level of agricultural prices and Trotsky compared the growing gap between agricultural and industrial prices to the blades of a pair of scissors.

By the time of Lenin's death industry was well on the way to recovery and the economic 'scissors crisis' was largely over, but socially the policy remained deeply divisive. Rumours circulated that NEP really stood for 'New Exploitation of the Proletariat', many members of which remained frustrated with the slow progress towards socialism and detested the new breed of Kulaks, retailers and traders known as Nepmen.

DIVISIONS IN THE PARTY

Their transformation from a party of revolutionary opposition to one of be-leaguered government had a massive impact upon the Bolshevik Party. Within months of taking power, debate and internal democracy became an impossible luxury. By 1921, the official instrument of government—Sovnarkom—had been sidelined by the smaller and more cohesive Politburo and Ogburo, which lay at the heart of a single-party state that dealt with dissent through summary executions during the civil war.

Nevertheless, the growing power of the state only served to aggravate divisions within the party. During the period of War Communism, the Workers' Opposi-tion, led by Shiliapnikov and Kollantai, opposed the reduction in the power of the Trade Unions and the Workers' Councils. The Democratic Centralists resented the 'dictatorship of party officialdom' and had called for more involvement in the decision-making process by rank-and-file communists.

The Decree on Party Unity (1921) banned formal factions, but the partial revival of capitalism in the NEP that same year created still deeper divisions. The right-wing of the party—led by Bukharin—vigorously defended the gradual, peasant-based socialism of the NEP. The Left Communists, however, quickly came to feel that more emphasis needed to be placed on a programme of massive and rapid industrialisation if the regime was to survive. They were represented most power-fully by Trotsky and his 'platform of 46', who described the NEP as 'the first sign of the degeneration of Bolshevism'.

Lenin tried his best to keep the two wings of the party together by refusing to make clear whether NEP was a short-term tactical retreat or represented a radical rethinking of communism, but this merely postponed rather than avoided internal party conflict. In some of his speeches and writings, War Communism was dismissed as the product of 'desperate necessity' and the NEP was presented as 'a radical modification in our whole outlook on socialism'. At other times, he presented War Communism as an ideologically motivated attempt to introduce 'the communist principles of production and distribution by direct assault' and described the NEP as a short-term tactical retreat ('Let the peasants have their little bit of capitalism as long as we have the power').

CONCLUSION

By 1922, when the USSR was formally proclaimed, it was clear that the Bolsheviks had succeeded in dealing with the immediate threats it had faced upon taking power. However, over the course of that year, Lenin suffered three strokes which left him partially paralysed and politically incapacitated. This served to highlight the cost at which success had been bought. As principles had been compromised and policies had become inconsistent, the party had become so divided that Lenin had dispensed with debate and democracy and relied upon brute force and personal dictatorship to hold the regime together. In the short term, this meant that the party rapidly fragmented following his illness, allowing Stalin to play factions off against each other in order to secure his own ascendancy. In the longer term, it set a tragic ideological precedent which the 'man of steel' was to exploit with disastrous effects for the Russian people in the years following Lenin's death. Far from 'withering away' as Marx had envisaged, the state had become all-powerful. Lenin had replaced one dictatorship with another.

FURTHER READING

Robert Service, *Lenin; A Biography* (Macmillan 2000)

Steve Smith, *The Russian Revolution—A Very Short Introduction* (OUP, 2002)

Michael Lynch, *Reaction and Revolutions: Russia 1894–1924* (Hodder and Stoughton, 3rd edition, 2005)

ISSUES TO DEBATE

- **Were Lenin's policies characterized by principle or expediency?**
- **To what extent did Lenin lay the foundations of Stalin's dictatorship?**
- **To what extent had Lenin built a communist state by the time of his death?**

TIMELINE

1903 Lenin writes *What is to be Done?*, stating that a dedicated minority, not a mass movement, had the most chance of realizing revolutionary change.

1917 February: Tsar overthrown by Provisional Government; October: Provisional Government overthrown by the Bolsheviks.

1918 January: Constituent Assembly summoned. Promptly dissolved when the Bolsheviks gain only a quarter of the seats. All opposition parties banned.

March: Treaty of Brest-Litovsk ends the war with Germany but on humiliating terms. Russia's former allies send troops to fight in the escalating civil war.

Summer: 'Red Terror' unleashed by the CHEKA following an assassination attempt on Lenin.

1919 Height of the Civil War. Bolsheviks attacked by the three armies of Denikin, Kolchak and Yudenitch.

1920 White armies defeated, but at massive social and economic cost. Numerous peasant uprisings and the beginnings of a famine that will reach its height the following year.

1921 Kronstadt Mutiny shows depth of disillusionment with the Bolshevik regime. Lenin responds by (a) Passing a Decree on Party Unity, and (b) Replacing War Communism with the NEP.

1922 Lenin suffers three strokes which leave him partially paralysed and politically incapacitated.

1923 Party fragments. Its greatest thinkers—Trotsky and Bukharin—are polarised by the NEP, allowing those in the centre to seize the initiative.

Stalin forms a triumvirate with Zinoviev and Kamenev and rapidly builds up a power base through his position as General Secretary.

1924 January: Lenin dies.

Reinventing Stalin[*]

By Rebecca Reich
The New Leader, March/April 2005

When it comes to buying souvenirs from the former Soviet Union, Russians like to say that Vologda is the home of fine lace while Tula is where you buy molded honey cakes and brass samovars. For portraits of Josef Stalin, though, the best place to go is Tbilisi's bustling Rustaveli Avenue, where framed photographs of the dictator are hawked on the sidewalk beside gold-plated icons of the Virgin Mary and Jesus Christ. There he is, just as Georgians remember him—proudly dressed in military uniform and putting a match to his trademark pipe.

Up north in Russia's capital, portraits of Stalin are still a rare sight, but the dictator's gargantuan esthetic is making headway. Just a short metro ride from Moscow's downtown, the Don-Stroi Construction Company is rearing what it bills as Europe's tallest residential building, a massive eighth sister to the seven gothic skyscrapers Stalin erected across the city. Last summer, Olympic team sponsor Zolotaya Bochka advertised its beer with neo-Socialist Realist billboards picturing a perfect gold-medalist physical specimen and the patriotic slogan, "Your Victory is Our Reward." It also is certainly significant that President Vladimir V. Putin, in the buildup to his attack on big business and his campaign to centralize power, reintroduced the Soviet national anthem in 2001 with new words by its original librettist.

A good deal of attention has recently been devoted to nostalgia for the Stalin era, and understandably so. Despite the intense rejection of Stalinism that followed Nikita S. Khrushchev's 1956 denunciation, Russian society has yet to kick the giant off his pedestal and turn the icon back into a man. A December poll by the independent Levada Center found that 21 per cent of the Russian population believes Stalin was a "wise leader who brought the USSR to power and prosperity." In the wake of the botched market reforms of the 1990s and the destabilization caused by the Chechen conflict, that legacy, however misperceived, has become increasingly attractive not only to the predictable diehards still around from the good old days, but to the discontented segments of the younger population. Stalin, who was larger than life while head of state, has been subjected to multiple interpretations and commentaries over the 52 years since his death, and being banned from public sight has only raised his voltage. Neo-Communists and nationalists who invoke his image know very well how effectively symbols from the past can be transformed to suit contemporary purposes. After all, they learned the art from Stalin himself.

It is the master of reinvention and nostalgia that Oxford-Russian history professor Robert Service brilliantly brings to life in *Stalin*, his authoritative new biography (Harvard, 715 pp., $29.95). Using archival sources that have only recently become available, Service captures the sorcery of a dictator who set out to change himself and his country by reinterpreting deeply inbred social convictions. There may never have been another ruler who placed such an emphasis on breaking with the past while constantly drawing on his own background. Stalin made little distinction between his personal and political life, and as Service demonstrates in this balanced, tightly written work, it is necessary to consider each in the context of the other. Never abandoning his wide-angle lens, Service shows how Stalin's experiences of religion, nationalism, peasant lore, and imperialism became the channels through which he funneled his radical agenda. Stalin set out to smash Russia's traditions. What is surprising, as Service repeatedly points out, is that he was fundamentally so traditional himself.

Stalin understood the language of religion because he had spoken it from his earliest youth. Born in 1878, the son of an alcoholic cobbler with a history of business failures and a penchant for violent outbursts, Josef Vissarionovich Dzhugashvili, as he was christened, would likely have remained in his Georgian hometown of Gori were it not for his mother's determination to have him enter the priesthood. By all accounts he was a believer as a boy, attending church regularly and even leading the choir. But Tbilisi, where he began studying at age 15, was a hotbed of nationalist stirrings, and its Russian-dominated Orthodox seminaries were, as Service puts it, "the finest recruiting agency for the revolutionary organizations." First Stalin turned to patriotic verse ("Flower, oh my Georgia!" was a line from a poem of his printed to wide acclaim in the local literary magazine *Iveria*), but he quickly moved on to Marxism, dropping out of the seminary just before graduation to become a full-time revolutionary.

Although the religious motifs that Stalin absorbed as a boy were later to be recycled in his cult, the future dictator played with feelings of nationalism early on. The leader who was to gain infamy for arresting and deporting entire populations once actually enjoyed a moderate's reputation for his demand that the new Soviet government guarantee autonomy to its ethnic minorities and his insistence that the era of empire had ended. Appointed People's Commissar for Nationalities Affairs after the 1917 Revolution, he briefly opposed Lenin's plans to create an infinitely expandable federation of republics administered from Moscow, fearing a resurgence of the resentment against the capital that had sparked his own political agitation.

Yet even as he reassured the Soviet Union's minorities that the days of Russification were over, he increasingly anchored himself in patriotic Russian themes. Anything having to do with the toppled tsarist rule was anathema in the early 1920s, but by the mid-1930s, Service notes, hard-line rulers like Ivan the Terrible and Peter the Great were hailed as administrative and economic innovators. In 1943, to rally the country against the Germans, Stalin relaxed his stranglehold over the Orthodox Church. And, at a Red Army banquet celebrating its victory, he raised a toast to the Russian people, singling them out as "the leading force of the Soviet Union among all the peoples of our country."

The nature of Stalin's own national identity has long been a subject of debate, with assertions that he was a Georgian chauvinist pitted against evidence of his Russian bias. Service maintains that he was neither a Georgian nor a Russian nationalist, but a "fluid, elusive mixture of both," and that fluidity is exactly the point. For Stalin, the imagery of nationalism, like that of religion and imperialism, was personal, but at the same time universally applicable. "It is doubtful that Stalin felt a need to fix a national identity for himself in his own mind," says Service. "Rather his priorities were focused upon ruling and transforming the USSR and securing his personal despotism."

The author does not simply dismiss Stalin as a cynical figure whose system of beliefs was motivated exclusively by a quest for power. He does credit him with an ideology. It is, however, an amalgam of selected Marxist and nationalist tendencies that could be picked over privately to suit his political needs and remade publicly to maintain his cult status. Stalin understood self-reinvention in his bones, having been exposed at an early age to the formulaic hagiographies of Orthodox saints. When Lenin died in 1924, Stalin immediately began deifying him. It was Stalin who spearheaded the macabre idea of embalming Lenin's body for public viewing in Red Square. Likewise, it was Stalin who edited Lenin's writings to bring them into almost prophetic alignment with the new regime. The precedent of sculpting a Soviet icon out of the raw material of a life proved so effective that one of the first de-Stalinizing actions taken by the Party Presidium after Stalin's own death in 1953 was to scatter his library and incinerate many of his personal writings.

Still, the religious force of Stalin's cult was such that any successor seeking validation had to climb aboard. Even as his papers were destroyed after his death, members of the Party Presidium vying for leadership had his body embalmed and placed next to Lenin's. It was the natural culmination of what Khrushchev was to call Stalin's "cult of personality." Through art, cinema, the press, and literature, Stalin reinvented himself by subjecting his image to a strict set of criteria that had its rival only in the iconographic inflexibility of the Orthodox Church. Indeed, as Service observes, if Marx' Das Kapital and Lenin's works functioned as the Gospels for the Soviet congregation, then Stalin's official biography, released in 1938, took the place of the Acts of the Apostles.

The more the cult was forced on the public, though, the less it actually revealed of Stalin. Service devotes an engrossing chapter to the fundamental austerity of what he dubs the "cult of impersonality." By withholding personal information to the point of appearing to be more divine than human, Stalin perfected the aura of mystery that had worked so well with the Romanov tsars. On a practical level, his removal from the public eye allowed him to play down his ethnic origins by, for example, avoiding public speeches that would highlight his Georgian accent, which he feared might cause resentment among the Russian population. But Service leaves no doubt that Stalin was also playing for imperial effect. "To Stalin's eyes, the mentality of most Soviet citizens had not yet been transformed by the October Revolution," he writes. "They needed to be ruled, at least to some extent, in a traditional way. And this meant they needed a 'tsar.'"

Service speculates that Stalin's early introduction to the fixed imagery of the Orthodox Church may well explain "the extraordinarily detailed control over publicly available material" on him. If so, Service adds, "it must have reinforced the predisposition of the Marxist-Leninist doctrinaires to secure fidelity to the texts of Marx, Engels, Lenin, and Stalin to root out any trace of heterodoxy." The word "predisposition" is key. Stalin thought of himself as an ideologue, and though in reality he regularly adjusted his ideology to the political situation, he never stopped believing in it as a religious body of law.

Perhaps only someone touched by old-fashioned fanaticism could have pushed for so radical a break with the past. True, other Bolsheviks agreed that the former way of life required violent overthrow. But it was Stalin who had the idea of using the bad old past to bring modernity about. Even as he subjected all sectors of the economy to state control, even as he collectivized peasant farms and consigned millions of citizens to labor camps, he kept his population in check through a black-and-white reinvention of traditional beliefs. "Without using the term," Service writes, "Stalin suggested that black magic had to be confronted if the forces of good—Marxism-Leninism, the Communist party and the October Revolution—were to survive and flourish."

Of course, not all of Stalin's reforms could be sugarcoated with tradition; he quite chillingly resorted to violence when people stood in his way. Beginning in the early 1930s, he systematically eradicated vast sectors of the population that could serve as witnesses to the bygone ways. A similar fate met those he saw as obstacles to his personal reinvention—particularly people who had been close to him in his youth. When his sister-in-law Anna Alliluyeva included some all too humanizing anecdotes about him in a memoir she had received permission to publish in 1946, Stalin had her sentenced to 10 years of labor despite the fact that her family had sheltered him on his return from exile in 1917. "The problem presented by the Alliluyev's was that they knew him so well," says Service. "He wished to float free of his personal history. Increasingly he opted for the status of state icon at the expense of a realistic image of himself."

But, as Service stresses, Stalin's major objective in implementing terror was not to protect his reinvented identity; it was to save his own skin: "Chief among his considerations was security, and he made no distinction between his personal security and the security of his policies, the leadership and the state." Service dismisses arguments that the intensification of arrests in the late 1930s was motivated by the need for added slave labor, pointing out that far fewer people would have been killed if this were the case. In fact, Stalin had good reason to fear his population, which had revolted under repressive rulers in the past and was proving resistant to his brutal policies. Moreover, he felt himself to be in constant danger, and since for him the personal was political, danger to himself meant danger to the country.

One of the tasks of a biographer—especially a biographer of a figure with Stalin's criminal record—is to identify the critical turning points in his subject's career. Much has been made of the connection between the 1932 suicide of Stalin's second wife, Nadya Alliluyeva, and the subsequent outbreak of the purges. Service sees things differently, calling Alliluyeva's suicide a profound shock to Stalin yet one that merely pushed him further down a familiar path. Stalin, according to Service, had always been violent. The author creates a convincing composite portrait of the prepubescent tough who tied a pan to a cat's tail and kicked a boy who could dance better than he; the young revolutionary who advised Lenin in a letter to give members of a rival political group "a right good thrashing straight in their gobs—and without respite"; the Civil War militant who torched villages that failed to comply with Red Army demands; and the emerging dictator who began his collectivization drive by demanding quotas of grain at gunpoint.

By Service's assessment, the hypersensitive and naturally vengeful Stalin fed his propensity toward violence on a diet of distorted Georgian tribal machismo and Bolshevik justifications for terror. Each offense he personally incurred was stored away and eventually avenged as an offense against the state. As Service sees it, Stalin's indiscriminate terrorizing of his own population was not very different from what we define as terrorism today. Moreover, Lenin and Trotsky had theorized the use of violence to achieve political aims long before Stalin set the standard. In contemporary terms, terrorism is usually portrayed as being inflicted from the outside on an innocent population, but Stalin, whom Service calls the "Great Terrorist" in a meaningful update on Robert Conquest's term for the purges, held on to power by inflicting terror from within.

Keenly aware that by putting a human face on the monster he is exposing himself to charges of being an apologist, Service nevertheless perseveres in setting the record straight in this comprehensive and landmark biography. "To explain is not to excuse," Service declares while describing the brutal collectivization campaign; "Stalin was as wicked a man as has ever lived:' But it would be delusional and dangerous, he argues, to group figures like Stalin in a separate species to whom normal standards do not apply. Stalin would never have risen to power if his uncanny human intuition had not enabled him to reinvent himself repeatedly by manipulating traditional social themes. And he would never have committed his horrific crimes were it not for his singularly vicious nature and grandiose conflation of himself with the state.

By painstakingly deconstructing Stalin's personal reinventions and self-created legacy, Service takes an important step toward revealing the man behind the myth. The more the tyrant is exposed for who he was, the harder it will become to wax nostalgic for his times.

3

From Soviet Union to Soviet Collapse

Worker and Kolkhoz Woman, a stainless steel sculpture by Vera Mukhina, was unveiled as part of the Soviet Pavillion at the 1937 World's Fair in Paris, France. It has since been relocated to Moscow, Russia.

The Coat of Arms (also know as the State Emblem) of the Soviet Union was used from 1923 to 1991. The design incorporates the famous hammer and sickle as well as the Red Star, symbols that became synonymous with the USSR.

The hammer and sickle represent the working classes—the hammer evoking the urban industrial laborer, and the sickle the rural agricultural worker. The Bolshevik Revolution gave birth to this symbol, which was also used in the Soviet flag.

Editor's Introduction

Vsya vlast Sovietam was a Bolshevik slogan meaning, "All power to the Soviets!" The Soviets were councils of workers, and one of the chief aims of the Bolshevik Revolution was to imbue the proletatriat—the working class—with the economic and political might they had so long been denied. From its inception in 1922 to its collapse in 1991, the Soviet Union claimed to stand for this principle. How effectively Soviet policies reflected this commitment, however, is another matter. The articles in this chapter provide an overview of the Soviet era, covering the end of World War II through the fall of communism. It was a complex time—one that saw the Soviet Union emerge from the ashes of the war as one of the world's two superpowers. Although it lasted only 70 years, the USSR had a profound impact on world politics, and its legacy can still be felt nearly two decades after its demise.

In the first article, "Russia Reflects on Sixty-Five Years Since the Soviet Union's World War Two Victory," Alexander Mekhanik considers the motives of those countries that fought Nazi Germany. He dismisses the idea that the USSR acted solely out of a desire to control Eastern Europe, writing that Soviet communism, unlike Adolf Hitler's fascism, "reflected classic values," the same sort that drove France, Great Britain, and the United States into World War II. Pointing out that none of the participating nations—not even the United States—were paragons of democracy, Mekhanik calls the conflict "the only war in history that was fought against absolute evil, a fight that united idealists defending their ideals, cynics defending their interests, and even scoundrels trying to incinerate their sins in the flames of a great struggle."

The author of the subsequent selection, "Stalin Denounced by Nikita Khrushchev," writes of a controversial speech delivered at the Kremlin, the seat of Soviet rule, on February 14, 1956. Three years had passed since the death of Joseph Stalin, and Khrushchev, his successor, sought to distance the Soviet Union from the "cult of personality" that had enabled his predecessor's brutal reign. Khrushchev blamed Stalin for many of the nation's problems, and in the wake of his speech, the government released thousands of political prisoners jailed during the Stalin era.

In the next piece, "When the Cold War Almost Turned Hot," Albin F. Irzyk provides a firsthand account of the Berlin Crisis of August 1961, a time he calls "by far the tensest period of the Cold War up until then." Irzyk was a U.S. soldier stationed on the border between East and West Germany. From this vantage, he watched and waited as a battle group of roughly 1,500 American soldiers rumbled toward Berlin, where communist leaders had just built a wall dividing the city in two. The Berlin Wall's construction came on the heels of a contentious meeting between Khrushchev and President John F. Kennedy in Vienna, Austria, and it appeared the two superpowers were heading toward an armed showdown. Luckily, the U.S. convoy reached Berlin without incident, leaving Irzyk's men "weak with relief," spared from fighting a potential World War III.

In the following article, "Saving Russia's Armpit," Anne Applebaum describes her visit to Vorkuta, a cold, desolate coal-mining town located north of the Arctic Circle. Originally one of Stalin's prison camps, Vorkuta grew during the 1960s and 1970s into a proper city. The transformation was the result of government spending Applebaum deems wasteful and inefficient, as the annual cost of heating the frigid city exceeded the value of its coal. While Russia is now encouraging residents to leave the city, some cling stubbornly to civic pride. Applebaum calls the city "the Soviet Union in miniature," adding, "Objectively speaking, it's an awful place, but people lived in it, people got used to it—and now they don't want it to change."

In the next selection, "Death of a Writer," Applebaum turns her attention to famed Soviet dissident Alexander Solzhenitsyn, author of *Gulag Archipelago*, a once-controversial text detailing the Soviet concentration camp system. While Applebaum questions Solzhenitsyn's late-life nationalism and support of former Russian president Vladimir Putin, she praises his work, writing, "It was not his personality, but his written language that forced people to think more deeply about their values, their assumptions, their societies."

When Mikhail Gorbachev became Soviet leader in 1985, he initiated many radical reforms, including increased freedom of speech. In addition, he pulled Soviet troops out of Afghanistan, where they had been engaged in a costly counterinsurgency campaign since 1979. These actions signaled the start of the movement that would ultimately lead to the dissolution of the Soviet Union. In this chapter's final entry, "When Gorbachev Took Charge," Archie Brown argues that if Gorbachev had not been selected to lead the USSR, the country might not have liberalized—or collapsed—the way it did.

Russia Reflects on Sixty-Five Years Since the Soviet Union's World War Two Victory[*]

By Alexander Mekhanik
Expert Magazine, February 26, 2010

Something has changed in Russia. Twenty years after the collapse of the Soviet Union and the values on which society was based—and after two decades of hard times—the search is on for a firm footing in values and ideology. Attention has focused on the Second Word War, especially the question of what we were fighting for.

It seems, in Russia and in the rest of the world, that there are two points of view about the war. The first holds that Stalin's regime was undoubtedly tyrannical, but the war was fought for humanitarian values and freedom. The Soviet Union made a decisive contribution to the victory of these values, though it was certainly no showcase for them.

The second may be called the revisionist one, that the Second World War was in fact two wars: the one on the Western Front, a battle for democratic ideals and freedom; the other, on the Eastern Front, between tyrants seeking to oppress and enslave nations.

One Russian political analyst has even written that, while the Western allies were fighting for democratic ideals, most people in the Soviet Union had little idea of either democracy or Nazism, and were simply fighting for the Motherland. And even then they thought long and hard before fighting: Stalin's regime had so "exhausted" them that many were ready simply to surrender. This, in part, explains why Russia lost the early stages of the war.

Most Soviet citizens fought simply for their Motherland, with no thought of ideology; the same can be said about most people in the anti-Nazi countries and those who fought in the Resistance. It is true that all the enemies of Germany and Japan also lost ground in the early stages of the war.

* This is an abridged version of an article that originally appeared in *Expert* magazine, No.44(681) November, 16–22, 2009 and was republished by Russia Now in the supplement in *The Daily Telegraph* on February 23, 2010.

If one pursues the logic further, then, evidently, the French, as well as the Czechs, Belgians, Dutch and others, had been "exhausted" by democracy. That isn't too far from the truth: democratic positions, as we now know, were seriously undermined throughout Europe as a result of the First World War and the Great Depression. This preordained the victory of the fascists and the Nazis in Italy and Germany.

One shouldn't forget that the younger Soviet generation supported the regime because it had allowed them to have educations and careers that before had been off-limits to them. They were fighting, if you will, for the Soviet Dream, for anyone having the chance to become, if not general secretary of the Communist Party, then at least a marshal or a people's commissar.

Who was the backbone of the Resistance in France? Supporters of de Gaulle and the communists. De Gaulle could not be called a consistent democrat. In his youth he was, after all, close to the right-wing thinker Charles Maurras.

The countries that conducted a real underground partisan battle and put up a genuinely fierce resistance to the Germans were ones that had not been especially democratic before Nazism: Poland, Yugoslavia, Albania and Greece. Resistance leaders in these countries, such as Josip Tito and Enver Hoxha, could hardly be called democrats.

Indeed, only a small group of countries were then democracies, and far from contemporary notions of what a true democracy should be. Think of segregation in the United States; think of the state of human rights in British, French and other European colonies. In Eastern Europe there was real democracy only in Czechoslovakia: in Poland you had the Sanacja regime; in Lithuania Smetona's dictatorship; in Latvia Ulmanis's dictatorship; in Hungary you had the dictatorship of Horthy; and in Romania that of Antonescu.

Indeed, it's not a question of the moods of the warring countries, their citizens and leaders, or of their political systems: it's a question of the objective nature of a war which, from the point of view of the anti-Hitler coalition, was a war to preserve humanitarian and democratic values; a war for freedom in the highest sense of the word. This does not change the nature of the Soviet regime and its crimes, or the crimes of the English and the French in their colonies, or the discrimination against blacks and the lynch mobs in the US.

The question of what the communists were fighting for or, more broadly, the question of the values of communists in the USSR and in Europe is far more complex. The Russian Revolution was brought about by people who believed that the road they had chosen was the only possible road to a consistent democracy combining political and social freedoms.

During the Second World War those same people believed that they were fighting for their ideals. This is the fundamental difference between communism and fascism/Nazism, which in principle rejected democracy as an institution. One has only to compare the works of classic communists, from Marx to Lenin, with those of fascists/Nazis, such as Maurras, Mussolini, Hitler, et al.

It is not just the attitude toward democracy; it is the common spirit of universalism, humanism and cosmopolitanism that distinguished classic communism from the spirit of antihumanism and chauvinism in fascism. Despite all the transformations, Soviet communism in those years still reflected classic values.

However one feels about the Molotov-Ribbentrop Pact, it did not run counter to the logic of the behaviour of leading countries in Europe at the time toward fascist Germany. From Britain to Poland and from Norway to Greece, all were trying to come to an understanding with Hitler behind each other's backs and at each other's expense.

First, the socialists and liberals of France, conservatives and labourites in Britain, and their European colleagues betrayed the Spanish Republic led by fellow socialists and liberals by allowing it to be torn apart by German and Italian fascists.

Then England and France, along with Poland and Hungary, betrayed Czechoslovakia. And between these betrayals they closed their eyes to Hitler's annexation of Austria. What could the Soviet leadership expect from such players? Another betrayal.

When France and England (after Germany invaded Poland) declared war, they were "just pretending". Small wonder that this war came to be known as the phoney war. This, evidently, is what Stalin was afraid of when he concluded his pact with Hitler: in the West there would be a pretend war, but in the East there would be a real one.

To all appearances, Stalin foresaw an extended war in the West and did not want to be left alone with Hitler. A highly rational, if not always highly moral, foreign policy combined with a domestic policy that was irrational in its terrorism: that was the trademark Stalinist style.

If the irrational anti-Semitism of the Nazis can be attributed to centuries-old prejudices peculiar to all of Europe, then the Stalinist terror cannot be attributed to anything but fear: fear of the ruling classes of old Russia that had suffered defeat in the Civil War; fear of the enemies real and imagined in one's own party; fear of the anarchic element in the peasantry, and so on. These fears were in part justified, but they assumed a paranoid form.

Responding to criticisms that he and Khrushchev did not do enough to expose Stalin's crimes, former first deputy premier Anastas Mikoyan reportedly said: "We couldn't do that because then everyone would have known what scoundrels we were."

That, too, is the difference between communism and Nazism: the communist scoundrels understood who they were because they realised the gulf separating them from the ideals they revered; the Nazis liked being scoundrels—that was their ideal.

Many historians and politicians in the new countries that rose from the ruins of the Soviet Union justify the struggle of Ukrainian nationalists and Lithuanian guerrillas on two fronts during the Second World War (against the Nazis and the communists) by saying that neither side in this "clash of tyrants" was better than the other; that these members of small nations were simply fighting tyranny. This is disingenuous: similar formations fought on the side of the Nazis and only towards the end of the Third Reich did they attempt to feign resistance.

The Second World War was no ordinary war. It was possibly the only war in history that was fought against absolute evil, a fight that united idealists defending their ideals, cynics defending their interests, and even scoundrels trying to incinerate their sins in the flames of a great struggle.

Together, they were all, like all the people who fought in that war, defending their Motherland, their life and their home in the present and the future—freedom for themselves and all mankind.

Stalin Denounced by Nikita Khrushchev[*]

February 25, 1956

History Today, February 2006

The Twentieth Congress of the Communist Party of the Soviet Union assembled in Moscow in the Great Hall of the Kremlin on February 14th, 1956. It was the first since the death of Josef Stalin in 1953, but almost nothing was said about the dead leader until, in closed session on the 25th, 1,500 delegates and many invited visitors listened to an amazing speech by Nikita Khrushchev, First Secretary of the party, on "The Personality Cult and its Consequences".

Khrushchev denounced Stalin, the cult of personality he had fostered and the crimes he had perpetrated, including the execution, torture and imprisonment of loyal party members on false charges. He blamed Stalin for foreign policy errors, for the failings of Soviet agriculture, for ordering mass terror and for mistakes that had led to appalling loss of life in the Second World War and the German occupation of huge areas of Soviet territory.

Khrushchev's audience heard him in almost complete silence, broken only by astonished murmurs. The delegates did not dare even to look at each other as the party secretary piled one horrifying accusation on another for four solid hours. At the end there was no applause and the audience left in a state of shock.

One of those who heard the speech was the young Alexander Yakovlev, later a leading architect of perestroika, who recalled that it shook him to his roots. He sensed Khrushchev was telling the truth, but it was a truth that frightened him. Generations in the Soviet Union had revered Stalin and linked their lives and hopes with him. Now the past was being shattered and what they had all lived by was being destroyed. 'Everything crumbled, never to be made whole again.'

It was an extraordinarily dangerous and daring thing for Khrushchev to do. Solzhenitsyn believed that he spoke out of 'a movement of the heart', a genuine impulse to do good. Others have pointed out, more cynically, that it tarred other party leaders with the Stalinist brush, to the ostentatiously repentant Khrushchev's advantage. It deflected blame from the party and the system on to Stalin's shoulders. A few months later it was announced that the congress had called for measures 'for removing wholly and entirely the cult of the individual, foreign to Marxism-Leninism . . . in every aspect of party, governmental and ideological activity.'

The speech was reported in the foreign media the next day. In March the Central Committee had the text distributed to the party branches, where it was read out. Inside the Soviet Union it would help to create greater freedom, in time. Plenty of Stalinist henchmen and functionaries were still determined to resist de-Stalinization, but thousands of political prisoners were released and others posthumously rehabilitated. Abroad, Khrushchev's words cut the ground from under the feet of Communist party members and left-wing intellectuals who had spent years denying reports of what was going on in the Soviet Union. Many party members left in disgust.

At the party congress in 1961 Khruschev repeated his attack on Stalin's memory, this time in open session, and other speakers denounced Stalin's crimes. The late leader's body was removed from its place alongside Lenin in the mausoleum in Red Square, and the names of Stalingrad and other such places were changed. When Khrushchev fell from power in 1964, he became an un-person, but was not executed, imprisoned or even banished to Mongolia. The Soviet Union had changed.

When the Cold War Almost Turned Hot[*]

By Albin F. Irzyk
Army Magazine, July 2004

Many words have been written, documentaries produced and books published about the Cuban Missile Crisis of October 1962. Yet an extremely dangerous situation not nearly as well known but of critical import prevailed not in Cuba, but in Europe a year earlier, in 1961. As in 1962, a direct and troubling face-off occurred between the United States and the Soviet Union. It became known as the Berlin Crisis. That situation came to a head and reached a crisis point in August of that year. It became by far the tensest period of the Cold War up until then. The Russians and Americans could have come as close to World War III as they did a year later. Despite the seriousness of the situation, relatively little is known about the details of that historic episode, and comparatively speaking, little has been written about it.

Before discussing that troubling and dangerous situation, some background information is appropriate. Early in the month of August, as it had for more than a decade, my command, the 14th Armored Cavalry Regiment, was broadly deployed along the East-West German border, better known as the Iron Curtain. The 14th was a light, fast, mobile armored force of more than 4,500 men that was a combined arms team. It was equipped with tanks, jeeps, mortars, helicopters and fixed-wing aircraft. Its regimental headquarters was located at Fulda, little more than eight miles from the border and about 60 miles northeast of Frankfurt. Elements of the regiment were spread widely along the border with a squadron to the north, one in the center and another to the south, and an attached squadron even further to the south.

The 14th shouldered tremendous responsibilities, for the missions assigned to it were critically important. The regiment had two main missions. First, it was responsible for conducting ground and aerial surveillance of more than 165 miles of that border—the Iron Curtain. Second, it was the NATO trip wire.

---

* Published by the U.S. Department of Defense.

The border over which we had to conduct surveillance separated the west from the east—U.S. troops from those of the Soviet Union. The border markings consisted of small stones imbedded in the ground that went north and south in a very irregular pattern. Since they lay along open terrain, through woods, gullies and ridges, they were difficult to follow and identify. To make the border more distinctive, more readily recognized, prominent five-foot-high, red-topped white wooden poles were installed.

For the Soviets the purpose of the border was not only to separate us from them, but by erecting an impenetrable barrier it also would prevent East Germans from fleeing to the West for sanctuary. (Over the years, many East Germans were killed or captured attempting to penetrate that barrier.) There were several elements to the barrier located just inside the East zone. The Soviets installed observation towers at strategic locations that were always manned and included automatic weapons capable of producing deadly and withering fire along the border to the north and south of the towers. In addition, they installed a steel mesh fence (iron curtain), barbed wire, mines and mortars, and maintained a regularly ploughed strip about five-meters wide (ostensibly to show footprints if East Germans had attempted to flee). For the Soviets, it was a protective barrier from both the West and East.

We performed our surveillance missions on the ground with jeep patrols and in the air with helicopters and fixed-wing aircraft. The jeep patrols rode the border day and night, during all types of weather—rain, sleet, bitter freezing winter days, hot stifling summer days. Sundays, Thanksgiving and Christmas were merely duty days.

Because many places along the border were inaccessible to jeeps, troopers frequently had to dismount and walk or crawl to appropriate vantage points. It was here that large numbers of U.S. and Soviet soldiers were lined up close to one another, literally face-to-face. It was not unusual to find a trooper peering out, only to find opposite him a Russian peering in.

Augmenting the jeep patrols, observation posts were also used for border surveillance. These were placed at strategic locations that provided a particularly good look into the east and were well concealed. Such outposts were often manned for some hours and provided an opportunity for more lengthy and detailed observation. Both the jeep patrols and the placement of observation posts had an irregular pattern and any kind of set schedule or routine was avoided. The responsibilities of the troopers of the 14th were demanding, dangerous, critical and sensitive. Their operations were as close as one could get to combat without actually being in it.

One permanent observation post was established early on and remained in place until the end of border duty. It would be known as O.P. Alpha (Observation Post Alpha). It provided the best and most breathtaking view of the Fulda Gap. From O.P. Alpha one could look for miles in all directions, particularly to the hills and mountains to the east, but most impressively one almost believed that if he reached down he could touch the broad, beautiful valley that flowed from the east right into the center of the 14th's positions.

The eyes that penetrated most deeply into the Soviet sector were located in the helicopters and fixed-wing aircraft that flew the border. Only inclement weather coming from the hills and mountains to the east prevented daily aerial patrols. Those were conducted by extremely skilled pilots. The border was difficult to follow as it zigzagged through all types of terrain, often with sharp deviations. Because of this challenge, before they were cleared to fly the border, pilots had to complete a thorough and detailed period of instruction and orientation. They flew the border time and time again, accompanied by an instructor, before they were permitted to fly it alone. The pilots fully realized that if they strayed across the border to the east side, they could receive hostile fire and create an international incident. Each helicopter and plane flew with an observer. As the pilot kept his eyes intently on the course he was flying, the observer's eyes stared widely and deeply to the east. The purpose of the ground and aerial patrols was to detect any unusual movement or activity across the border and to note any suspicious physical changes that had been made.

For the 14th Armored Cavalry Regiment to be called the NATO trip wire was not hyperbole but a truism. The regiment's mission placed it firmly and directly astride the famous, fabled, historic Fulda Gap. It was at this point that the East butted farthest into West Germany. This was the ancient invasion corridor which had served as the strategic East-West passage for six centuries. In 1961 it was still the likely invasion route into Western Europe for Soviet Bloc forces. This is the frontier where it would happen. The Fulda Gap is a series of river valleys running north and south with distinct hill masses and several open passes running through the hills that create the Gap and that wind like a huge serpent, twisting here and there to avoid rivers and forests. The gap broadens into an exceedingly wide ten-mile-long valley north of a town called Rasdorf. This valley is capable of accommodating vast numbers of mechanized and motorized vehicles. Dominant hills—known as the Three Sisters—create a natural line of defense. From O.P. Alpha near Rasdorf, the panorama that unfolds is truly spectacular.

The troopers of the 14th had no illusions about the criticality and importance of their trip-wire mission and its ramifications. Every man in the regiment was fully aware that if the Soviets decided to attack and send their hordes across the border, we would be the first of the U.S. and Allied forces to be fired upon—thus, the trip wire. It would immediately signal to the United States and the world that the West and East were at war.

Because ours was a small and relatively light force, it was a foregone conclusion that we had absolutely no chance of stopping such an onslaught and would rapidly be overrun. Realistically, our mission was to delay their advance and gain time by fighting fiercely, imaginatively, courageously—even to the last man. By slowing the enemy and gaining time, it would enable heavier forces behind us, the first of which was the 3rd Armored Division, to close up, pick up and join in the fight.

At that time Gen. Lauris Norstad, commander of NATO forces, had under his command 22 divisions with several that were badly understrength. Conversely, the Russians had a massive ground force. According to NATO intelligence estimates, the Soviet Bloc could field 60 powerful divisions almost immediately and 130 within a month. That is an absolutely staggering statistic. Thus, at least on paper, it would have been no contest.

To prepare for the eventuality and execution of our mission, we at the 14th had painstakingly examined, over a period of time, virtually every foot of terrain along and behind the border. From such extensive reconnaissance efforts we selected the absolutely best defensive positions, designated specific units that would occupy and fight from those positions and determined the fastest, quickest and best routes to them. As part of their training, units moved frequently to their positions until every man was as familiar with them as with the back of his hand.

A real test occurred once a month. We were alerted by 7th Army Headquarters to move to our tactical positions with a simple call to the regimental duty officer. The alert would come on any day of the month and at any hour—day or night. The most demanding test came when the alert was called during the early hours of the night—1:00 A.M. to 2:00 A.M. Upon receiving the call, the duty officer had to get the word immediately to the far-flung squadrons and separate companies and receive an acknowledgment. At every location, lights went on, alarms sounded, troopers were routed out of beds in barracks, homes and apartments. There was furious and frenzied activity. Every individual, wherever located, would immediately dress in his combat gear, which was always ready. Troopers on foot at a gallop or in cars would race to the motor pools. In no time engines were running and gear was being stowed. Each unit reported to regiment when it was assembled and moving to its positions. It reported again when it was fully deployed and occupying those positions. The moment the last unit was in place, the regiment notified 7th Army. That headquarters timed the exercise from the moment the regimental duty officer had acknowledged the call until the final regimental report was received. That concluded the alert.

Those monthly alerts were realistic, superb exercises and tests. During each alert, the regiment tried to improve on its previous times, always hoping to set a new record. This self-imposed competition contributed greatly to constantly maintaining its fighting edge.

Regardless of whether it was day or night in cities such as Fulda, Bad Hersfeld or Bad Kissingen, the windows of German homes would be wide open and its occupants would be leaning out of those windows, as the tanks, jeeps and mortars raced to their defensive positions and again when the troops returned.

Dependents—wives and children—were very much a part of the regiment. Because they lived in such close proximity to the border, they were every bit as much at risk as their soldier husbands and fathers. Plans and procedures for them were in effect in case they had to flee on short notice. Every family had to have its survival provisions ready. These consisted of footlockers in basements containing food, liquids, clothing, medicine, flashlights and sanitary products—items essential to survive for a time in the event they were hastily displaced. Randomly, regimental military personnel inspected homes to ensure that their evacuation stores were ready and adequate for that family. Automobiles were required to always have their gas tanks at least half full. Plans for the evacuation of noncombatants were kept up-to-date and were occasionally rehearsed. All dependents knew how and where to go. The wives were jocularly referred to as the "border belles."

Because of the criticality and sensitivity of the role the 14th was performing, members of the regiment had an unusual and heightened interest and awareness of national and international events. By August the troopers of the 14th were well aware that 1961 had already been a very eventful year and had all the earmarks of becoming even more eventful. On January 20, a young John F. Kennedy was inaugurated as our 35th President. He quickly received his baptism of fire as our Commander in Chief. On April 19, the ill-fated, disastrous operation known as the Bay of Pigs occurred. Shortly after that, the President manfully took personal responsibility for the abortive invasion of Cuba.

In early June, he had his first big test on the world's diplomatic stage in Vienna. He met face-to-face with America's prime Cold War adversary, Nikita Khrushchev. On June 3 at the American Embassy, and extending into June 4 at the Soviet Embassy, over two lunches, the two leaders had 11 hours of what turned out to be a contentious, bitter, verbal duel.

Khrushchev had been pictured in American newspaper stories as colorful, impetuous, unpredictable—even irrational—a kind of buffoon. Kennedy quickly found such a characterization extremely faulty. What Kennedy confronted was instead, an impressive, formidable adversary not to be trifled with. This Soviet leader was extremely well-informed, had a broad and deep knowledge of history and was a skilled debater who could thrust forth with telling points and present logical and powerful arguments.

For Kennedy, discussions with that man were the "hardest work in the world." Try as hard as he might, Kennedy just could not find an "area of accommodation." At one point during the discussions, Khrushchev leaned hard on Kennedy, declared that he had decided to sign a peace treaty with East Germany by December and stated that his decision was firm and absolutely irrevocable. (So much for accommodation.) To that declaration Kennedy responded "If that is true, it is going to be a cold winter."

As their meeting was drawing to a close, the subject discussed was Berlin and the words about it were dark and bleak. The atmosphere during those closing moments was gloomy, depressing and discouraging. What troubled Kennedy greatly was the realization that Khrushchev really meant what he said when he had boasted that he intended to bury us.

As the two antagonists walked from their meeting to the front door of the embassy, they did not speak. The atmosphere was frigid. There were no smiles, back slapping or hearty handshakes. Their final act together was just that—an act, a brief pause for a hasty photograph and an equally hasty and perfunctory handshake.

Kennedy without a doubt was greatly depressed by his first encounter with the enigmatic Khrushchev, and because of the Soviet leader's uncompromising attitude, Kennedy believed that U.S. and Soviet relations were profoundly grave. There were indications that Khrushchev left Vienna still believing that Kennedy was weak and inexperienced.

Subsequent to the Vienna meeting, the Soviet leader continued to maintain his very belligerent posture. Later in June, Kennedy also flexed his muscles by rejecting some demands made by Khrushchev. A noticeable hardening of the Soviet line continued into early July. On July 8 the Soviet leader suspended planned troop reductions.

By July 25 the Berlin situation had grown to such proportions and intensity that President Kennedy decided that he had to talk to the American people once again. That evening at 10 P.M. he addressed the nation and stressed the need for partial mobilization and psychological preparation for a Berlin showdown. He asked Congress for an additional $3.25 billion of appropriations for the current fiscal year for the armed forces and an increase in the Army's total strength from 875,000 to approximately one million. He declared, "We are clear about what must be done—and we intend to do it." He continued by adding, "I hear it said that West Berlin is militarily untenable. And so was Bastogne. And so, in fact, was Stalingrad. Any dangerous spot is tenable, if men—brave men—will make it so."

He closed by saying, "We have previously indicated our readiness to remove any actual irritant in West Berlin, but freedom of that city is not negotiable. . . . The world is not deceived by the communist attempt to label Berlin as a hotbed of war . . . We seek peace—but we shall not surrender."

As the days passed, the situation in Berlin grew from troublesome, to tense and then to chaotic. It was reported that the fear of their future had 1,500 East Germans a day fleeing across the border with another 1,000 being pulled off commuter trains and jailed by communist police. John J. McCloy, Kennedy's disarmament advisor, returned to the United States from a meeting with Khrushchev, reported that the Soviet leader was in a totally belligerent mood and seemed absolutely intent on extracting what he called the "rotten tooth" of Berlin.

Fear that the East Germans would close the Berlin border caused immense consternation; the escapees became a flood, and then it happened. On Sunday, August 13, East German communist leader Walter Ulbricht began building a wall along the border. Work on this grotesque, incongruous enterprise began at 2 A.M. Large numbers of cargo trucks dumped every imaginable item that could form a barrier—concrete pillars, stone blocks, barbed wire-and the tools, picks and shovels to install them. By dawn the city was scarred and seared by a truly ugly wall that had seemed to erupt instantly out of nowhere.

It was not too many hours later, before noon, that I received information that East Germans were at work in East Berlin just inside their border constructing a barrier that would soon be recognized worldwide as the Berlin Wall.

To us on the border, that was a totally unexpected, incredible development, and we instantly recognized that the actions in Berlin were presenting an uncertain, critical and potentially explosive situation. I immediately dispatched the information to all elements of the regiment.

I instructed all commanders to be prepared on a moment's notice to drop whatever was on their schedules and on my order to move without delay to their deployment positions. My immediate and great concern and my big question was—what action would our forces in Berlin take to try to stop or dismantle the construction? Such a confrontation, without question, could easily lead to very serious consequences. We at the regiment began holding our breaths waiting for an answer to our question. The answer was not long in coming, and that answer was—nothing.

The American response was silence. It appeared that no one in Washington provided advice or suggested any immediate action or move. Even West Berlin Mayor Willy Brandt had no idea what to do right then. Military commanders never seriously considered knocking down the wall. They were well aware that it was being installed on rightful communist territory, which they legally occupied, and that if we moved against the wall, we would be invading that territory and inviting serious trouble. It presented a real political and military dilemma. We soon learned that President Kennedy finally decided that our nation would do nothing about the wall.

We on the border were left hanging. We were convinced that the situation was anything but over, and we believed instinctively that something more was going to happen, so we went about our tasks with a most uneasy feeling, still holding our breath and waiting for the shoe that would surely drop. We, of course, had been fully aware that tensions had been progressively building since Khrushchev and Kennedy had met in Vienna. The recent actions in Berlin had greatly exacerbated those tensions. We remained in an animated state for about three days and then I received the startling information from a staff officer at corps headquarters that a belligerent Khrushchev was threatening to close U.S. ground access to Berlin. If this threat were carried out, it would be a momentous, earthshaking development. The only way U.S. ground elements could move from West Germany through East Germany to Berlin was through an established, single 110-mile corridor. That passage was the Helmstedt-Berlin Autobahn. Helmstedt, the jumping-off place, sat on the border separating the British zone from the Soviet zone. It was located between two large cities—Braunschweig to the northwest in the British zone and Magdeburg to the southeast in the Soviet zone. With passage along this axis closed, the United States would be left with but two choices, both of which were dangerous and potentially cataclysmic: to use military muscle to try to force open the passage or, in order to avoid such a major confrontation, to be reconciled to initiating an airlift as Truman had in 1948–49.

With that news it appeared that the shoe had, indeed, dropped. I spent only a moment speculating. My wartime Army commander, Gen. George S. Patton Jr., had preached, "Do something, now!" Without hesitation I ordered the elements of my regiment to move at once to their operational positions. As our vehicles moved through the streets of the German cities, the inhabitants, as always, were hanging out of their windows. This time their faces showed puzzlement, anxiety and even fear. Somehow, intuitively, they recognized that this was not a normal alert, that something important was afoot. Before we departed, our families were also alerted to be ready in the event we were forced to implement the plan for the evacuation of noncombatants.

I reported to corps headquarters that my regiment had moved and was in its forward positions. I quickly learned that with tension there had also been some confusion. I was now informed that Khrushchev had not made an overt threat to close the Helmstedt-Berlin corridor and that thus far there had been no interference with access. A moment later, however, I learned that I had made the right call. I was provided with surprising and astonishing news—the kind that is totally unexpected. President Kennedy had made a critical decision, but one fraught with danger. He had decided that he would send a U.S. battle group, consisting of about 1,500 American soldiers, to Berlin along the Helmstedt-Berlin Autobahn.

It appears that the President had grown weary of Khrushchev's belligerency and bombast. In a sense he would be calling Khrushchev's hand. He was completely within his rights. With the wall going up and with the residents of Berlin living in an intensified atmosphere of uncertainty and fear, he was ready to demonstrate dramatically that there were rights that he considered basic to Berlin; access from West Germany to the city was vital, and under no circumstances would those rights be given up or stolen away.

Kennedy was well aware that this would be a real test of communist threats, and specifically, a head-on test of the crucial rights of access. Such a deliberate move, he recognized, [could] be viewed at least as an unnecessary irritant, or more important, as a veiled threat. He was under no illusions. He knew that if our troops were halted or interfered with, it meant that the absolute and sacred right of access was being denied to us and shooting could be the result.

From then on, because of the vital and critical importance of our mission, I began to receive regular reports from higher headquarters, which enabled me to be on top of the news as it was breaking. I soon learned that because troops in the forward positions and already facing the communists could not be spared, the troops selected for the Berlin mission were those stationed in the western part of the U.S. zone. Making the journey would be the 1,500 men of the 1st Battle Group, 18th Infantry of the 8th Infantry Division stationed in Mannheim. That city was nearly 400 miles away from the entry point at Helmstedt. The unit, however, was right on an autobahn, would be able to move out immediately and could ride an autobahn all the way to Helmstedt. On Friday, August 18, we were notified that Gen. Bruce C. Clarke, commander of U.S. Army troops in Europe, had selected Col. Glover S. Johns Jr. to lead the American battle group along that 110 miles of communist territory between West Germany and West Berlin. Col. Johns was selected, undoubtedly, because he had a fine record as a field commander during World War II. He was the author of a book, *The Clay Pigeons of St. Lô*, about his experiences. He seemed an excellent choice to lead such a sensitive expedition.

Now the only question that remained was—when? It was not long before we began receiving the answer to that question. We learned that Col. Johns received verbal orders late on Friday evening. By 5:30 A.M. on Saturday morning, his troops had received an orientation about the mission, had been fed breakfast and were ready to roll the 400 miles of their approach march. Gen. Clarke was on hand as the force moved out. He sent Lt. Gen. Frederic J. Brown, V Corps and my direct commander, to Helmstedt in his command train, which was fitted with the latest communications equipment and would enable Gen. Brown to send periodic reports about the moving column. The march to the jumping-off point was long and time-consuming. By this operation the United States was telegraphing its next move. This gave the Russians considerable time to chew on it, and if they were contemplating some kind of action, this surely provided a tempting challenge for them. If they waited and did nothing as the battle group moved from Mannhein to Helmstedt, that would surely be a good omen. Initial concerns were ultimately allayed, for the battle group reached Helmstedt without incident and bivouacked for the night at an airfield.

Everything was now on a hair-trigger alert. Clarke could communicate with Norstad in an instant if he needed a response from him or the President. All forces in Europe had been alerted and instructions issued to them. Norstad was prepared to implement plans for air and ground support regardless of how limited or extensive.

Then came the news that brought goose pimples and butterflies in our stomachs. The battle group would kick off at 6:00 A.M., Sunday, August 20, for the 110-mile test ride to Berlin.

On the border, in our deployed positions, tension that had been increasing by the hour now reached an unbelievable pitch. It became so tight and crisp that it virtually crackled. We were holding our breaths. It was not inconceivable that we might soon be in a firefight, so we were leaning well forward in our foxholes. We tried to visualize the possibilities and probabilities. The convoy could proceed to Berlin without any attempt to stop it. The convoy could be stopped by a physical roadblock covered by military troops and ordered to return to the west, or it could be fired upon by Russian forces, perhaps including tanks. If either of these two provocations occurred, what would be the actions of the U.S. forces? What orders had Col. Johns received from the President? If he had been told that his mission was to get to West Berlin and to shoot it out if necessary, World War III could well be hanging in the balance. If U.S. forces returned the fire, the Russians, with massive troops nearby and at the ready, could escalate the situation by moving to the west in strength.

We learned later that President Kennedy and his immediate staff were even more concerned than we were, if that was possible. It was said that back at the White House "tension hung in the corridors like a ground mist before sunup." One member of that staff later declared, "It was a much greater crisis than people know. Talking to President Kennedy then was like talking to a statue." There was a feeling there, as on the border, that the mission could escalate into shooting. An advisor declared, "If a single day can be pointed to when the President felt the nation was entering the danger zone, it is August 20 when the troops raced those 110 miles into West Berlin." It was Kennedy's most anxious moment during the prolonged Berlin Crisis.

The first news was good news. We learned that the lead elements left Helmstedt and moved out onto the autobahn without incident heading for the Berlin Gate. Unit after unit followed unhampered. We received periodic reports that all was well, and as they ate up the miles without incident, tension eased immeasurably. Then came the electrifying news that we had breathlessly awaited. The lead elements had just entered West Berlin.

We learned somewhat later that the operation had been carefully planned, scheduled and timed so that Vice President Lyndon B. Johnson and Gen. Lucius D. Clay, President Kennedy's direct representatives, would be on hand to show the flag to the Berliners, to greet Col. Johns and his troops and to remain until every man had moved safely into West Berlin. For Vice President Johnson it was a momentous day as thousands upon thousands of West Berliners greeted him and the U.S. battle group. Johnson cried out, "This is the time for confidence, for poise and for faith—faith in ourselves. It is also a time for faith in your Allies, everywhere throughout the world. This island does not stand alone." President Kennedy had graphically and decisively accomplished his mission of raising the spirits of the residents of Berlin and had brought them reassurance, confidence, optimism and even great excitement. Most important, he had courageously showed Khrushchev the hand that he was playing.

The world heaved a great sigh of relief. On the border, when the 14th Armored Cavalry Regiment received the news that it was all over, there was a collective gush of breath; it was as though the helium escaped simultaneously from a thousand balloons. We were like the rubber band that had snapped and was lying wrinkled and listless. The tension that had been so tight for so long had in an instant completely vanished. We were literally weak with relief.

A now unfettered, jubilant but whipped and completely wrung-out group of 14th Armored Cavalry Regiment troopers disengaged from their forward positions and in record time were heading back home. An unbelievable week with endless possibilities, many of them truly alarming, ended on an absolutely upbeat note. As always, the Germans were hanging out of their windows, but this time they cheered the returning warriors. They were keenly aware of the tense situation that had prevailed to the east and knew full well that they had been very vulnerable and that had events taken a different course, they, too, would have had to contend with the boots, wheels and tracks of Soviet hordes.

Fortunately, that would never happen.

Saving Russia's Armpit[*]

By Anne Applebaum
Slate Magazine, August 20, 2001

As one might have expected, the 10th anniversary of the Communist coup against Mikhail Gorbachev—whose defeat led directly to the breakup of the Soviet Union—is being marked, in the West, by a mixed bag of intelligent comments, where-are-they-now articles, and the odd spot of dramatic TV footage. Rather than joining this onslaught of theoretical journalism, I suggest, instead, that it might be worth sparing a moment for Vorkuta, where I recently happened to be. Vorkuta is a city built beside a coal mine, north of the Arctic Circle, in barely habitable, treeless tundra. Vorkuta is also the Soviet Union in miniature. Objectively speaking, it's an awful place, but people lived in it, people got used to it—and now they don't want it to change.

Untypically, on the day I arrived in Vorkuta, the temperature was climbing into the 70s. The week before, I was told, it had been near freezing—and not long after I left, it dropped again. There are years when the Arctic summer lasts two weeks, and years when it lasts six weeks. In that short period of time, the city's 200,000 inhabitants are to be found strolling the streets of their city, basking in its perpetual daylight: This is the reward they get for living the other half of the year in perpetual darkness.

True, they can't stroll very far: Vorkuta is built upon permafrost, which in summer turns into a virtually impassable, mosquito-infested swamp. Nor can they drive anywhere, since Vorkuta and its famous coal mines are not accessible by car: One gets there by train (very crowded) or by plane (very expensive). Nor even, one would imagine, ought the inhabitants of the city to get much pleasure out of contemplating its architecture—let alone its history. Vorkuta's first 23 settlers arrived in 1931, via the waterways that run from the Arctic Sea, bringing their wooden picks and shovels with them. This being Stalin's Soviet Union, these 23 original settlers, were, of course, prisoners, and their leaders were, of course, secret policemen. Over the subsequent two and a half decades, a million more prisoners passed through the city's coal fields, one of the two or three most notorious hubs of the gulag, the vast labor camp system that once stretched from the Soviet-Finnish border to the Pacific Ocean.

And yet—*"Kak vam nravitsa nasha Vorkuta?"* I was constantly asked while I was there: "How do you like our Vorkuta?" It is hard to imagine the contemporary inhabitants of Auschwitz asking visitors to share their civic pride, but those who live in Vorkuta do expect praise for their sprawling city. For Vorkuta was not shut down when Stalin died. On the contrary, throughout the 1960s and '70s, the Soviet authorities built shops and swimming pools and schools, the better to attract inhabitants. They flattered and feted the city's highly paid miners, telling them they were Soviet heroes of labor. As a result, the city's inhabitants believed themselves to be patriots, willingly enduring the harsh Arctic conditions in order that the Motherland might have coal. That the price of heating shoddy Soviet apartment blocks for 11 months of the year is astronomical, that the coal from the mines was worth less than the cost of maintaining the buildings and the street, none of that was ever taken into consideration.

Alas, the truth is that Vorkuta, is—and always was—utterly unnecessary. The miners could have been flown in and out on two-week shifts, as they are in Canada or Alaska, spending half their time with their families in the south. Why build kindergartens and university lecture halls in the tundra? Why build a puppet theater? Once constructed, however, such institutions aren't so easy to dismantle, particularly given the rhetoric that was lavished upon them. In the company of the daughter of former prisoners, I walked around the ruins of the city's geological institute—a once-solid structure, complete with a columned, Stalinist portico, a red star on its pediment—and listened to her rail against the "thief-democrats" and "greedy bureaucrats" who had, rather sensibly, decided to shut the institute down. If your whole life has been associated with a place, even a place widely famed for atrocity and stupidity, it is hard to admit that it ought to be shut down.

Although they don't quite come out and say it, the bureaucrats in the regional capital, Syktyvkar, know this perfectly well. "Vorkuta will always exist," one of them told me: "Forever!" He banged his fist, a touch over-dramatically, on the table. Then he proceeded, more rationally, to agree that it might have been wiser to adopt a different system of exploiting the coal. He also explained that the Russian government is in fact trying to persuade people, especially pensioners and couples with young children, to leave the city, the better to reduce its size and the expense of maintaining it. There is, he told me, a pattern. First, those willing to move are offered flats in more southerly parts of the country. Then, they are helped to move.

But then—they come back. In fact, he said, the majority come back. Whether unable to find jobs, unable to make friends, or unable to tear themselves away from a place that was once so widely praised and celebrated—they come back. In Vorkuta, a young woman with two small children—a classic candidate for resettlement, and herself the granddaughter of prisoners—told me with wide eyes how much she loves her city. "I have been other places, but nowhere else is as good as our Vorkuta." She showed me the ordinary violets she cultivates in summer—inside, in plastic pots—because nothing but weedy wildflowers grow in the courtyard of her falling-down block of flats during the short Arctic summer.

Of all the obstacles confronting those economists and politicians who would sincerely like to reform Russia, none is more formidable than this: the power of habit. Vorkuta, like the Soviet Union, ought never to have been built in the first place. It required slave labor to construct and an enormous propaganda machine to maintain. From a purely economic and practical point of view, it ought to be dismantled. But it will take more than 10 years—more than a generation—to accustom its inhabitants to something else.

Death of a Writer[*]

By Anne Applebaum
Slate Magazine, August 4, 2008

Although more than three decades have now passed since the winter of 1974, when unbound, hand-typed, samizdat manuscripts of Alexander Solzhenitsyn's *Gulag Archipelago* first began circulating around what used to be the Soviet Union, the emotions they stirred remain today. Usually, readers were given only 24 hours to finish the lengthy manuscript—the first historical account of the Soviet concentration camp system—before it had to be passed on to the next person. That meant spending an entire day and a whole night absorbed in Solzhenitsyn's sometimes eloquent, sometimes angry prose—not an experience anyone was likely to forget.

Members of that first generation of readers remember who gave the book to them, who else knew about it, and to whom they passed it on. They remember the stories that affected them most—the tales of small children in the camps, or of informers, or of camp guards. They remember what the book felt like—the blurry, mimeographed text, the dog-eared paper, the dim glow of the lamp switched on late at night—and with whom they later discussed it.

In part, his Soviet readers responded so strongly because Solzhenitsyn—who died on Sunday at 89—was simultaneously very famous and strictly taboo. Twelve years earlier, the Soviet regime had serendipitously allowed him to publish, officially, the first fictional account of Stalin's concentration camps—*A Day in the Life of Ivan Denisovich*. It was also the last: Too honest for the Soviet Union's leaders at the time, the book, though a publishing sensation, was quickly banned along with its author, whose later works would be "published" illegally—or abroad.

It didn't matter: Even Solzhenitsyn's expulsion from Russia in 1974 only increased his notoriety as well as the impact of *The Gulag Archipelago*. That book, though based on the "reports, memoirs, and letters by 227 witnesses," was not quite a straight history—obviously, Solzhenitsyn did not have access to then-secret archives—but, rather, an interpretation of history. Partly polemical, partly auto-biographical, emotional and judgmental, it aimed to show that, contrary to what many believed, the mass arrests and concentration camps of the Soviet Union were not an incidental phenomenon but an essential part of the Soviet system—and that they had been from the very beginning.

Not all of this story was new: Credible witnesses had begun reporting on the growth of the gulag and the spread of the terror from the time of the Russian revolution. But what Solzhenitsyn produced was simply more thorough, more monumental, and more detailed than anything that had been produced previously. It could not be ignored or dismissed as a single man's experience. As a result, no one who dealt with the Soviet Union, diplomatically or intellectually, could ignore it. So threatening was the book to certain branches of the European left that Jean-Paul Sartre described Solzhenitsyn as a "dangerous element." The book's publication certainly contributed to the recognition of human rights as a legitimate element of international debate and foreign policy.

In later years, Solzhenitsyn lost some of his stature, thanks partly to Soviet propaganda that successfully portrayed him as a crank and an extremist, but thanks also to his own failure to embrace liberal democracy. He never really liked the West, never really took to free markets or pop culture. When the Soviet Union finally collapsed in 1991, he went back to Russia, where he was first welcomed and then forgotten. In a Russia that is no longer interested in examining its history, he came to seem outdated, a spokesman from an irrelevant past. Even his Russian nationalism, now a popular cause, had something crusty and old-fashioned about it. His vision of a more spiritual society, of Russia as an alternative to the consumerist West, doesn't hold much appeal for the supercharged, superwealthy, oil-fueled Russian elite of today. His apparent endorsement of ex-President Vladimir Putin seemed more like an old man's foible than a serious change of heart.

In the week of his death, though, what stands out is not who Solzhenitsyn was, but what he wrote. It is very easy, in a world where news is instant and photographs travel as quickly as they are taken, to forget how powerful, still, written words are. And Solzhenitsyn was, in the end, a writer. A man who gathered facts, sorted through them, tested them against his own experience, composed them into paragraphs and chapters. It was not his personality, but his written language that forced people to think more deeply about their values, their assumptions, their societies. It was not his TV appearances that affected history—it was his written words.

His manuscripts were read and pondered in silence, and the thought he put into them provoked his readers to think, too. In the end, his books mattered not because he was famous—or notorious—but because millions of Soviet citizens recognized themselves in his work. They read his books because they already knew that they were true.

When Gorbachev Took Charge[*]

By Archie Brown
International Herald Tribune, March 11, 2010

When the Soviet leader Konstantin Chernenko died on the evening of March 10, 1985, and Mikhail Gorbachev was elected by the Communist Party's Central Committee as its general secretary less than 24 hours later, few realized that this presaged serious reform.

And no one, including Mr. Gorbachev himself, realized just how far that reform—known as perestroika (reconstruction)—would go and what would be its consequences.

Yet the choice of Mr. Gorbachev 25 years ago was of decisive importance. We know the views of every other member of the Politburo at the time of Chernenko's death—from their memoirs, interviews and the official archives—and not one of them would have undertaken radical reform of the Communist system or transformed Soviet foreign policy in anything like the way Mr. Gorbachev did.

There was no shortage of pundits in 1985 ready to declare that since no reformer could ever reach the top of the political ladder in the Soviet Union, it would be foolish to expect other than cosmetic change from Mr. Gorbachev. International relations specialists, including ex-foreign ministers, lined up to say that Andrei Gromyko would still be running Soviet foreign policy, so we could expect no change there.

Mr. Gorbachev had not been chosen because he was a reformer. Apart from a significant speech in December 1984, he had offered few clues to his Politburo colleagues as to how reformist he might be prepared to be. He had kept his more radical views to a very narrow circle.

Within it was Alexander Yakovlev, who at that time was about number 500 in the formal Soviet hierarchy. Such was the accelerated promotion Mr. Gorbachev gave him, by June 1987 he was in the top five. During those years Mr. Yakov-

* Permission granted by author. This work originally appeared in the *International Herald Tribune*, March 10, 2010. Archie Brown is Emeritus Professor of Politics at Oxford University, UK, and author of "The Rise and Fall of Communism", Ecco, New York, 2009.

lev was an influential ally in the radicalization of the Soviet reform agenda. Mr. Gorbachev's own ideas, given his institutional power, mattered even more. They underwent further speedy evolution while he held the highest office within the Soviet state.

Mr. Gorbachev was chosen by the Politburo, and endorsed by the Central Committee, for three main reasons. The first was that with Soviet leaders dying in quick succession, annual state funerals had become an embarrassment. Even within the aged oligarchy, some could see the need for a younger and more vigorous leader. Mr. Gorbachev, who had celebrated his 54th birthday just one week earlier, exuded mental and physical energy.

Second, although Mr. Gorbachev had enemies within the leadership, they did not have a plausible alternative candidate. Furthermore, Mr. Gorbachev was already the second secretary of the Central Committee and, given the hierarchical nature of the Soviet system, he was able to seize the initiative.

Later he was to be accused of indecisiveness, but there was nothing hesitant about his actions on the day Chernenko died. He convened and chaired a Politburo meeting that very evening and was appointed to head the funeral commission. When Leonid Brezhnev and Yuri Andropov died, that role had been allotted to the person who subsequently became general secretary. Thus, Mr. Gorbachev was preselected as party leader within hours of his predecessor's death.

The foreign policy change that followed was dramatic. Far from continuing to dominate Soviet foreign policy, Gromyko—who had been foreign minister since 1957—was moved from that office within four months of Mr. Gorbachev's accession and replaced by a neophyte in international affairs, Eduard Shevardnadze.

Within a year of becoming Soviet leader, Mr. Gorbachev had changed the entire top foreign policy team and had begun to implement what was called the New Thinking. It involved acceptance that real security meant mutual security and interdependence, agreement on arms reductions, withdrawal from Afghanistan (one of Mr. Gorbachev's aims from the outset, and fully realized by early 1989), and constructive engagement with the West. Ronald Reagan, who had not met any of Mr. Gorbachev's predecessors, had a summit meeting with Mr. Gorbachev in every year of his second term.

The most momentous change of Soviet foreign policy was the reversal of the Brezhnev doctrine, whereby the Soviet Union had arrogated to itself the right to intervene in any Warsaw Pact country in which Communist power appeared to be threatened.

In the summer of 1988 and at the United Nations in December of the same year, Mr. Gorbachev declared that the people of every country had the right to decide for themselves in what kind of system they wished to live. The huge implications for Eastern Europe, and the fact that Mr. Gorbachev meant what he said, were demonstrated in the course of 1989.

Domestically, growing freedom of speech and publication was accompanied by institutional reforms. The most remarkable manifestation of the former was the serialization in a major Soviet journal of Solzhenitsyn's "The Gulag Archipelago" in 1989. The most momentous example of the latter was the decision in 1988 to move to contested elections for a legislature with real power.

In March 1989 those elections—for the Congress of People's Deputies—were held. Although they were only semi-free, they marked a qualitative break with the past. Scores of millions of Soviet citizens were able to watch live television coverage of real debate during assembly proceedings, including criticism of the K.G.B. and the party leadership.

Those elections also, however, marked the beginning of the phase of perestroika when it ceased to be a revolution from above and became a movement from below that neither Mr. Gorbachev nor his increasingly agitated conservative Communist opponents could control. But it was the new tolerance, radical reform and changed international climate that had raised expectations that could not be satisfied.

Had any other member of the Politburo been chosen as leader in March 1985, the society would not have been politicized and revitalized. Highly authoritarian regimes, when prepared to use all the levers of coercion at their disposal, have ways other than liberalizing reform of staying in power.

4

After the Fall:
Post-Soviet Russia

Courtesy of the U.S. Department of Defense. Photo by SSGT. F. Lee Corkran

On November 9, 1989, the Berlin Wall was demolished. While this moment marked the symbolic end of the Cold War, it would take two more years for the Soviet Union to dissolve and for the Cold War to officially draw to a close.

Elements of Company C., 2nd Battalion, 18th Infantry Regiment, 170th Brigade Combat Team, of the U.S. Army readies to march in Red Square as part of a full dress rehearsal for the Victory Day Parade in Moscow, Russia. The Victory Day Parade is held every year, on May 9, to commemorate the end of World War II and the victory of the Soviet Union over Nazi Germany. In 2010, on the 65th anniversary, Russia's allies marched in the parade for the first time.

Editor's Introduction

The Soviet Union officially dissolved in December 1991, months after a failed *coup d'état* launched by communist hardliners. The coup—which was put down by popular resistance and effectively led to the transfer of power from Mikhail Gorbachev to Boris Yeltsin—was a last-ditch effort to preserve an empire long in decline. For years, the USSR had been plagued by corruption and inefficiency, and in 1989, it lost its grip on the Eastern Bloc, watching as Poland, Hungary, East Germany, Bulgaria, Czechoslovakia, and Romania deposed their communist governments.

On top of that, some Soviet republics had begun to resist the central government, which was weakening due to democratic reforms instituted by Gorbachev. Within two years of the fall of the Berlin Wall, the once-mighty Soviet empire was no more. This chapter covers the events leading up to and following the USSR's break-up.

John O'Sullivan focuses on the fall of the Soviet Union in this chapter's first article, "The Road from 1989." The collapse was a gradual process, O'Sullivan writes, beginning even before 1984, when the United States' successful positioning of long-range missiles in Europe signaled victory in the Cold War. In the Soviet Union, years of inefficient economic policy and poor planning had taken their toll, as had the failed war in Afghanistan. Following the "velvet," or nonviolent, revolutions in Eastern Europe, it was only a matter of time before the USSR met a similar fate. O'Sullivan looks at why the region mostly avoided bloody conflict and considers how history might have been different had the collapse occurred sooner.

In the wake of the USSR's dissolution, Boris Yeltsin, the first leader of the new Russian Federation, had the unenviable task of picking up the pieces. The former superpower was shattered, and Russia was contained within its own borders. In "Russia's Flawed Hero," the next selection, Lynn Berry reviews *Yeltsin: A Life*, a biography of the leader. The author of the book, Timothy J. Colton, sees Yeltsin as a great man, a "hero in history" who, despite his shortcomings, set Russia on a course toward democracy and a free-market system.

In the next entry, "Forged in Fire: Witnessing the Rise of Iron Rule in Russia," Fred Weir mourns "Russia's best hope for democracy," which he insists died in October 1993, when Yeltsin used military force to settle his longstanding disputes with the parliament. Since the Soviet collapse, the president and parliament—both democratically elected—had been fighting over who would steer the ship of state. With the "mini-civil war," as Weir terms it, Yeltsin was able to concentrate power in his own hands. Top-down rule has proved popular, Weir writes, because of "relatively good governance" and the financial boom brought about by Russia's energy sector.

In the next article, "The Kremlin Begs to Differ," Dimitri K. Simes and Paul J. Saunders examine some of Russia's most pressing problems. The authors quote Winston Churchill, who described Russia during World War II as "a riddle, wrapped in a mystery, inside an enigma." That assessment holds today: corruption is rampant in Russia's political system and hinders progress and economic growth. The parliament lacks power, and the executive branch operates free from checks and balances. The authors focus on the complex relationship between President Dmitry Medvedev, a leader who has been slow to institute change, and Prime Minister Vladimir Putin, who preceded Medvedev as president and still enjoys widespread popular support. While Putin—who many see as more powerful than Medvedev—has been accused of stripping away civil liberties, many Russians appear willing to exchange personal freedoms for economic prosperity and a restoration of Russian influence abroad.

In "The Next Silicon Valley: Siberia," the subsequent selection, Brett Forrest visits Novosibirsk, a Siberian city home to a thriving information-technology sector. The city's tech prowess dates back to the early 1960s, when Soviet officials built Akademgorodok, a secluded enclave for the nation's best and brightest scientists. After the fall of communism, the city's scientists had little choice but to take jobs with private companies. This shift has attracted such corporations as Intel, spurring hopes that Russia's economic future lies in technology.

In the final piece in the chapter, "Russia and the U.S. Sign Nuclear Arms Reduction Pact," Peter Baker and Dan Bilefsky discuss a treaty that, despite calling for "only modest reductions in the actual arsenals maintained by the two countries," could pave the way for further, more meaningful disarmament. The pact is symbolic of improved relations between the two nations, which had butted heads over Russia's 2008 war with neighboring Georgia and U.S. plans to build a missile-defense system in Europe. Despite disagreeing on these issues, both sides are committed to curtailing Iran's nuclear ambitions.

The Road from 1989[*]

By John O'Sullivan
National Review, November 23, 2009

On Inauguration Day 1989, National Review gave a celebratory dinner in Washington at which the guests included Jeane Kirkpatrick, Bill Safire, and the Soviet ambassador and his wife. Contrary to stereotypes, the ambassador was charming and his wife both charming and attractive. But what the ambassador said went beyond charm. He remarked, apparently in passing, that the Soviet Union had no interest in what kind of regimes existed in Eastern Europe. They were independent countries. What kind of government they had was a matter for the voters.

We had just heard what became known as the Sinatra Doctrine: They can do it their way. Safire took out his notebook and pen. He wanted to take down the lyrics.

"Does that mean they can leave the Warsaw Pact?" asked Jeane suspiciously, probably recalling that it was Hungary's decision to do so that had made a Soviet invasion inevitable.

"We would be sorry if they did so," replied the ambassador suavely, "but that's really a matter for them, not us." So the Brezhnev Doctrine "once a socialist country, always a socialist country"—no longer applied either. When the ambassador left for his next dinner—his wife told me apologetically that they had three that night—we all fell to discussing the significance of his remark. Was it true? And even if it was, why had he told us? What was going on?

Of those present, I had the least excuse for being skeptical or surprised. Shortly before the dinner, our first issue of 1989 had hit the newsstands with a cover story by our roving correspondent, Radek Sikorski (now Poland's foreign minister), with the title "The Coming Crack-Up of Communism" and a picture of Lenin under shattered glass. There had been other forecasts of a Soviet collapse too—notably, Andrei Amalrik's book *Will the Soviet Union Survive Until 1984?* Above all, we had just won the Cold War. Not everyone quite realizes that because we tend to think that the collapse of Communism and the end of the Cold War were the same thing. In fact, the Cold War really ended in 1984—score one for Amalrik—when America's cruise and Pershing missiles were successfully stationed in Europe despite a massive "peace" campaign against their installation.

Gorbachev went to Geneva and Reykjavik with the intention of getting an arms-reduction agreement that would allow Moscow to argue that the Cold War had ended in a draw. He failed to get such an agreement because Reagan refused to abandon strategic missile defense. So he returned to Washington a year later and made all his previous concessions without getting his quid pro quo. America won the Cold War at that point.

But Soviet Communism still ruled a large part of the world. Most observers in 1987 and 1988 expected that the two blocs would continue a peaceful competition of systems more or less indefinitely. It would not be hard to carry out a thought experiment—there's a different one below—about a world in which that happened. In such a world, socialism would not be a synonym for economic waste and collapse. European social-democratic parties would not have embraced the market (however inadequately). Moscow would regularly seek export credits and other subsidies. Etc., etc.

So what turned the Soviet defeat of 1984–86 into the Soviet dissolution of 1989–91? Take a look at the opening paragraph of Sikorski's article:

> An elderly woman in a peasant scarf lights a candle and kneels piously at the altar in the Vilnius Cathedral—recently restored to the Catholic Church after decades of serving as a Museum of Atheism. A food queue several dozen strong stands pliantly in the dawn cold in front of a shabby state monopoly store in Moscow. Deputies of the Supreme Soviet of the Estonian Republic spectacularly declare for genuine autonomy, defying the line from Moscow. In Yerevan soldiers enforcing the state of emergency keep themselves warm around a fire next to a snow shrouded tank.

If I could not read plainly that this piece was published in January 1989, I would guess that it describes 1990 to 1991, after the fall of the Berlin Wall. Everything Sikorski writes about in that passage is taking place not in one of the USSR's restive Eastern European neighbors but within the borders of the USSR itself. He depicts dissolution under way. The rot has already set in: widespread economic inefficiency, nationalist uprisings everywhere, military failure in Afghanistan, the Kremlin's growing inability to finance anti-American subversion, its similar impotence in the face of Solidarity's rebellion, the evaporation of the perestroika illusion, and—not surprisingly—the collapse of elite morale within the party. Around this time, political philosopher John Gray returned from a visit to Poland with a new joke: The Communist party held a competition to recruit new members. If you recruited one new member, you got a vacation on the Black Sea; two, and you could resign from the party yourself; three, and you got a written certificate testifying that you had never been a member. The joke was told to Gray by a member of the Polish Central Committee. Communism was definitely over—it was itself a joke.

But what would replace it—especially in Eastern Europe—Gorbachev seems to have intended to replace the hardliners there with some form of local perestroika.

His former college roommate, a Czech, later arrived in Prague to help the velvet revolution move towards the "socialism with a human face" of 1968. But he was shouted down when he slipped unwittingly into leftist jargon. 1968 represented a socialist simulacrum of freedom. By 1989 Eastern Europeans wanted something better and more real. The tectonic plates of politics were shifting. An earthquake was simply a matter of time. The earthquake, when it came, was a picnic. And it marked the return to European history of the Hapsburgs.

On Aug. 19, 1989, a "pan-European picnic" was held near the town of Sopron on the Austria-Hungary border by Hungary's four opposition parties, under the joint patronage of Otto von Hapsburg and the Hungarian reform communist Imre Poszgay. Hungary had already started to demolish its fortified border with Austria. East Germans now took the opportunity to flee in large numbers. By September the Hungarian government gave up all pretense of guarding the border, despite protests from East Germany's dinosaur leader, Erich Honecker. The Iron Curtain was trampled down by an exodus of refugees from all the Eastern-bloc countries except East Germany. And in November that final domino fell when, in an entirely fitting epilogue to Communism, the Berlin Wall fell too—because the bureaucrats in charge of it couldn't make sense of their orders.

All these revolutions were "velvet" (i.e., non-violent), except for the revolution in Romania, which was a fraudulent pantomime camouflaging a struggle for power between hardline and perestroika Communists, and thus very bloody indeed. With Eastern Europe now independent and heading for democracy, Gorbachev told Thatcher that his willingness to appease stopped at the Soviet borders. In fact, Communism continued to unravel, ending in the farce of the failed counter-coup.

Gorbachev deserves credit for not sending in the tanks, but it was not entirely a question of moral restraint. In Yugoslavia, the Communists did fight—disguised as nationalists launching wars against Slovenia, Croatia, Bosnia, etc.—to hold on to power; but they failed. There was simply no longer any fight in Communism. It was exhausted—and it left behind a series of exhausted nations and bankrupt economies. What would happen next?

Before examining what did happen, it may be useful to look at what failed to happen. Western observers in 1989 and 1990 feared that Eastern Europe and Russia would develop along the lines that actually characterized Yugoslavia: There would be border disputes, attacks on minorities, anti-Semitism, even fascism and civil wars. Some of these, such as anti-Semitism, did crop up—but, disconcertingly, in Western Europe and on the left rather than in Eastern Europe and on the right. Between 1989 and 2000, Eastern and Central Europe escaped most of the ills forecast for them and introduced democracy and market economics with a good deal of social pain but with relatively little upheaval. Most are now established market democracies, some facing real difficulties in the world recession, but none looking likely to abandon the political and market reforms they embraced in the Nineties.

How is this success to be explained? The first explanation is that NATO, under U.S. leadership, promised them entry into the alliance if they reformed themselves. This was a powerful incentive. Poland, Hungary, the Czech Republic, et al. wanted U.S. protection against Russia, to be sure, but they also wanted to be "normal" countries inside "Europe." "Europe"—meaning in this context both the European Union and the Western European members of NATO—was less keen. It was nervous about angering Russia by moving NATO to its borders, and it wanted to concentrate on "deepening" the EU with stronger political integration rather than "widening" (and perhaps weakening) it with new members.

It was the U.S., under presidents of both parties, that pushed the unwilling Europeans into NATO expansion. The prospect of NATO membership persuaded the Eastern Europeans to modernize their economies and reform their political systems along liberal lines. That success gave the Europeans the justification for expanding the EU eastwards as well. By the early 21st century, Eastern and Central Europe, including the Baltic states, were full members of both "Europe" and "the West."

A second explanation is that the free-market reforms worked. All the countries that adopted them have prospered after early setbacks—and in general, the more thoroughgoing the reforms (Poland, the Czech Republic, Estonia), the stronger the economic revival. Some countries are suffering in the current recession; some over-borrowed (Latvia, Hungary) and are facing a painful financial readjustment; and there has been a modest intellectual reaction against "neo-liberalism" or "market fundamentalism" in the region (encouraged by local boy George Soros). But no politician with realistic hopes of office proposes to reverse the market reforms. They know from bitter experience the truth of the devastating retort by Columbia University's Jagdish Bhagwati to his colleague Joseph Stiglitz:

> Stiglitz made a much cited claim that the current crisis was for capitalism (and markets) the equivalent of the collapse of the Berlin Wall. Now, we know that all analogies are imperfect, but this one is particularly dicey. When the Berlin Wall collapsed, we saw the bankruptcy of both authoritarian politics and an economics of extensive, almost universal, ownership of the means of production and central planning. We saw a wasteland. When Wall Street and Main Street were shaken by crisis, however, we witnessed merely a pause in prosperity, not a devastation of it.

The experience of Central Europe in particular underscores this truth, since in Poland there has not even been a pause in prosperity. It is the only EU country not to have experienced recession.

A third explanation is that those on both sides of the 1989 barricades showed restraint before, during, and after the velvet revolutions. Beforehand the Communist authorities in Hungary and Poland sought a compromise peace with their dissident opponents in the hope (subsequently realized) that they would be able to participate and even regain power in any new democracy. Afterwards the new democrats sought, with a few exceptions, to preserve this "social peace" by not pursuing justice (let alone revenge) against the people and parties who had misgoverned them for half a century. Few indictments have been brought even against police torturers; fewer have succeeded; and attempts to restore property to its owners or restrict the political offices open to former officials have been kept to a bare minimum by the courts. Some ill consequences have flowed from this restraint—see below—but it did at least ensure that the new democratic order was very quickly accepted by entire societies. There were no outlaws nursing resentment and plotting return.

Finally, a different kind of restraint—the restrained diplomacy of the Bush administration and its major allies—helped to bring about the dissolution of the Soviet empire, the absorption of a united Germany into NATO, and the creation of a free Europe right up to (and into) the borders of the USSR, all without inviting massive bloodshed. In part this was because the peoples behind the Iron Curtain took their revolutions further and faster than governments and diplomats really thought possible or perhaps even wanted. Gorbachev hoped the revolutions in Eastern Europe would go no further than perestroika or "socialism with a human face." Many Western politicians, notably President Bush in his "Chicken Kiev" speech, similarly wanted the Soviet Union to remain intact. It was a known quantity in international affairs—a force for "stability." Who knew what Ukraine or Georgia would get up to?

This caution failed in the end; the empire struck out; everywhere peoples forced governments to give them the independent democracies they wanted. During the crisis, however, this restraint reassured the Kremlin that the West was not planning to exploit the crisis to obtain a more conventional kind of victory. And that, paradoxically, allowed the Kremlin to be more—well, more liberal in its response to the multiplication of rebellions.

For these and other reasons, 1989 and 1991 produced the most significant and beneficial peaceful political change in history. Not only did those years see the liberation of millions of people who only ten years before had been living under what looked like durable oppression, but their secondary effects included the globalization of markets and a marked rise in living standards for *billions* of Asian workers. With such results it is hard to cavil.

Yet within Europe itself there were failures of policy and imagination that have lingered to disturb the apparently peaceful continent. Some "market" reforms included corrupt privatizations that in effect handed massive economic and financial assets to Communist apparatchiks. They quickly became capitalist oligarchs. Shadowy networks between them, their former intelligence services, and the Russian FSB meant that they retained a sometimes unaccountable power and position under the new democracies. That in turn fostered cynicism among the populace. There is a widespread sense of a moral vacuum at the heart of a democracy sundered from justice—coupled with anger that no one has been made to pay for the horrendous crimes of Communism.

This failure to de-Communize has come back to haunt Europeans in international affairs as well as in domestic ones. When Yeltsin tried to hold a constitutional trial of the Communist party—something that might have exorcised the Communist demons—he was discouraged from conducting such a "witch hunt" by the West. One result is the qualified attempt in Russia today to rehabilitate

Stalin. Another result is in Western Europe, where the Left still resists the attempt of the Baltic states to obtain a reckoning for one of the largest mass murders in history. But the most ominous result lies in foreign policy.

Because Soviet crimes were never established beyond doubt in a court of law, as Nazi crimes were condemned at Nuremberg, many Russians have the sense that their nation is an innocent victim of Western deceit and bullying. They sympathize with Vladimir Putin's description of the fall of the Soviet Union as "the greatest geopolitical catastrophe of the century." They have accordingly embraced a grievance mentality in foreign affairs. And today Russians are easily tempted to support a foreign policy that, in the words of the Eastern European intellectuals who wrote an open letter to President Obama earlier this year, "challenges our claims to our own historical experiences . . . asserts a privileged position in determining our security choices . . . uses overt and covert means of economic warfare, ranging from energy blockades and politically motivated investments to bribery and media manipulation in order to advance its interests and to challenge the transatlantic orientation of Central and Eastern Europe."

Could it have been different? Let's try a thought experiment: What if the events of 1989 and 1991 had occurred in 1986 and 1988, when Reagan was still president and Thatcher still enjoyed a firm grip on power? Would the outcomes have been significantly different?

We have some idea of what Thatcher might have attempted because, in her 1996 reprise of Churchill's Fulton speech, she outlined a full program of post–Cold War institution-making. It included the admission of Central and Eastern Europe's new democracies into NATO, the abandonment of any separate European "defense identity," and the creation of a transatlantic free trade area encompassing the former Soviet satellites. It was a thoroughgoing Atlanticist program that would have united Europe economically but—quite explicitly—under American political and diplomatic leadership.

Reagan would probably have agreed. But he would also have seen that such a program needed both European acquiescence and a means of soothing Russia's sense of defeat and humiliation. How? Well, Reagan might have celebrated victory over the Soviet Union in the festive (a.k.a. "triumphalist") way that the Bush administration avoided doing—yet treated Russia as among the nations liberated by the Soviet collapse and Russians as the first victims of Soviet oppression. We can glimpse how Reagan might have attempted this from the imaginative and generous speech he gave to the students during his 1988 visit to Moscow University.

But speeches and public-relations gestures would not have been enough. Reagan would have seen that a grand strategic offer was needed to convince the Russians that he was not seeking their surrender in disguise. Might he then have suggested that Russia join NATO and other institutions of Western cooperation—something that Yeltsin himself floated in the early, heady days of post-Communist euphoria? If such an offer had been made and accepted, the Western Europeans would have been unable to resist the tsunami of popular enthusiasm that would then have followed. Concentrating on "deepening" the EU when Reagan and Yeltsin were shaping a new free world from Vladivostok to Vancouver (and not just over water) would have looked like the pettiest kind of envious irrelevance. A very different and more united Europe and West would then have emerged in the 1990s.

Fanciful? Without any doubt. Counterfactual history is little more than an intellectual game to remind us that actual history was not necessarily inevitable. There were other possibilities—roads not taken. Had this particular road been taken, of course, it might have led to a very different destination from that outlined above. It would certainly have negated some of the benefits that emerged from the actual history of the day. For instance, Timothy Garton Ash in *The New York Review of Books* argues persuasively that it was the Bush administration's diplomatic restraint in 1989 and 1991 (rooted in an underestimation of what would happen) that enabled the Soviet Union to retreat and collapse without massive bloodshed. Events would presumably have taken a different course if a policy shaped by Reagan's more adventurous outlook had been pursued. We shall never know.

What we do know, however, is that the current situation of a Europe increasingly divergent from the U.S. but divided between its own East and West on how to deal with a revanchist Russia is the outcome of the cautious "realism" of Western governments in 1989, 1991, and the years following. Their peoples were braver and more imaginative, and they deserved better. But perhaps that thought is secondary to a permanent truth: However sensibly we act, history will always throw up unpleasant surprises.

Russia's Flawed Hero[*]

By Lynn Berry

The Wilson Quarterly, Summer 2008

When Boris Yeltsin died on the afternoon of April 23, 2007, CNN and the BBC immediately interrupted their programming to run nonstop coverage of his life and legacy, but the Russian channels, all under Kremlin control, did not seem to know quite what to say. They did not even report his death until more than two hours later.

The master of the Kremlin at the time, Vladimir Putin, had built his popularity in part by perpetuating the myth that he had saved Russia from the horrors of the Yeltsin years. Many Russians look back on the 1990s as a time of economic collapse, social misery, and national humiliation. But some, including much of the Moscow intelligentsia, remember Yeltsin as the man who gave them freedom and hope. They mourned not just Yeltsin but the final realization that the democratic rights he had handed them had been all but snatched away.

By evening, Putin seemed to understand that he could not allow Yeltsin's death to become a rallying point for his opponents. He arranged for his predecessor to lie in state in the grand Cathedral of Christ the Savior and to be buried in Novodevichy Cemetery, the leafy resting place of Russia's heroes. When Putin finally spoke publicly, he announced a day of national mourning for Yeltsin with words of praise, albeit indirect: "A new democratic Russia was born during his time, a free, open, and peaceful country." Thus began the cautious official reassessment, even co-option, of Yeltsin's legacy.

The role of Russia's first president in the country's transformation remains controversial both within Russia and abroad, as Timothy J. Colton acknowledges in his biography. The man will be forever remembered for climbing onto a tank in August 1991 to valiantly defend democracy and also for embarrassing his compatriots three years later when he tipsily conducted a German band outside Berlin's city hall. He was committed to freedom of speech but shelled a defiant parliament into submission. He freed market forces but allowed a group of loyal bankers and businessmen to grow fabulously rich as ordinary citizens paid the cost of economic reform.

Still, Colton, a professor of government and Russian studies at Harvard, says he has come to see Yeltsin as one of history's great men. For all his foibles and mistakes, Yeltsin put his country on the path toward democratic politics and market-based economics, and he did so while largely avoiding the apocalyptic scenarios of anarchy and civil war. He was a "hero in history—enigmatic and flawed, to be sure, yet worthy of our respect and sympathy."

Colton's biography is the first major assessment to come along since Leon Aron's *Yeltsin: A Revolutionary Life*, which went to press shortly before Yeltsin unexpectedly stepped down from Russia's presidency in the final hours of 1999. It benefits from the passage of time and perspective afforded by Putin's eight subsequent years as president. Colton's research included what he describes as "eye-opening" interviews with Yeltsin, his family members, and about 150 others. He also had access to declassified files from Soviet archives and new memoirs by former aides and other political players of the time that shed light on Yeltsin's life.

Colton says he set out to write a book about Yeltsin's leadership in the 1990s, but the further he got, the more he wondered what had molded the man who would rise through the communist system to become its "hangman." The result is that the chapters on Yeltsin's family, childhood, and early career as a construction boss in Sverdlovsk provide some of the most engaging reading of the book.

Yeltsin grew up in a self-reliant family in the Ural Mountains. His paternal grandfather, a "self-made man, a backwoods capitalist," suffered under Joseph Stalin for the crime of owning a farm, a mill, and a smithy. A dispossessed kulak, he died a broken man when Yeltsin was five. Yeltsin's maternal grandfather, a master carpenter, and his wife also were driven from their home, and when Yeltsin was a boy his father spent nearly three years in a labor camp for "anti-Soviet agitation and propaganda."

Because he had relatives who were persecuted during the Stalinist repressions, Yeltsin was neither permitted nor particularly inclined to join the Communist Party as a young man. He did so only in 1961, at age 30, after the Khrushchev thaw made it possible, and with the aim of advancing his career in the construction industry. A natural leader, he soon moved into the regional party nomenklatura.

Colton finds harbingers of Yeltsin's future rebellion in his behavior as Sverdlovsk party boss in the late 1970s and early '80s. Yeltsin encouraged entrepreneurial initiative in the state sector and thought it economic nonsense to control prices in the farmers' markets. Even his hair seemed "suspiciously long" for a party member in good standing. While Yeltsin believed in the ideals of communism and had no "metaphysical thirst for reform, democracy, or the market," he had a visceral sense that the Soviet system had lost its way. "The bacillus was there, gnawing away at Yeltsin *before* he left for Moscow in 1985," Colton writes.

Mikhail Gorbachev brought Yeltsin to Moscow to help carry out perestroika, but they soon clashed. Yeltsin turned on him at a Central Committee meeting in

1987, spontaneously taking the floor to accuse the party of bungling the promised reforms and kowtowing to Gorbachev. Colton calls this Yeltsin's secret speech, a bombshell comparable to Khrushchev's address denouncing Stalin in 1956. Yeltsin later tried to patch up his relationship with Gorbachev, who wavered before stripping him of his position as Moscow party boss. Had they reached a compromise, Yeltsin told Colton in 2002, history might have been different.

Shunned by the Soviet establishment, Yeltsin shifted the action to the Russian republic. He won a seat in 1990 in the new Russian Congress of People's Deputies, which elected him speaker. Gorbachev tried to prop up his own position by introducing a Soviet presidency, but refused to submit to a popular vote, even though, at the time, he would have won, a decision Colton describes as a "blunder of biblical proportions."

The Russian republic then held a general election for its own president, which Yeltsin won with 59 percent of the vote, thus gaining the legitimacy of a democratically elected leader that Gorbachev had allowed to pass him by. After his defiance of the bungled coup of August 1991, Yeltsin's victory was complete and the fate of the Soviet Union was sealed.

As president of a newly independent country, Yeltsin set out to free the economy from the control of the state. But the lifting of price controls led to soaring inflation, wiping out the savings of ordinary Russians. Outdated factories languished as state subsidies and contracts dried up. Colton defends Yeltsin's reforms, claiming that the economic slump was not as bad as usually depicted. And when Yeltsin stepped down, Russia had a market economy that was beginning to see the strong growth that has continued to this day.

Colton also challenges other common perceptions of the Yeltsin presidency. While Yeltsin did overindulge in alcohol, his drinking was not central to his public role, and few realized that, after a series of heart attacks, he virtually stopped in 1996. In his second term, heart disease weakened but did not incapacitate Yeltsin, who "rationed his effort and expended it purposefully." Colton dismisses as not credible persistent accusations that the Yeltsins accepted bribes from a Swiss construction company hired to renovate the Kremlin. Contrary to what many believed at the time, Yeltsin did not surrender control to what was known as the Family, a group of insiders that included his daughter Tatyana Dyachenko and oligarch Boris Berezovsky. Yeltsin chose Putin not because Berezovsky or anyone else put him up to it, but because Yeltsin himself thought Russia needed a leader with a "military manner" who could consolidate political authority. But Colton is convinced Yeltsin would have reversed the decision later if he'd had the chance.

The Yeltsin that emerges in Colton's book is a powerful man of sharp political instincts and the courage to act on them. He generously gives away his wristwatches. He habitually snaps pencils in frustration. He remains loyal to friends from his hometown but promotes young economists to help run Russia. He makes mistakes, then apologizes to his fellow Russians for them.

Frequently, Colton sets Yeltsin off against Gorbachev, his chief rival. Born a month apart, the two men could not have been more different. While Yeltsin, the grandson of kulaks, was 30 when he received his party card, Gorbachev, a third-generation Communist, joined in his early 20s, when Stalin was still in the Kremlin. Yeltsin's instincts, Colton says, were feline, while Gorbachev's were more canine— "trained, trainable, tied to the known and to the previously rewarded."

But it is in the comparisons to Putin, in most cases unstated, that Yeltsin truly shines. Yeltsin was roasted in the media over the brutal war he unleashed in Chechnya in 1994, but he did not try to silence his many critics or stop journalists from investigating alleged corruption, accepting the need for political debate and an independent press. "For the first sustained period in modern times, Yeltsin's Russia was to be a land without political censors, political exiles, or political prisoners," Colton says. Under Putin, this all changed. National television stations were deployed as propaganda tools of the Kremlin, and journalists who angered those in power lost their jobs and, in some cases, their lives. Berezovsky leads a long list of Russians who sought asylum abroad to avoid politically motivated criminal charges, and Russia's prisons and mental hospitals once again began to collect political dissidents.

In stepping down on New Year's Eve 1999, Yeltsin said he was confident that Russia would never return to the past and would "proceed only forward." He then famously asked Putin to "take care of Russia." Putin let him down. With Putin's installation this spring of his own handpicked successor, Dmitry Medvedev, a man who promises to fulfill "Putin's Plan" and has made the former president his prime minister, Putin still rules.

But Colton concludes that there is still hope for a democratic Russia. Yeltsin gave Russians a personal independence that they will not easily relinquish. His economic reforms underlie the growth that has improved the lives of his compatriots, who mistakenly thank only Putin. In his book, Colton is kind to Yeltsin. History will be, too.

Forged in Fire[*]

Witnessing the Rise of Iron Rule in Russia

By Fred Weir
The Walrus, March 2009

Russia's best hope for democracy in our time died, and was buried in an un-marked grave, after a two-day wave of political violence in the streets of down-town Moscow in October 1993. I note this in retrospect, though it was clear to me at the time that former Soviet leader Mikhail Gorbachev's perestroika project, which aimed to create a modern system of divided government based on popular-ly elected institutions in what had been a monolithic one-party state, was expiring as armed militias supporting the Supreme Soviet, or the parliament, battled it out with police and special forces loyal to President Boris Yeltsin. Both he and the leg-islature had been freely elected, in 1990 and 1991 respectively, and they had stood together to withstand the ensuing military putsch launched by Communist Party diehards. Following the collapse of the Union of Soviet Socialist Republics just months later, however, they began to quarrel over many details, underlying which was the issue of who would hold supreme power: parliament or the president? No one, not even Yeltsin's American advisers, took this political gridlock for a sign of healthy democracy.

In September of '93, Yeltsin made the first move, ordering the parliament to disband and laying a paramilitary siege around the Russian White House, then the seat of the Supreme Soviet. Journalists were allowed to come and go, and I spent a lot of time inside the building's cell-like offices, interviewing some of the sev-eral hundred beleaguered parliamentarians who had stood their ground, drinking vodka at the surprisingly well-stocked bar (considering that Yeltsin had cut off the building's water and power supplies), and regarding it as yet another crisis in the ongoing drama of perestroika.

But on October 3, an unseasonably warm, sunny day, a huge pro-parliamentary crowd marched to the White House and slammed through police lines, which evaporated in a bloody melee. The officers withdrew, possibly under orders, but a few opened fire, and for the first time in my life I heard that whining hornet sound Kalashnikov slugs make as they fly through the air. I saw people killed, some torn apart by bullets, others trampled amid crowd surges. Huddled against the White House wall, under a balcony, I tried to scribble notes.

That evening, as the violence spread, pro-Kremlin police fanned out around Moscow to shut down the elected district councils, or soviets, that had been set up in the heyday of perestroika. Boris Kagarlitsky, a frenetically active deputy of the radical, left-leaning Moscow city soviet and a close friend, had spent the day in neighbourhoods like Oktyabrskaya, where a hulking statue of Soviet founder Vladimir Lenin overshadows the nearby Moscow police headquarters, trying to dissuade local pro-parliament activists from engaging in violence. But Kagarlitsky's name was on a list, and police seized him and handed him over to the security organs, who passed him on to some special cops, who held him for forty hours, beating his back and stomach with rifle butts, until Amnesty International pulled him out. (Kagarlitsky, who spent thirteen months in a Soviet jail in the early '80s, is the only Russian I know to have been arrested twice, under two different regimes, for exactly the same reason: he is a democratic socialist.)

The next day, a Russian Army armoured division entered Moscow and stormed the White House, setting it ablaze with tank fire. The parliamentary leaders surrendered and were hauled away to prison while other deputies and supporters found in the building were herded into a nearby football stadium for interrogation. Most later reported being beaten; a few were forced to kneel and threatened with a cocked rifle to their heads, in mock execution, sometimes repeatedly.

I knew there had been a fair bit of violence around the Soviet Union's periphery as the huge state collapsed, but this was the first time I'd experienced, with full adrenaline rush, the way angry speeches can turn into a storm of gunfire. I realized that the potential for it had always lurked just below the surface. I've seen a good deal more of it in the years since—it has erupted frequently in Vladimir Putin's new Russia.

But what is not present today is any struggle over the soul of Russian democracy. That was all settled in the mini–civil war of October 1993. In the weeks that followed, all of the perestroika-era soviets around Russia were forcibly closed down. Yeltsin used his triumph to rewrite Russia's constitution, vesting the lion's share of power in the Kremlin and reducing a new incarnation of parliament, the State Duma, to little more than a talking shop. "It was the end of the democratic experiment," says an older, somewhat more dour Boris Kagarlitsky, and the end of the great hopes Gorbachev had aroused in so many Russians.

Mine must be an unusual story. I came to Moscow over twenty years ago as a correspondent for the *Canadian Tribune*, the now defunct weekly newspaper put out by Canada's Communist Party. I was a third-generation red diaper baby from Toronto, and a long-time member of the party. My uncle, trained at the Lenin

School in Moscow in the 1920s as an agent of the Communist International, spent many years in the USSR. I'd visited a few times, had studied Russian history up to the graduate level, but never wanted to live there until Gorbachev came to power in 1985. The new general secretary, the party's first to be born after the revolution, talked unlike any Communist leader since the original Bolsheviks. Suddenly, there was the electrifying prospect of a socialism powered from below, a system focused on creative human potential rather than crop statistics. Optimists could imagine a Soviet Union that might actually compete with the West in ideas as well as nuclear missiles, a non-capitalist society that worked, or at least an example that might be productively debated to replace the albatross hanging around the neck of any Canadian who self-identified as a socialist. I grabbed the *Tribune* job as soon as it was offered to me.

When I arrived in Moscow in the fall of 1986, the place was still in Soviet deep freeze. One of the double-edged advantages to being a Communist correspondent was that one got to live, pretty much unsupervised, in regular Soviet housing. (Other foreigners, diplomats, and journalists were kept in special closed compounds and followed around by the KGB.) I recall nearly starving to death in my first couple of weeks because I couldn't figure out the system of multiple line-ups in Soviet grocery stores, or talk my way past the imposing doormen outside so-called restaurants, where the staff were engaged in many pursuits, not many of which involved attending to customers. But having few obstacles to fraternization with the natives, I found it surprisingly easy to make friends, who quickly conjured away those little mysteries for me. Within a year, I married Masha, a graduate student of history, and moved into her family flat in a huge grey tenement across the Moscow River from the Kremlin.

Just as quickly, I became convinced that the Soviet revolution, for all its ugliness, had succeeded in transforming Russia into a modern, urbanized, industrial society. Most people I met were highly capable, sophisticated professionals—the products of an extraordinarily effective system of mass education. The central problem, which Gorbachev identified, was that the regime dictated all terms of their public lives. That doesn't mean they lived in terror, as their parents had under Joseph Stalin. After being viciously clubbed with Kalashnikov rifle butts by Yeltsin's police in 1993, my friend Boris would sometimes speak nostalgically of his Soviet-era incarceration, and even of his KGB interrogator, "with whom one could discuss things intelligently."

People certainly had no fear of opening up in private, usually over lengthy, vodka-soaked meals at their kitchen tables. It was through many such boisterous yet often deeply philosophical discussions with friends that I learned just about everything I think I know about Russia, not least of which was that these people were perfectly capable of running their own lives and, by extension, their own country. Gorbachev's message resonated with me because that's exactly what he was saying almost as though he was trying to rule the country from one of those kitchen tables.

My own dispatches to the *Tribune* were mostly stories about how well Gorbachev's plan was working out. I travelled in cramped, smoke-filled Aeroflot jets across the Soviet Union, from Leningrad to Vladivostok, and everywhere found people waking up to new possibilities. The first miracle was the transformation of the Soviet media, which sprouted a full political spectrum almost from the moment Gorbachev began to relax censorship. Previously unheard-of political criticism and social investigation exposed the harrowing facts of Soviet history, most of which were easily found in any standard Western text on the USSR but were news to the Soviet public. "It was like sixty years of memory suddenly sprang into view. It was exhilarating," says Sergei Strokan, then an intensely idealistic young reporter for *Moskovskie Novosti*, the flagship of perestroika. "People would start queuing at 6 a.m. to buy a copy of our paper."

Gorbachev also moved to revive the existing Bolshevik system of legislatures at all levels, through open and competitive elections. In 1989, the Soviet Congress of People's Deputies was created, with one-third of its representatives chosen by the people. The body, scheduled to meet twice a year, pulled from its ranks a regular sitting parliament, the Supreme Soviet. I was thrilled to see a huge banner hanging across the Kremlin Wall with the old Bolshevik slogan "*Vsya vlast Sovietam!*" ("All power to the Soviets!"), which actually seemed to be coming true. The next year, a Russian congress (with its own Supreme Soviet) was elected entirely by popular mandate, and freely elected local soviets were springing up everywhere. Gorbachev bluntly told Communist Party functionaries that if they hoped to retain executive power, they'd have to get elected. I recall one particularly painful interview in Kaluga with a local party secretary, who sat white knuckled and red faced behind his desk, contemptuously ignoring my questions about his future plans, if any, to run for office.

Around this time, I also conducted two cross-Canada tours, to publicize the *Tribune* and my book of essays on Gorbachev's reforms. Even in the West, perestroika seemed to be a magic formula that disintegrated old sectarian lines on the left. I found myself chatting with Trotskyists without quarrelling over Stalin, and NDPers quizzed me earnestly about the potential of socialism. Indeed, just about everyone I met was intrigued by the momentous changes overtaking the old USSR.

At the Toronto headquarters of the Communist Party of Canada, however, there was also some disquiet at the processes in the USSR that were aggressively reshaping the views of history and definitions of socialism party members had long defended. I held a couple of private meetings in the book-lined office of the party's long time leader, Bill Kashtan, a grizzled, Soviet-trained apparatchik of my uncle's generation, who listened to my glowing reports of burgeoning people's power with narrowed eyes.

Perhaps I was naive, but it isn't as though I had failed to notice that the garden was crawling with snakes. I found highly organized, though democratically minded, nationalism in the Popular Fronts of the Soviet Baltics. Down in Uzbekistan, I was shocked to see women wearing the veil, discouraged since the 1920s, and even more so to hear a party satrap explain it to me as part of "perestroika's new opening to Islam." In the Caucasus, I encountered simmering ethnic hatreds. By loosening the grip of the Communist Party, Gorbachev had opened up possibilities, but these were taken very differently by peoples across the vast patchwork state that was the USSR.

Meanwhile, the Soviet economy was crashing. A lack of central planning had resulted in the foundering of industry, and massive shortages began to cripple life in the cities (e.g., those insufferable lineups at the shops). Gorbachev spoke in almost utopian terms of "workers' democracy"—turning the factories over to elected councils—but attempts to implement it merely aggravated the chaos. The only part of the economy that worked was the "co-operatives," basically private businesses, which quickly expanded beyond consumer services into manufacturing, banking, and farming. Most of my acquaintances, members of the educated elite, grew sick and tired of the lofty chatter in the "theatre of democracy," increasingly at odds with the dreary realities of life, while exposure to the West and the example of rich co-operative owners stimulated dreams of becoming successful Western-style businesspeople.

Sometime in the spring of 1991, I realized how far they had taken this. I was invited to a garden party at the country home of Andrei Brezhnev, nephew of former Soviet leader Leonid Brezhnev, in Zhukovka, an elite dacha settlement outside Moscow. One of the guests, whom I'd known for years as a functionary of the Komsomol (the Young Communist League) rolled up in a shiny white Volvo and told me he was now president of an import export firm. Another, whom I'd often dealt with as an official of the *Tribune*'s fraternal newspaper, the Soviet Communist Party organ *Pravda*, boasted that he'd just been hired at a private bank. A third, even more surprising because he was the son of renowned Soviet dissident Andrei Sakharov, leaned over the table and handed me a card that announced him as an "international business consultant."

I poured out my confusion over a bottle of vodka with Vladimir Pozner, a fellow red diaper baby who'd laboured much of his life in the bowels of the Soviet propaganda system, and then achieved a brief perestroika-era stardom in the West, as a Soviet spokesman who spoke flawless, New York–accented English. We sat on the terrace of his dacha, eating and drinking by candlelight, thanks to one of the frequent power outages. "Socialism and the Soviet Union are probably finished," he told me. "But we're a democratic country now, and nobody will be able to roll that back."

He turned out to be right (if too optimistic about the fate of democracy). By December, the balance of power shifted to the republics, and the USSR disintegrated into fifteen separate states. Gorbachev shuffled off into retirement, handing over authority to Russia's recently elected president, Yeltsin. Any semblance of socialism was junked by the acting prime minister, Yegor Gaidar, whose now infamous "shock therapy" campaign consisted mainly of liberating prices. Hence, one of the first post Soviet experiences fixed in Russians' memories is a hurricane of hyperinflation that wiped out savings and jacked the price of all but a few regulated goods (e.g., energy, housing, and bread) out of reach. I held an account in the Sberbank state bank with 1,000 rubles, which would have purchased a two week Black Sea vacation in the summer of 1991 but a year later was barely enough to purchase a Snickers bar.

Disillusionment with Yeltsin, who'd rashly promised to improve popular living standards within a year, came swiftly among ordinary Russians (though he retained the support of the liberal intelligentsia and the new business class). I recall the savage political jokes that proliferated in that dreadful winter of 1992. "You know, everything our old Soviet leaders told us about communism was false," says one friend to another. "But everything they told us about capitalism was true." Or another: What has Boris Yeltsin accomplished in one year that the Communists couldn't do in seventy years? He's made communism look good.

But the democratic system created by Gorbachev staggered on. Russia's Congress of People's Deputies continued to meet in the Kremlin Palace, and in late '92 it forced the removal of Gaidar and required Yeltsin to appear regularly before the Supreme Soviet to explain Kremlin policies. The relationship between the president and parliament, in particular its vain and ambitious chairman, Ruslan Khasbulatov, quickly soured. I remember running into Yeltsin in a Kremlin corridor after he'd given a darkly threatening address, warning "extreme measures" if parliament didn't start co-operating with him. His bodyguards pushed me and several other reporters out of the way, but the burly leader weaved toward us and embraced a startled Swede of his acquaintance, whom he dragged away for what we later heard was "a few drinks" in one of the ornate anterooms.

The main thing Yeltsin and the parliament fought over was the shape of constitutional reform. The system set up by Gorbachev was highly unstable, with no clear division of powers between the grafted-on presidency and the soviet-style legislature, and a parliamentary committee chaired by Yeltsin was tasked with drafting a new basic charter for the country. Its main author was the committee's executive secretary, a brilliant, bespectacled legal scholar named Oleg Rumyantsev. When first elected to the Supreme Soviet, Rumyantsev was described in a glowing article by then *Washington Post* correspondent David Remnick as "the James Madison of Russia." But as the confrontation deepened and the Bill Clinton administration in the US unambiguously took Yeltsin's side, Russia's parliamentarians morphed into "hard-liners" and "communist holdovers" in most Western press coverage. Yeltsin's domestic supporters, unfortunately parroted at the time by many of my Western journalistic colleagues in Moscow, claimed that the parliament's constitutional reform project aimed to reduce Yeltsin to a mere symbol, like the Queen of England. Yeltsin, who broke with the parliamentary reform committee and published his own super-presidential constitutional draft in April 1993, argued that Russians needed a single strong leader. "Two bears can't share the same cave," he famously remarked.

When the final showdown came in October, Rumyantsev was dragged from the White House by troops and handed over to the police, who beat him badly, much like the treatment Boris Kagarlitsky was receiving on the other side of town. His opposition knocked out, Yeltsin wasted no time in redesigning the country's institutions, and its basic charter, into the neoczarist shape they've held ever since.

As became clear amid the muted eulogies and angry street commentary at the time of Yeltsin's funeral in 2007, most Russians now blame the old leader for a decade they associate with economic decline, social decay, political drift, and national disgrace. Few, at least in Russia, praised him as any sort of democrat. It seems odd to me, then, that the man Yeltsin hand-picked to succeed him in 1999, ex–KGB agent Vladimir Putin, has been singled out by Western pundits as the main culprit in Russia's regression into an authoritarian state. Putin, an able man with a genuine, often-expressed passion for modernizing Russia's economy and military forces, inherited an office with full power to effectively renationalize key segments of the economy, take over media outlets, end popular elections for regional leaders, and make war.

If Russians have been quiescent—even dutifully marching to the polls to endorse Putin's own hand-picked successor, Dmitry Medvedev, last March, and then standing by late in the year as Medvedev pushed through constitutional changes that could see Putin re-elected in 2012—it's because the Kremlin's decisive leadership has been undeniably popular. Relatively good governance, combined with windfall oil and gas revenues in recent years, prompted an economic boom that brought prosperity to millions of Russians and is only lately beginning to peter out. My own family just moved into a house we constructed on the site of our Soviet-era dacha in Razdori, a small village near Moscow, and life has generally become far more comfortable. Among other delights, Boris Kagarlitsky, who now heads an institute that studies global social movements, sometimes meets me for an American-style lunch and leftish political conversation at the Starlite Diner, near the giant Lenin statue where he was arrested fifteen years ago. But most of my friends smile bitterly at official rhetoric that describes the political system as "democracy with Russian specifics."

The constitution written by Oleg Rumyantsev, which would have given Russia a modern government with effective checks and balances, went up in flames with the White House in 1993. The last time I met the scholar, about five years ago, he was standing alone at a sumptuous buffet in the posh downtown Moscow apartment of the black Russian TV presenter Yelena Khanga, granddaughter of American Communists who came to the USSR in the 1930s. As soon as he saw me, Rumyantsev, still tall, gaunt, and intense, held up his hand. "I don't discuss politics anymore," he barked. "It's a dead end. I'm a corporate executive now, and that's how I make my contribution."

The Kremlin Begs to Differ[*]

By Dimitri K. Simes and Paul J. Saunders
National Interest, November/December 2009

Twenty years after the fall of the Berlin wall, Russia remains as Sir Winston Churchill described it: "a riddle, wrapped in a mystery, inside an enigma." Russia's complexity has contributed to an American debate in which policy preferences too often shape analysis rather than analysis driving policy. It's not a sound basis for decisions when key American interests and goals are at stake.

One doesn't need to be a Russian domestic radical or a foreign Russophobe to see major flaws in the way Russia is ruled. The country's president, Dmitri Medvedev, has catalogued its problems: "an inefficient economy, semi-Soviet social sphere, fragile democracy, negative demographic trends and unstable [North] Caucasus," not to mention "endemic corruption" defended by "influential groups of corrupt officials and do-nothing 'entrepreneurs'" who want to "squeeze the profits from the remnants of Soviet industry and squander the natural resources that belong to us all."

Russia's problems are fundamental to its political system, which, while officially democratic, is perhaps best understood as popularly supported semiauthoritarian state capitalism. Russia is clearly not a Western-style democracy, though its citizens enjoy considerable freedom of personal expression, with the level of liberty inversely proportional to the potential impact of criticism. The state dominates "strategic sectors" of the economy like energy and defense, but political-business clans have retained much space to pursue their parochial interests, including through the state's administrative machinery. As throughout its history, Russia is dominated by a ruling class: originally aristocrats, then Communist Party *nomenklatura*, and now a combination of senior bureaucrats and business leaders, including former Soviet managers, ruthless-yet-effective younger entrepreneurs, and outright criminals who took advantage of the decay, collapse and anarchy of the 1980s and 1990s.

The question now is how long Russia's current political arrangements can hold. Corruption is deeply embedded and pervasive, affecting state and private enterprises along with the media and the courts, severely limiting Russia's modernization and sustainable economic growth. And with so much power concentrated at the top of the system, recent murmurs of a growing rift between President Medvedev and Prime Minister Vladimir Putin raise serious concerns about stability.

Moscow's arbitrary rule affects the people and state of Russia most of all, but it also presents a challenge to the United States. Russia is vital to American interests, and if the Obama administration has any illusions about the nature of Russian politics or, alternatively, surrenders to the long-standing temptation to act as a self-appointed nursemaid, it could severely damage our ability to work pragmatically with Russia to advance important U.S. goals.

It is difficult to overstate the role of corruption in Russia, which in many ways is the glue that holds together the disparate groups dominating Russia's current political system. The Russian state is organically linked to Russian companies, both overtly—through stock ownership and officials' simultaneous service on corporate boards—and covertly, through family ties and secret deals. At the upper levels, Russia's corruption takes the form of private stakes in state firms and profound conflicts of interest; at lower levels, simple bribery is more common. And the scope of corruption is expanding: according to official statistics, Russia's bureaucracy has doubled in size in the last ten years.

Those at the top have a relatively free hand to enrich themselves through insider dealing. Thus, notwithstanding Russia's extensive privatization, it is often difficult to distinguish between government-owned companies and large private conglomerates. Officials are deeply involved with both and the government often acts to protect both, though it is not always clear whether government actions are a result of state or private interests.

Because of corruption, Russia's political system is simultaneously very resistant to change and remarkably fragile. Extensive overseas portfolios and property held by Russian officials and oligarchs are a clear indicator of their own limited confidence in Russia's stability. There is an exuberant Russian presence in London, New York and on Mediterranean beaches that is totally out of line with the size of Russia's economy. The reluctance of major Russian firms to make long-term capital investments in their own country is further evidence of this mindset. If those who hold power still feel the need to hedge their bets, it is all the more true of international investors.

In addition, the uninhibited power of huge government-owned or government-connected firms to act against their competitors discourages both foreign investment and the development of small- and medium-size businesses in Russia. Though Gazprom has legitimately wanted Ukraine to pay its bills on time and in full, the resulting disputes took on a very different character when Russian officials became involved. In the end, the repeated crises damaged Moscow's reputation as a reliable energy supplier and a responsible European power. The Alfa Group's struggle with BP over control of their TNK-BP joint venture is another example in which well-connected Russian moguls allied with the state to apply pressure to their business partners. What would be routine commercial disagreements in other countries can rapidly trigger state intervention in Russia, usually to the disadvantage of foreign firms or others outside the system who lack effective protections or recourse.

Corruption and insider dealing can have tragic consequences in Russia, as they did in an August explosion at the Sayano-Shushenskaya dam in Siberia, when over seventy people were killed due to inadequate maintenance. Putin himself described as "irresponsible and criminal" an apparent maintenance contract with a fraudulent firm set up by top managers. Beyond limiting investments in safety and maintenance, however, irresponsibility and corruption have also strongly discouraged investment in other key areas. Russian firms happily squeeze out foreign investors but don't themselves put money into new equipment, training, or research and development. Despite recent increases, state investments in education, health, and science and technology are also inadequate for sustainable economic growth and to diversify beyond energy exports.

Here it is useful to compare Russia to China. China is less free than Russia according to Freedom House, and has a number of similar problems, but is considerably more attractive to foreign investors. The huge scale of China's market is a major inducement, but Beijing's greater willingness to accept international rules and its much more strategic approach to cultivating foreign investors—whose presence China's leaders view as essential to meeting their development goals but energy rich Moscow has seen as easily replaceable—also make a big difference.

It will not be possible to modernize Russia without a genuine effort to eliminate corruption—and this includes at the top. Corrupt conduct is not simply tolerated, but a way of life with profound political implications. Any opening in the political system that would allow corruption to be exposed could potentially decimate Russia's elites—and they know it. Everyone who is involved in corruption whether directly or indirectly (by failing to act on knowledge of corrupt acts) may be in legal jeopardy and is therefore a stakeholder in the current system. Russia's weak media and biddable court system and parliament prevent corrupt elite actions from coming to light and ensure few if any consequences.

The media face direct state interference and engage in constant self-censorship as well. The central government effectively controls television news broadcasting, with the exception of minor cable channels, and blocks critical reporting that questions official policy. Moscow newspapers enjoy wider freedom to debate policy, and papers like *Novaya Gazeta* and *Nezavisimaya Gazeta* regularly challenge government decisions. But they reach only a small audience, and regional papers are usually more cautious, especially in dealing with local officials. The internet is quite free, though also limited in reach because of its low penetration in Russia. Media that cross the government face harassment through tax inspections and lease problems, to name only a few of the potential consequences. More chilling are the fates of leading investigative journalists like Anna Politkovskaya, Yuri Shchekochikhin and others who have been murdered or died in suspicious circumstances after pursuing major corruption investigations or challenging senior officials. All of this creates a climate of intimidation.

What Dmitri Medvedev has frequently described as the easy manipulation of the judicial system makes impotent yet another potential check on elite power and corruption. Interference in the courts by the government and private companies is a common practice rather than an exception, and the weak judiciary helps to maintain Russia's political status quo by derailing serious efforts to change it. This creates an environment in which the Russian leadership lacks important information and independent analysis when making key decisions. Moscow's control mechanism blocks this critical input and feedback.

The subservient political system merely adds another layer of top-down control. Russia's formal political system is built around the concept of the "power vertical" introduced by then-President Vladimir Putin and still in effect today. In brief, the power vertical concentrates power at the top by subordinating the country's entire government apparatus to its leaders and ensuring that any and all decisions are their prerogative. While the president and prime minister do not make every policy choice, they retain the right to make (or retroactively question) any particular decision.

Governors and other regional leaders are nominated locally but selected by the presidential administration in consultation with the prime minister's office; mayors are elected through processes that are easily manipulated, as demonstrated by the recent election in Sochi, where opposition candidates were marginalized or disqualified. Pro-government candidates at all levels routinely enjoy considerable advantages, including ready access to television, ease in getting permits for rallies and campaign donors recruited by the regime.

Local leaders—especially those in Russia's ethnically based regions, such as Chechnya's President Ramzan Kadyrov—have what resembles feudal autonomy so long as they remain outwardly loyal to the federal government and can maintain control of their domains. Kadyrov in particular is a striking case, a former rebel turned minidictator who embraces polygamy and honor killings. Yet with his brutality Kadyrov has, at least until recently, maintained stability in Chechnya—allowing Moscow to withdraw Russian troops and remove the issue as a domestic political irritant.

Moscow Mayor Yuri Luzhkov is another interesting example. Luzhkov was attacked as corrupt by the pro-Kremlin media when he and former–Prime Minister Yevgeny Primakov led a key challenge to Putin's ascension to power. Luzhkov subsequently failed to endear himself to the federal government's officials as the leader of a political-business clan that did not share the capital city's spoils sufficiently with federal bureaucrats. But Putin came to appreciate Luzhkov after his firm response to protests in the wake of a 2005 decision to reduce social benefits to retirees, veterans, the handicapped and, remarkably, even the police by providing regular benefit payments instead of free services. The Moscow mayor proved that he knew how to run his city when the chips were down. All this goes to show the conduct top officials are willing to tolerate from regional leaders so long as they deliver what counts.

While in theory a separate branch of government, Russia's legislature is in reality subordinate to its top leaders. The executive branch decides which parties hold what number of seats in the State Duma and the Federation Council and can ensure the passage of virtually any legislation. Members of parliament are permitted to lobby for their constituents by trying to secure federal-budget funds or other benefits, but have only a marginal role in policymaking.

The political parties themselves are created and destroyed from above rather than from below. There are only four parties represented in the State Duma, and three of them are creations of the Russian government. United Russia was established explicitly to serve as Russia's ruling party and a vehicle to bring Putin to power. After remaining aloof as president, Putin now leads the party, which holds a supermajority sufficient to amend the constitution. Whenever it matters, United Russia can count on the votes of the Liberal Democratic Party (LDPR), which according to insider accounts was established in part by the Soviet KGB to serve as a nationalist pseudo opposition.

The presidential administration openly served as the principal architect of Just Russia, a center left party assembled as a social-democratic alternative to United Russia. Just Russia repackaged and expanded a previous government-inspired opposition party, Rodina (Motherland), itself created as a nationalist and populist alternative to the Communists, but ultimately destroyed when the party and its leader Dmitry Rogozin proved too successful for their own good. The regime's demonization and subsequent rehabilitation of Rogozin as Moscow's ambassador to NATO once he was no longer a threat illustrates Russia's political hardball.

Only the Communist Party—which traces its origins to the Soviet period— appears to be a genuine mass party with a degree of independence. Despite this, the Communists are well aware of the limits of their power and consequently they remain unambitious: they know that the party depends on the government for its national and local registration, for access to television and for relatively easy fundraising. The Communist Party is not a toy of the Russian government, but neither is it an engine of regime change.

Parties outside the parliament have even less impact. Russia's democrats have failed to capture the public imagination—and not only because of government pressure and limits on their activities. Most pro-Western reformers were never able to successfully demonstrate that they represented the interests of ordinary people or to establish patriotic credentials with a population that remained proud and suspicious of the West. Radical Russian democrats ridiculed fear of NATO enlargement when most opposed it, dismissed concerns over U.S. missile defenses that others stoked, and in some cases supported Georgia's perspectives when Russia and Georgia were at war. More recently, democratic opposition politician and former–Prime Minister Mikhail Kasyanov supported the expulsion of Russia's delegation from the Parliamentary Assembly of the Council of Europe—a position with which very few of his fellow citizens could identify. Russian parties that appear insufficiently patriotic are marginalized, while those that embrace nationalism—like Eduard Limonov's rabidly xenophobic and anti-Western National Bolshevik Party—have greater appeal.

Despite its unattractiveness to outsiders, Russia's system of control from above and corruption throughout produces little discontent. Many feel a degree of comfort with strong leaders and a degree of discomfort with democratic freedoms. So long as Russia's citizens reap real benefits from the current arrangement, most see little need to question it.

At its deepest, this is a matter of history. There is less demand for an alternative in part because neither of Russia's two experiments with democracy was stable or successful in Russian eyes. The first experiment, between February and October of 1917, led rapidly to a "dual power" arrangement between Alexander Kerensky's Provisional Government and the Communist-dominated Soviets that degenerated into revolution, collapse and totalitarianism. The second, which began with Gorbachev's perestroika, fell apart as Yeltsin turned democratization to his own purposes and allied himself with separatist elites in order to unseat Gorbachev, splintering the USSR in the process. Yeltsin's aggressive pursuit of radical economic reforms despite popular opposition led him to rely increasingly on revitalized security services, the oligarchs and oligarch-controlled media for political backing. After this, most Russians welcomed Putin's imposition of order.

Russia's present political system is also at least partially attributable to Vladimir Putin and his allies in the security services, who have displayed both a ruthless instinct to establish control and a suspicion of anything they do not control. As president, Putin demolished the national political pretensions of the oligarchs and out-of-control governors (which helped bring an end to the semianarchy of the 1990s), but he could not bring himself to encourage civil society or free markets or to establish alternative centers of influence. From this perspective, Russia's current semiauthoritarian system is not entirely the product of a deliberate process but also the result of a vigorous effort to rein in previous abuses unaccompanied by anything else. It is authoritarianism by default.

At the same time, Russia's democratic leaders have failed to unite and failed to excite. In private conversations, many of Russia's post-Soviet democrats acknowledge that their own limited appeal was a major factor in their failure to win continued representation in the Duma in 2003. Electoral manipulation and skewed media coverage made the task much harder, but the democratic parties themselves clearly also fell short.

Without strong and unified public pressure for change, and with few mechanisms to voice those concerns should they arise, a near-term move toward further openness can come only from the top. No polls thus far show widespread public dissatisfaction with how Russia is governed, nor do any suggest that democracy is a priority for a majority or even a sizable minority of average Russians. More important for most is the fact that real incomes in Russia doubled during Vladimir Putin's two terms as president and poverty dropped by half. Wages and pensions were paid on time, and grew faster than inflation. GDP rose by 70 percent, though Russia has since been hit hard by the current crisis.

Yet even the economic downturn has had a muted political impact. Unlike during the 1998 financial meltdown, Russia today holds considerable gold and hard-currency reserves that it has been able to spend to address emerging problems or potential sources of upheaval and to protect private interests, including by bailing out many of the country's business leaders. Revealingly, though Putin publicly humiliated metals magnate Oleg Deripaska and chastised the local leaders of Pikalevo, a one-factory town near Saint Petersburg, for failing to pay their employees, he ultimately resolved the dispute to Deripaska's advantage by providing state funds to help the plants at the center of the crisis. While the former oligarchs have been shut out of high politics, they remain quite capable of advancing their concrete interests. And Russia's government can thus far afford to satisfy both the economic elite and the public.

This relative wealth and public apathy produce a degree of political stability in Russia. And because those at the top of the power vertical clearly understand that maintaining everyone's well-being is a necessary precondition of avoiding upheaval, they tend to prefer maintaining calm by tolerating the financial-industrial barons and ensuring a decent standard of living for the rest of the population. So absent a continued and more serious financial crisis that drains Russia's reserves, the status quo is likely to hold.

That is, unless the talk of competition between Putin and Medvedev has some real heft. A genuine struggle could tear both the corrupt elite and the power vertical apart, with unpredictable consequences.

Since most power rests at the top, any uncertainty there shakes the entire system. How much influence and ambition Medvedev and Putin possess, and the intentions of each, will powerfully shape how Russia evolves.

But the Medvedev-Putin dynamic is less than clear. Medvedev, the one most challenging to the status quo, is sending mixed signals about his intentions while Putin appears somewhat ambivalent about protecting his primacy. So far, Medvedev seems to be more talk than action. Though he speaks graphically about Russia's challenges and failings, he seems unprepared to act on these sentiments.

This may mean that he enjoys less than full authority, as many have suspected. As one senior official who knows both well put it privately, Putin has a "higher potential" to persuade Medvedev when the two differ. Medvedev has so far been cautious and pragmatic, openly stating that he has no plans to replace the government, therefore minimizing the chances for any fight with Putin over the fate of particular ministers or, of course, over Putin's own role. Revealingly, he has also avoided making significant changes in his own senior Kremlin staff. Khrushchev and Gorbachev learned Stalin's lesson that "cadres decide everything" and moved very quickly to bring in their own people, like Gorbachev's liberal adviser Aleksandr Yakovlev. Medvedev has talked about personnel policy but has done little.

However, judging Medvedev on the basis of his current conduct may be unwise. Russia's still-new president has clearly grown, impressing his foreign counterparts with his confidence and command of the issues. Like many others who have met him, we also noted Medvedev's evolution before and after he became president. Moreover, his behavior in Russia makes sense—he is in no position to challenge Putin directly, and alienating the prime minister prematurely would not advance his career or his agenda.

Thus it should be no surprise that Medvedev has signaled plans to move slowly in attempting to introduce change. He justifies this by referring to mistakes of the past rather than his current constraints: "not everyone is satisfied with the pace at which we are moving," he wrote, adding that he will "disappoint the supporters of permanent revolution" because "hasty and ill-considered political reforms have led to tragic consequences more than once in our history."

Yet despite Medvedev's careful politics, he is clearly trying to establish both his authority and identity, demonstrating a degree of political courage and independence. After Putin declared "we're people of the same blood, with the same political views," the Russian president commented that "we'll have a test to see whether we have the same blood type," an obvious effort to define himself distinctly from his mentor and senior partner. While Putin remains publicly unperturbed, Medvedev's growing assertiveness has clearly not gone unnoticed by the prime minister's supporters. As one close Putin associate put it to us, "at a minimum Medvedev is allowing his ambitious advisers to play a very dangerous game. Vladimir Vladimirovich's [Putin's] patience is not unlimited."

Still, Medvedev's advisers seem optimistic about his prospects and apparently do not fear open retaliation. Igor Yurgens, who leads the Institute of Contemporary Development, which Medvedev chairs, has openly suggested that Putin has outlived his usefulness and should not run again for the presidency, lest he become a new Leonid Brezhnev, the ailing Soviet leader who presided over the country's stagnation in the 1970s and early 1980s. The fact that Medvedev occasionally differs with Putin creates political space that did not previously exist. Medvedev must know this and, at a minimum, is allowing his advisers to criticize Putin and Putin's team while signaling in his own public statements that the two have different views. According to Yurgens, there is now a full-blown "clash of interests" between "conservatives and statists on one side and liberals on the other."

Medvedev's constituency—"the liberals"—seems built around Russia's educated, urban middle and upper classes. It includes some tamed oligarchs who made peace with Putin, but who still resent having been cut down to size, as well as Westernized elites and professionals. Many were educated or have a presence overseas and see integration into the global economy as among Russia's important national interests. They also see themselves as part of a transnational elite—a few are a part of that coterie that have property and bank accounts overseas—and would suffer both financially and psychologically from Russian self-isolation.

Putin, for his part, enjoys considerable authority because of the strong support of the so called *siloviki* (former KGB men and military types) in the security ministries, his economically driven popular legitimacy, his reputation for machismo and decisiveness, and a widespread sense of Russia's renewed stability and global influence. He has also grown. Appointed by Yeltsin's inner circle, including the un-savory tycoon Boris Berezovsky, who now lives in exile in London, Putin rapidly demonstrated that he was not the tool they sought and became a genuine leader. In the eyes of most Russians, he restored order, prosperity and dignity to their lives and their country, even if many outsiders believe he benefited from high energy prices and U.S. and Western distraction in Iraq and Afghanistan. Relatively few Russians are concerned about the gradual loss of freedom during his rule; Putin gave them what they wanted in exchange for what they didn't think they needed.

Importantly, most Russians believe that Putin cares about their country and cares what its people think. While no longer president, Putin continues to convey the image of a "good czar"—a national leader with clear power, charisma and a certain mystique. When polled, a majority or plurality of Russians regularly state that it is Putin who rules the country, with a smaller group saying that Putin and Medvedev share power, and only a slim share arguing that Medvedev alone is in charge. Strikingly, an August poll by the respected Moscow-based Levada Center found that some 52 percent of Russians credited Putin with leading Russia through the crisis relatively unharmed, compared to just 11 percent who praised Medvedev. When assigning responsibility for the economic hard times, 36 percent blamed "the government," 23 percent blamed Medvedev and only 17 percent blamed Putin.

Many Russian liberals recognize Putin's power and see no path toward reform without him. Yevgeny Gontmakher, who is also affiliated with the pro-Medvedev Institute of Contemporary Development, wrote that Russia needs "modernization with the prime minister" because "we do not have another person capable of somehow influencing the situation." Both Medvedev and his advisers also seem to fear moving too quickly and impulsively, reluctant to be crushed under the wheels of history like Kerensky and Gorbachev by unleashing a process that would develop its own momentum, not only bringing very different people to power (in today's case, possibly virulent left-leaning nationalists), but also creating considerably more upheaval than planned, and risking Russia's collapse or disintegration. Gontmakher writes that Russia has two options: "a ruthless mutiny" that he believes would not succeed or "some kind of modernization from above."

Much hinges on the relationship between Medvedev and Putin, which is perhaps Russia's most carefully kept secret. Medvedev says that they meet only once per week, a fact his partisans share to dispel the notion that the president receives regular guidance from Putin. Both frequently cite Russia's constitutional division of labor, which puts the president firmly in charge of foreign and security policy and leaves the economy and social issues to the prime minister. However, each routinely acts to blur the lines; Medvedev summons ministers who report to Putin to issue public instructions on the economy, while Putin often takes a visible role on security and foreign-policy issues, such as last year's war with Georgia, the decision to apply to the WTO as a customs union with Belarus and Kazakhstan (announced just days after Medvedev's advisers said Moscow would continue with its previous approach), and high-profile foreign trips, like a 2009 visit to Poland around the seventieth anniversary of the Molotov-Ribbentrop Pact and the German (and Soviet) invasion. Nevertheless, without knowing what understandings may exist between them, it is difficult to be certain what behavior and statements to ascribe to a good cop/bad cop routine, to personal ambitions or to real policy differences.

Both Medvedev's intentions and Putin's potential responses are unclear. After all, it was Putin who spent eight years systematically eliminating or weakening any potential rivals in Russian politics only to create just such a rival when he left the presidency to become prime minister. Medvedev's supporters clearly hope that the prime minister will be prepared to fade away after receiving appropriate assurances. Putin's confidants deride this as "daydreaming," arguing that their man is reenergized and sees a continuing mission for himself in Russian politics.

The big unknown is whether Putin has a sufficient lust for power to fight back if Medvedev appears successful and loyal at the same time. If so, Putin seems unlikely to be as inept as the Soviet Union's so called "anti-party group" that tried to remove Khrushchev in the 1950s or the anti-Gorbachev coup plotters of 1991.

Some Russian pundits suggest this will all come to a head with Medvedev and Putin running against one another for president in 2012. This seems unlikely. Russian politics have so far been decided before rather than during its elections and this probably will not change in the next three years. There is also no clear institutional base for Medvedev in an electoral competition against Putin. Putin chairs the United Russia party, and among the other parties in the Duma, only Just Russia could conceivably be an appropriate home for Medvedev. But Just Russia remains loyal to Putin and is both fairly weak and less supportive than United Russia of the Western-style reforms that Medvedev's camp seems to want. Thus, for Medvedev to build an institutional base, he would more likely have to be a divider rather than a uniter, splitting apart Russia's elite, its government and the United Russia party—something many will resist and many others will fear. The steady approach of 2012 and the preelection decisions it will force only fuel the tension in the Medvedev-Putin relationship—and add to Russia's uncertainty. And while Putin remains dominant thus far, his power has never been seriously challenged.

Political and economic liberalization in Russia would advance American interests and improve U.S.-Russian cooperation. However, real political conflict or a stalemate in Russia will likely be a problem for the United States as well. This is not an argument for stability for the sake of convenience in U.S. policy; it is simply a statement of fact. Political competition in Russia creates pressures to take harder lines in defining Moscow's positions and goals and can even lead to dangerous Russian actions. U.S. officials, members of Congress and others will take note of these attitudes or actions and react. At the same time, domestic uncertainty in Russia only increases the difficulty that outsiders have in understanding its government decision making and predicting Moscow's conduct—which in turn undermines American policy.

This situation means that taking sides in Russia's internal political debates could come at a great cost. This is a central lesson of the 1990s, when American support for Boris Yeltsin—who many thought was a pro-Western democrat despite early signs to the contrary—in fact persuaded most Russians that Washington was more interested in ensuring that Moscow's leaders remained weak and compliant than in helping the country's citizens or preserving democracy.

Another reason to avoid taking sides is the murky relationship between domestic reforms and foreign policy in Russia. Russia's past is replete with rulers who supported both ambitious internal reforms and aggressive foreign policies, ranging from Czar Alexander II (who freed the serfs but pursued wars in the Balkans and the Caucasus) to Soviet leader Nikita Khrushchev (who led the post-Stalin thaw but provoked the Cuban missile crisis). It also includes a few pragmatic autocrats like Alexander III, who reversed many of his father Alexander II's reforms but was careful to avoid reckless foreign pursuits.

With all the uncertainty about Russia, it may be helpful to focus on what the country is not. First and foremost, Russia is not a country governed by a messianic ideology and is neither intrinsically antidemocratic nor anti-Western. Secondly, however, Russia is not a nation of altruistic do-gooders upon whose support the United States can rely when its interests and priorities differ from Washington's. Here it is useful to recall Churchill's entire quote: "I cannot forecast to you the action of Russia. It is a riddle, wrapped in a mystery, inside an enigma; but perhaps there is a key. That key is Russian national interest."

Russia's domestic situation will be an obstacle to cooperation in some areas, but not in others. For example, Russia does not particularly seem to care how its foreign partners run their countries. Moscow has worked quite successfully with democracies such as Germany and Italy, demonstrating that Russia does not have a problem with democratic governments as such. In fact, Russia's leaders seem to have gotten along much better with German Chancellor Angela Merkel than Belarusian strongman President Alexander Lukashenko, with whom they have frequent public spats. Conversely, contrary to Georgian President Mikheil Saakashvili's assertions, Russia's problem with Georgia is not its democracy but its hostile conduct. When Saakashvili acted on his sometimes-authoritarian instincts in Georgia, he received no credit for it in Moscow.

Similarly, Russia's internal politics will not prevent its leaders from cooperating pragmatically with the United States on issues like arms control and nonproliferation when they view such efforts as promoting their interests. Nor will it prohibit Russia from becoming an American partner on some issues at some times, or from viewing partnership with the United States as sufficiently serving its national interests to influence other calculations.

Ultimately, of course, Russia's domestic practices present the greatest obstacles to Russia itself, which severely limits foreign investment, modernization and the country's integration into the international system without making real changes. This will in turn affect not only Moscow's hard power but also its soft power. So while Vice President Joseph Biden's recent blunt assessment of Russia's decline may have been exceedingly undiplomatic—and mistaken in its conclusion that Moscow would have no choice but to cooperate with Washington—it was not fundamentally incorrect if Russia does not alter its course. While Medvedev has promised to do this, he admits that little has happened even in the wake of Russia's dismal performance in the global financial crisis.

Russia has been a difficult interlocutor since its independence nearly two decades ago and is unlikely to become an easier one anytime soon. But for all of its faults—and they are many—Russia is not inherently an American foe. Russia's leaders may be ruthless, but they do not need foreign enemies. With care and determination, the United States can work with Moscow to advance important national interests.

The Next Silicon Valley

Siberia*

By Brett Forrest
Fortune, March 23, 2007

Time passes slowly in Novosibirsk. In front of the opera house on Red Prospect, skateboard kids skid off the plinth of the Lenin statue, chewing on Afghan nuswar, which calibrates the brain to a low buzz. Rusted auto husks and the tilting chimneys of roadside hovels appear to have slouched into poses over many decades. At the boat hotel on the Ob River, the cook does not hurry with the kasha. The capital of Siberia, Russia's third-largest city, Novosibirsk in winter offers few explicit charms.

But travel beyond the slot halls of downtown, past wild dogs patrolling wild weeds, past Tajik road crews in orange jump suits, and a hub of activity rises from the woodland. In this place, where capitalist opportunity has overcome post-Soviet dreariness, time moves at the pace of obtainable dollars.

This is Akademgorodok—Academy Town—where Russian high tech booms. Action in IT , pharmaceuticals, metallurgy, and fossil fuels is making Novosibirsk, tucked away in a remote tract of Russia, a hive of outsourcing. Private high tech in Akademgorodok has expanded from a $10 million business a decade ago to a $150 million industry last year, with the number of firms growing at a rate of 15% annually. Akademgorodok won't pass for Silicon Valley. But there is enough upside and softly priced expertise for Intel, IBM, and Schlumberger to make camp here in what is called the Silicon Forest. Russia's federal government has also taken note, backing the construction of a new $650 million technology business district. And in an odd signal of Akademgorodok's broadening reach, a local IT firm is producing a web portal for Oprah Winfrey.

Russian science and technology present an unusual mix of critical thinking, developmental breakthrough, and professional hunger born of the proximity of actual hunger. "Inside Intel we have an expression," says Steve Chase, president of

Intel Russia. "If you have something tough, give it to the Americans. If you have something difficult, give it to the Indians. If you have something impossible, give it to the Russians."

The story begins in 1958, when leading figures in the Soviet scientific apparatus secured Nikita Khrushchev's backing to establish a town devoted entirely to pure science. The idea was to collect many of the country's top scientists in a single location deep in the Siberian woods, far from prying eyes and metropolitan distractions. By 1963, building crews had completed Akademgorodok, a scholastic and research entity 20 miles outside Novosibirsk. Within a few years, a university had opened, and its graduates were being plugged into the dozens of institutes dedicated to advanced research—a Soviet approximation of Cambridge, Mass.

In much of the world, moving to Siberia wouldn't be regarded as an especially brainy plan of attack. But that is just what many of the Soviet Union's greatest scientific minds decided to do, and to a large extent willingly, lured by the promise of new housing and professional advancement. For 30 years, Novosibirsk was one of the smartest cities in the imperium, a collective of academics who put their minds to everything from nuclear physics to theoretical genetics, from the space program to the weapons aimed at the great American evil.

And then the bottom dropped out.

When the Soviet state collapsed in 1991, the scientific community crumbled along with it. The salaries and status allotted to accomplished scientists vanished, as did a system geared toward nourishing young talent. Novosibirsk's Akademgorodok was left with thousands of scientists, a bruised mission, little money, and the overwhelming anxiety that attends the decease of a patriarch.

A walk through the Novosibirsk Institute of Automation and Electrometry is all it takes to see the neglect. Electrical wires hang from the ceiling like stray hairs across a tired forehead. Paint flakes from the walls; lights in the passageways flicker from dim to dark. For an institution that once sparred with the math department of MIT, the place could use a pick-me-up.

But when Mikhail Lavrentyev, a Siberian mathematician of lofty provenance, opens the door to a research lab, he reveals what is saving Akademgorodok from sliding into irreversible institutional decrepitude: one very spherical man and another with severely crossed eyes hunched over computer terminals. These two doctoral students are writing code for Intel.

Lavrentyev's grandfather, also Mikhail, was the prime mover in creating Akademgorodok. It was while working in the closed nuclear research town of Sarov that the elder Lavrentyev came upon the idea of creating an entirely new science town. It has been his grandson's fortune to oversee Akademgorodok's repurposing. "Akademgorodok was a new idea, multi-disciplinary, to give young scientists a real chance to develop ideas," Lavrentyev says. "But salaries in the '90s went south, and it became a problem for the academy. There became a clear choice when you finished your degree. Go to science, or go to business and immediately you have a reasonable salary."

So began the great hustle, as the pure scientists of Akademgorodok had to find a way to survive, commodifying and commercializing the high-tech expertise that once served the state. Many young scientists gravitated toward IT. Every year, Russia graduates as many scientific and technology specialists as India—200,000—although Russia is 80% smaller by population. Russia's software exports now exceed $1.8 billion annually, and the country is the third-largest software outsourcing destination in the world, after China and India. "In these other countries, there was no technological culture like we had in Soviet times," says Dmitry Milovantsev, Russia's deputy minister of information technology and communication, hinting at the country's potential.

A company called Novosoft launched Novosibirsk's IT wave in 1992, growing to 500 employees and eventually partnering with IBM. Novosoft splintered in the Internet bubble, the effects of which registered even in Siberia, although the firm maintains a significant presence. Other companies have made considerable strides since then, most notably SW Soft, an IT infrastructure company specializing in server software. Today, SW Soft has more than 10,000 international customers and has received funding from Insight Venture Partners and Intel Capital.

Large multinationals are also taking advantage of the changing climate. Intel opened an Akademgorodok office in 2004 and now employs 200 programmers who optimize microprocessors. IBM arrived first to the market in 2000, while Schlumberger has taken the lead in local investment, having purchased a plot of land on which it is building an R&D lab.

The low cost of rent, services, and salaries—roughly one-fifth of Western prices—appeals, but so does the manner in which the system molds its wards. "None of our programmers in Novosibirsk are programmers by education," says Intel's Chase. "They are physicists, chemists, biologists, mathematicians. They are first of all scientists. Secondly, they learn how to program, as an afterthought. This combination is extremely powerful."

IT offices are springing up on Akademgorodok's leafy lanes as well as in its industrial back alleys. The work has been easy to come by, and with good reason, for words such as "loans," "grants," and "investments" haven't a place in the local lexicon. "We're kind of spoiled in America," says James Smith, manager of emerging Internet technologies for IBM. "In Novosibirsk, they work from a different mindset. They need to generate capital if they're going to move forward and buy a house or build a business."

IBM now works with, among others, a Novosoft spinoff called Axmor, employing web mashup technologies—combining a spreadsheet, say, with a Google map—to create applications for clients in digital media and retail banking. Smith dispatches his marching orders from IBM's suburban campus in Raleigh. Axmor, meanwhile, finds itself in a renovated apartment complex on the edge of Akademgorodok, a pack of mongrels lurking about the entrance. Inside the office, two slender, sun-deprived code punchers are playing table-hockey.

Pavel Toponogov, Axmor's director, has turned a $30,000 investment into $1 million in revenue in just a few years. The bulk of work comes from outside Russia, much of it generated through Internet advertising. That is the way Harpo Productions, Oprah Winfrey's media company, hired Axmor to build a web portal. "We didn't really know who Oprah was," says Andrey Kanonirov, Axmor's IBM project manager, "but we know who she is now."

In Russia, outside of Moscow and St. Petersburg, hunting for computer service and parts is a game marked by retail incompetence and technical incompatibility, a product of last decade's models and the last regime's disregard for the wishes of the customer class. Not so in Novosibirsk. Walk into Technocity in Akademgorodok and not only will you encounter the kind of service that betrays the sales force's acquaintance with capitalist fundamentals, but you had also better hope that your own hardware is up to speed. With five-dollar haircuts and Bluetooth rigs jammed into their ears, the attendants will let you know that their merchandise moves so quickly that all they have is the newest of the new, about which they are highly conversant. As this sinks in, walk out the door and deposit a few rubles in the hand of a terrified pensioner whom society has cast aside.

There's a lot of that in this town, the up-to-date encased in the same old sausage skin, the ultramodern colliding with the outmoded. Developers at Broker Consulting Services design a Panasonic home-theater system in a building that once served as casing for a giant computer, in the days when mainframes were of such size. Laser Crystal Solutions, which grows crystals under a lucrative contract with a California photonics firm, operates out of a darkened longhouse. One of the top exporters in Akademgorodok, the Novosibirsk Institute of Nuclear Physics, houses an electron-positron collider that its 65-year-old director used during his school days. In a drafty hangar that was until recently inhabited by drunks and rodents, Screen Photo Electronic Instruments produces night-vision devices for a San Francisco company. "It's so cold here," says Vladimir Aksyonov, the general director, wrapped in a white lab coat, "there's nothing to do but work."

Even with less than ideal facilities, Akademgorodok presents a singular picture of Russia. A sense of purpose is difficult to ignore. "What you feel out there is pride," says Intel's Chase. "That's what their history is all about."

Before the railroad came to Novosibirsk in 1893, travelers endured a tenmonth journey to reach the area by horse cart from Moscow. Now, Dmitry Verkhovod interrupts a meeting to sign for an overnight package from Ozon, Russia's equivalent of Amazon.com. "Look at this," he says, tossing the package from hand to hand. "Even out here in Siberia, I can receive DVDs, books, music."

Verkhovod, deputy president of the Siberian branch of the Russian Academy of Sciences, is the man in charge of plans for Novosibirsk's one-million-square-foot business center, designed to alter the way Akademgorodok tech is turned into profit. "The history of Novosibirsk is a series of jumps like this," Verkhovod says, spreading architectural drawings across his desk.

First the rails came, the town sprouting up after engineers chose this barren spot for the Trans-Siberian Railroad to cross the Ob River. Then, during World War II, the state evacuated factories from European Russia to the safe harbor of Novosibirsk. Akademgorodok was the next major development. "This will be another jump," Verkhovod says. "Right now we don't have a way to commercialize our developments. The Novosibirsk Akademgorodok is a huge brand, and it has to be marketed."

Novosibirsk's tech center will be one of four in Russia, part of a plan President Vladimir Putin announced in Akademgorodok in 2005, on the heels of a trip to tech-savvy India. The complex will receive $100 million in state funding for infrastructure, with private firms kicking in the rest and receiving tax breaks in return.

High tech is the sort of thing the Kremlin would like to develop, understanding that natural resources can't last forever and brain resources need tapping. "We simply mustn't waste this chance," Putin declared. But Russia is still learning on the fly. The Ministry for Information Technology and Communications was established only in 2004. Deputy minister Milovantsev stresses patience. "It's not like building a house, where you put people in it and they're happy," he says. "Our goals are more distant."

Lenin once commented disapprovingly about the disposition of the Siberian peasant: wealthy, satisfied, uninterested in revolution. But there are revolutions of grapeshot, and those that employ more subtle means. In the tech revolution, Novosibirsk has shown itself to be more than game.

"My grandfather was a fighter," Lavrentyev says, emerging from his institute, braced against a cutting wind, wearing only a sport coat. Attached to his lapel is a small pin, a cameo of his grandfather. "I think he would appreciate worldwide high-tech brands like Intel and Schlumberger here. At the same time, I think he would want business to pay for using our brains."

Someone will always shell out for a scientific mind, be it the state, the private firm, or the publicly traded behemoth. In Akademgorodok, it has been a matter of shifting masters, and in various instances becoming one's own master. Back on the road to solvency, Lavrentyev turns away and walks up a boulevard named for his grandfather, a bust of the old man visible against the trees.

Russia and U.S. Sign Nuclear Arms Reduction Pact[*]

By Peter Baker and Dan Bilefsky
The New York Times, April 8, 2010

With flourish and fanfare, President Obama and President Dmitri A. Medvedev of Russia signed a nuclear arms control treaty on Thursday and opened what they hoped would be a new era in the tumultuous relationship between two former cold war adversaries.

Meeting here [Prague, The Czech Republic] in the heart of a once divided Europe, the two leaders put aside the acrimony that has characterized Russian-American ties in recent years as they agreed to bring down their arsenals and restore an inspection regime that expired in December. Along the way, they sidestepped unresolved disputes over missile defense and other issues.

"When the United States and Russia are not able to work together on big issues, it is not good for either of our nations, nor is it good for the world," Mr. Obama said as his words echoed through a majestic, gilded hall in the famed Prague Castle. "Together, we have stopped the drift, and proven the benefits of cooperation. Today is an important milestone for nuclear security and nonproliferation, and for U.S.-Russia relations."

Mr. Medvedev called the treaty signing "a truly historic event" that will "open a new page" in Russian-American relations. "What matters most is this is a win-win situation," he said. "No one stands to lose from this agreement. I believe this is a typical feature of our cooperation. Both parties have won."

The Russian president signaled general support for the American-led drive to impose new sanctions on Iran, saying that Tehran's nuclear program has flouted the international community. "We cannot turn a blind eye to this," Mr. Medvedev said, while adding that sanctions "should be smart" and avoid hardship for the Iranian people.

Mr. Obama said he expected "to be able to secure strong, tough sanctions" on Iran during the spring.

The apparently warm relationship between the two presidents was on display as they entered the hall to trumpet music. They whispered and smiled with each other in English as they sat side by side signing copies of the so-called New Start treaty, then traded compliments during a follow-up exchange with reporters.

Mr. Obama called the Russian a "friend and partner" and said "without his personal efforts and strong leadership, we would not be here today." For his part, Mr. Medvedev said the two had developed a "very good personal relationship and a very good personal chemistry, as they say."

While the treaty will mandate only modest reductions in the actual arsenals maintained by the two countries, it caps a turnaround in relations with Moscow that sunk to rock bottom in August 2008 during the war between Russia and its tiny southern neighbor, Georgia. When he arrived in office, Mr. Obama made restoring the relationship a priority, a goal that coincided with his vision expressed here a year ago of eventually ridding the world of nuclear weapons.

Even as the two presidents hailed the treaty, however, they found no common ground on American plans to build an anti-missile shield in Europe to counter any Iranian threat. Mr. Obama refused Russian demands to include limits on missile defense in the treaty, nearly scuttling the agreement. In the days leading up to the ceremony here, Russian officials alternately claimed the agreement would bind the program or complained that it did not and threatened to withdraw if it went forward.

The treaty, if ratified by lawmakers in both countries, would require each country to deploy no more than 1,550 strategic warheads, down from 2,200 allowed in the Treaty of Moscow signed by President George W. Bush in 2002. Each would be limited to 800 total land- , air- and sea-based launchers—700 of which can be deployed at any given time—down from 1,600 permitted under the Strategic Arms Reduction Treaty of 1991, or Start.

Because of counting rules and unilateral reductions over the years, neither country would have to actually eliminate large numbers of weapons to meet the new limits. Moreover, the treaty does not apply to whole categories of weapons, including thousands of strategic warheads held in reserve and tactical warheads, some of which are still stationed in Europe.

But the treaty would re-establish an inspection regime that lapsed along with Start last December and bring the two countries back into a legal framework after years of tension. Moreover, both sides hope to use it as a foundation for a new round of negotiations that could lead to much deeper reductions that will cover weapons like stored or tactical warheads.

The first task for Mr. Obama after returning to Washington will be persuading the Senate to ratify the new treaty and advisers planned to head to Capitol Hill on Thursday, even before his return, to brief Senate staff.

Ratification requires a two-thirds vote, or 67 senators, meaning the president needs at least eight Republicans. The White House is counting on the support of

Senator Richard G. Lugar of Indiana, the senior Republican on the Foreign Relations Committee and one of his party's most respected voices on international affairs, to clear the way.

But it could still have to contend with skeptics like Senator Jon Kyl of Arizona, the Republican whip, who have expressed concern about limiting American defenses. And the polarized politics of Washington heading into a mid-term election are volatile, meaning a vote could be delayed until after the election, which would further put off other elements of Mr. Obama's anti-nuclear agenda, such as consideration of the Comprehensive Test Ban Treaty.

The White House wants a vote by the end of the year and Robert Gibbs, the president's press secretary, reminded reporters on Air Force One during the flight here that past arms-control treaties have received near unanimous votes. "We are hopeful that reducing the threat of nuclear weapons remains a priority for both parties," he said.

But what he did not note is that the Senate has also rejected an arms control agreement in recent times, refusing to ratify the test ban treaty when it was originally brought up in 1999. Moreover, it took three years in the 1990s to ratify the first Start follow-up treaty, known as Start 2, which never went into force because of a dispute over Russian conditions attached during its own ratification process.

Mr. Obama hopes to use the trust built during the treaty negotiations to leverage more cooperation from Moscow on other issues, most notably pressuring Iran to give up its nuclear program.

Speaking after signing the treaty with Mr. Medvedev, Mr. Obama said the United States and Russia were "part of a coalition of nations insisting that the Islamic Republic of Iran face consequences, because they have continually failed to meet their obligations" under international rules governing the use of nuclear materials.

"Those nations that refuse to meet their obligations will be isolated, and denied the opportunity that comes with international integration," he said. Iran maintains its nuclear program is for civilian purposes, but the United States and its western allies suspect Tehran wants to build a nuclear weapon.

Warmer relations with the Kremlin worry American allies in Central and Eastern Europe, which were already concerned that Mr. Obama's decision last year to scrap Mr. Bush's missile-defense plan in favor of a reformulated architecture was seen as a concession to Moscow.

Hoping to soothe those concerns, Mr. Obama plans to have dinner Thursday night in Prague with 11 leaders from the region, including the presidents or prime ministers of Bulgaria, Croatia, the Czech Republic, Estonia, Hungary, Latvia, Lithuania, Poland, Romania, Slovakia and Slovenia.

Similarly, Mr. Obama made sure before leaving Washington to speak by phone with President Mikheil Saakashvili of Georgia to reassure him of American support. He will meet separately with Czech leaders on Friday morning before returning to Washington.

5

"A Riddle Wrapped in a Mystery": Inside Contemporary Russia

Courtesy of Sergey Feo

Buildings under construction at the Moscow International Business Center (IBC) district. The Moscow IBC, also known as Moscow City, is a commercial district that opened in 1992.

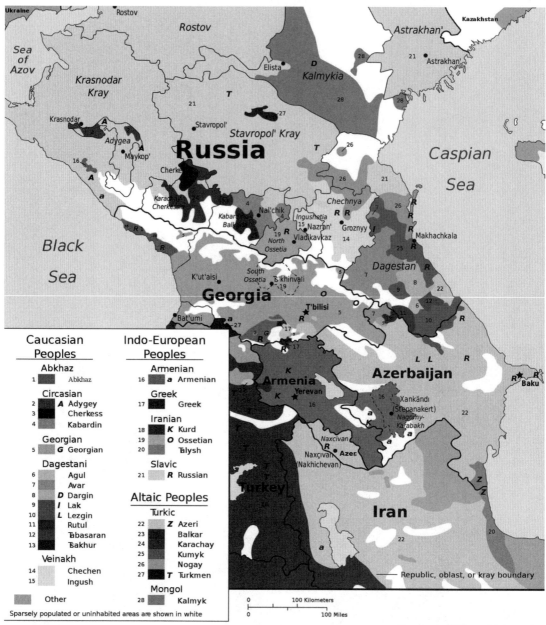

Caucasian Peoples

Abkhaz
1   Abkhaz

Circasian
2   **A**   Adygey
3   Cherkess
4   Kabardin

Georgian
5   **G**   Georgian

Dagestani
6   Agul
7   Avar
8   **D**   Dargin
9   **I**   Lak
10   **L**   Lezgin
11   Rutul
12   Tabasaran
13   Tsakhur

Veinakh
14   Chechen
15   Ingush

    Other

Indo-European Peoples

Armenian
16   **a**   Armenian

Greek
17   Greek

Iranian
18   **K**   Kurd
19   **O**   Ossetian
20   Talysh

Slavic
21   **R**   Russian

Altaic Peoples

Turkic
22   **Z**   Azeri
23   Balkar
24   Karachay
25   Kumyk
26   Nogay
27   **T**   Turkmen

Mongol
28   Kalmyk

Sparsely populated or uninhabited areas are shown in white

— Republic, oblast, or kray boundary

0   100 Kilometers
0   100 Miles

Courtesy of Temo Blumgardt

A map of the ethnic groups in the Caucasus region. The Caucasus Mountains starddle the border betwen Asia and Europe and contain the nations of Chechnya, Ingushetia, Dagestan, Adyghea, Kabardino-Balkaria, Karachai-Cherkessia, North Ossetia, Krasnodar Krai, Stavropol Krai, Armenia, Azerbaijan, and Georgia.

Russia has often had tense relationships with its southern neighbors, especially Georgia. A war broke out in 2008 over the disputed area of South Ossetia, a predominantly Russian enclave that falls within Georgia's borders. Russia intervened to protect South Ossetia, which had declared independence from Georgia in 1990, sending troops across the border. The five-day war ended in a cease-fire, although Russian troops remained in the area.

Editor's Introduction

> "I cannot forecast to you the action of Russia. It is a riddle, wrapped in a mystery, inside an enigma; but perhaps there is a key. That key is Russian national interest."
>
> *-Winston Churchill*

Nearly two decades after the Soviet collapse, Russia remains an enigma. Geographically vast, ethnically diverse, and governed by somewhat opaque rulers, it is a nation of contradictions and ambiguities—an erstwhile superpower struggling to reassert its global importance. Whereas Americans see things as "black and white," according to a source quoted in writer Martin Cruz Smith's "Moscow Never Sleeps," one of the pieces included in this, the fifth and final chapter, Russians have learned to see "a gray area perhaps 80 percent" of the time.

The articles in this chapter seek to illuminate this gray area, telling the tales of modern Russians in a range of situations. In "Moscow Never Sleeps," the first entry, Smith hits the town with the city's young millionaires and billionaires, sipping champagne in exclusive nightclubs and watching as Ducati motorcycles zip around the Garden Ring, a de-facto raceway for the nouveau riche. In Smith's version of Moscow, the police are ineffective and bribery is commonplace. While the haves live the good life, he writes, the have-nots stumble drunk through Komsomol Square, better known as Three Stations, where gangs and prostitutes exemplify the prosperous city's dark flipside.

Compared to Smith's extravagant clubbers, the Russians described in Julia Ioffe's "The Moscow Bombings Don't Matter," the next selection, are a resigned, sober lot. Mere hours after a series of March 2010 subway bombings perpetrated by Chechen separatists, many residents of Russia's capital simply resumed their daily routines, seemingly unfazed by the attacks. Russians are used to such violence, Ioffe suggests, arguing that the bombings will neither lead to a third war with Chechnya nor undermine the credibility of Prime Minister Vladimir Putin, who remains a more trusted figure than President Dmitry Medvedev.

In "Why Are Chechens So Angry?" the following article, Oliver Bullough explains the centuries-old conflict between the Russians and Chechens, an Islamic people based in the Caucasus Mountains. The two sides have been fighting on and off since 1721, and given the recent spate of terror attacks, an end to hostilities is nowhere in sight.

With "Send Me to Siberia: Oil Transforms a Russian Outpost," the subsequent selection, Paul Starobin considers life in one of Russia's eastern regions. Notoriously frigid and barren, Siberia has at least one thing going for it: crude oil—and lots of it. Thanks to Siberian reserves, Russia has surpassed Saudi Arabia as the world's leading oil producer. While the oil boom has revitalized Siberia's cities, it has also led to charges of widespread corruption—particularly as the Kremlin has sought to gain control of the industry.

Staying in the east, *Observer* writer Luke Harding situates himself on the Russian-Chinese border, the focal point of "Russia Fears Embrace of Giant Eastern Neighbour," the next piece. Harding traces the complex history of Russian-Chinese relations and highlights the ways in which citizens of the two countries are increasingly intermingling, both socially and economically. The improved informal relations come as the two nations move in different directions, Harding writes, with Russia's global influence seemingly waning and China's very much on the rise.

Switching back to the west in "Restlessness in Russia's Western Outpost," the following selection, writer Michael Schwirtz visits Kaliningrad, a city physically and culturally apart from the rest of the country. Situated between Poland and Lithuania—both members of the European Union—Kaliningrad has become a hotbed for anti-Kremlin sentiment. As Schwirtz explains, residents long for a more European way of life. Although they enjoy greater freedoms than those in Russia proper, they're frustrated by their city's decrepit infrastructure and overburdened by Moscow's high import tariffs. "We live within the European Union," a café owner tells Schwirtz. "But it turns out that we live behind a fence."

Focus next shifts back to the east, as writer David Quammen looks at the Kamchatka Peninsula, the setting for this chapter's final article, "Where the Salmon Rule." This far-flung eastern territory is a key breeding ground for many varieties of salmon, whose unique life cycle involves swimming out into the Sea of Okhotsk or Pacific Ocean, spending two to five years awaiting sexual maturity, and then returning home to lay eggs. This process, which is crucial to Kamchatka's ecosystem, is being threatened by overfishing and egg poaching, Quammen writes. While the local government, in partnership with private environmental organizations, has instituted measures for protecting the salmon, the effectiveness of these efforts remains to be seen.

Moscow Never Sleeps[*]

By Martin Cruz Smith
National Geographic, August 2008

At midnight the city is a brilliant grid of light that includes the gilded dome of the Cathedral of Christ the Savior, the Stalinist horror of the Ukraine Hotel, and a dark loop of the Moscow River. Downstream the lights of round-the-clock construction hang in the air while steel and concrete disappear. The clutter of the day is gone. The night brings clarity, and lights trace the future.

On Sparrow Hills, however, all eyes were on an unsanctioned rally of motorcycles: Japanese bikes as bright as toys, dour Russian Vostoks, "monster" Ducatis, Harleys with exhaust pipes of polished chrome. Hundreds of bikers and admirers filled the vista terrace to see machines that posed on their stands in the negligent fashion of movie stars. A Harley merely had to clear its throat to thrill the crowd.

Some bikes were so customized it was difficult to determine what they started as. A Ural that usually hauled sacks of potatoes in its side car had been transformed into a stealth-black predator bristling with rockets and machine guns. As the machine-gun barrels were chair legs and the handlebars were crutches, the effect was more theatrical than threatening. Despite the display of leather and studs, the same could be said of the bikers. I asked an ogre with a shaved head and bandanna what his day job was.

In a growl, "I sleep."

To which his girlfriend added, "Fievel's a computer programmer."

Geek by day, bandit by night.

My friend Sasha was along. Sasha is so soft-spoken he seems shy, when in fact he is a homicide detective who weighs his words. In the army he competed in biathlons, the sport of racing on skis with a rifle and then stopping to shoot at a target as his heart pounded against his ribs. He still has that calm.

We first met years ago in an Irish bar in Moscow. My highly intelligent colleague Lyuba and I were celebrating the end of two weeks of on-the-ground research and interviews for one of my novels. Sasha had just dragged some dead mafia from a swamp and was in no mood for fictional heroes. Now that he is married to Lyuba, he is forced to endure my constant questions, although he gripes that my Investigator Renko should be a regular detective like him.

Racing began across the boulevard. Competitors were a blur between spectators, the smaller bikes accelerating with a whine while the heavyweights produced a roar that made the ground tremble. The finish line was negotiable, anywhere from a hundred meters to a circuit of the Garden Ring, the peripheral road around the center of Moscow, where bikes could reach 120 miles an hour, depending on traffic. Car races also took place, or did until the crackdown after YouTube featured videos of drivers weaving in and out of Ring traffic at three times the speed limit.

A biker in a padded leather outfit—more a belief system than actual protection—mounted a Kawasaki, maybe 750cc. What did I know? I once rode a Vespa scooter from Rome to the south of Spain; that's the extent of my expertise, and I worried when a teenage girl wearing little more than a helmet hopped on behind. As soon as she had a grip, they glided toward the race lanes. The girl looked so frail I had to ask, Who is in charge? Where are the police?

Sasha pointed at a group of militia officers who stood bashfully to one side.

"It's out of their control."

The bikes blasted off the mark. In seconds the kids were taillights that faded away.

WHO IS IN CHARGE?

Vladimir Putin? His successor, Dmitry Medvedev? The legendary oligarchs? The KGB disguised as a kinder FSB? (There does seem to be an active or former secret agent on the board of every major company.) Well, as they say in Russia, "Those who know, know." What is certain is that Moscow is afloat in petrodollars; there are more billionaires in Moscow than in any other city in the world. More than New York, London, or Dubai. Millionaires are as common as pigeons. Together the rich and mega-rich constitute a social class who were loosely called New Russians when they first appeared in the 1990s. Half of them are survivors of industrial shake-ups like the "aluminum war" of ten years ago, when executives were killed left and right. Half have discovered that starting a bank is more profitable than robbing one. Half are young financial trapeze artists swinging from one hedge fund to another. (You can have three halves in Russia.)

But what a change. When I first visited Moscow in 1973, the entire population of the city seemed to retire to a crypt as soon as the sun went down. The few cars on the street were small, dyspeptic Zhigulis. A shop window display might be a single dried fish. Red Square was empty except for the honor guard at Lenin's Tomb, and billboards featured the stony visage of General Secretary Brezhnev. Banners declared, "The Communist Party Is the Vanguard of the Working Class!"

That was the world that today's New Russians grew up in, and it is no wonder that their repressed energy and frustration have erupted with a passion.

Russians are over the top. They're not "old money" hiding behind ivy-covered walls. In fact, they often refuse old money. It's new money, crisp American $100 bills flown in daily and spent almost as fast. Think about it. A billion dollars is a thousand million dollars. How do you celebrate success on such a scale? How much caviar can you eat? How much bubbly can you drink? Et cetera. That's why clubs were invented.

Clubs give the rich the chance to "flaunt it, baby, flaunt it," assured that "face control" will stop undesirables at the door. Face control is executed by men who in a glance can determine your financial profile and celebrity status. And whether you are carrying a gun.

The first sign that the GQ Bar was hot was the number of Bentleys and Lamborghinis lined up at the curb. I was visiting with writer Lana Kapriznaya and journalist Yegor Tolstyakov. Lana is dark haired, petite, about a hundred pounds, including cigarette smoke. She is an acerbic chronicler of the follies of New Russians. Yegor has a voice meant for a dirge, but see him, and he's smiling.

"Think of the GQ as a boy's club," Lana said. "A boy's club with bodyguards."

New arrivals were greeted by women who were beautiful on a surreal level. Big air kiss. Big air kiss. The GQ Bar is licensed by the magazine publisher Condé Nast International, which provides a steady supply of models who sip water at $20 a bottle and pick at Kamchatka crab, a giant crustacean served with six sauces. The interior design is out of Somerset Maugham, all dark woods and lazy ceiling fans. Not hungry? Nyet problem. GQ's VIP lounge is a watering hole for lions only. Here a man can sip Johnnie Walker Blue, light a Cuban cigar, sip a brandy, unwind, and make more money.

New Russians are social animals; they squeeze business and pleasure together the way Russian drivers squeeze five lanes out of four. The office is full of petty distractions: meetings, phone calls, endless details. Billion-dollar deals await the cool hours of the evening. There is a Russian tradition that you can't trust or do business with a man until you have been drunk together. Food, vodka, money, they go hand in hand.

More astonishing than the grooming of men is the transformation of women. In the few years since the collapse of the Soviet Union, Russian women have metamorphosed from hefty builders of socialism to tennis stars who stand a head taller than the general population. During the day, clones of Maria Sharapova move from spa to spa. At night, they go from club to club in the giddy hope of meeting their own millionaire.

While a GQ deputy director named Sergei gave us a tour, Lana described the buy list of a New Russian: "a flat in Moscow, a town house in Belgravia, a villa in St.-Tropez, a ski chalet in Courchevel, foreign schools for his children, foreign banks for his money, and, finally, a private jet to fly away in."

This is a sore point in Russia. Even in the worst days under Stalin there was a general sense of classlessness. People didn't have money, they had perks: a larger ration of sausage, an extra week at a sanatorium, access to foreign films. The New Russians have emerged in a cloudburst of dollars, and they are, in the eyes of most people, thieves. Their lifestyle is both envied and abhorred, and since Moscow is the center, there are imitations of its club scene across the country. It is fair to say that for many young Russians, clubs define the night.

Sergei described the clubbing schedule: 10 to 12 is for pre-party socializing in the restaurant, 12 to 4 for partying in the clubs, 4 to 6 for post-party cooling off. He informed me that when Mickey Rourke is in Moscow, he parties at GQ.

I can imagine Rourke partying until dawn. I imagine myself in bed, my head on a pillow.

We left GQ and hit a club that was launching either a new BMW or a new vodka or both. Then to a club in Gorky Park for a more democratic crowd where, besides playing Whac-A-Mole with a rubber mallet, you can walk on a man-made beach. Nice place.

Nonetheless, I felt that I was missing something. What was the very best club in Moscow? Which was the most fantastic?

"Well," Lana said, "there's Diaghilev."

"What makes it so popular?"

"No one can get in."

THREE STATIONS—PART ONE

If Diaghilev is Moscow's Mount Olympus, Three Stations is its lower depths. Officially Three Stations is Komsomol Square, but the locals know it by the railway terminals that converge there: Yaroslavl and Leningrad Stations on the north side and Kazan Station on the south. A statue of Lenin stands on a side plaza. The firebrand of the Russian Revolution holds the lapel of his coat with his left hand and with his right reaches for a back pocket. He appears to have just realized his wallet is gone. That's Three Stations.

Every day thousands of commuters arrive and pour out onto the wide pavement against a counterflow of traders dragging in suitcases stuffed with clothes and shoes for resale in the provinces. Street vendors offer rabbit fur hats, Soviet kitsch, roses wrapped in cellophane, pirated CDs. Tourists stagger under backpacks. Women from Central Asia brush by in voluminous skirts the color of poppies, while soldiers search for game arcades.

Every kind of face surfaces. Blue-eyed Ukrainians, hawklike men from the Caucasus, Uzbeks in caps, Mongolians, and especially Tajiks. A demographic time bomb facing Russia is its declining population and the influx of Tajiks, who are known to be sober, hardworking, and willing to do jobs Russians won't.

But at 2 a.m. the square was vast and still. The misty light of streetlamps revealed what the traffic of the daytime, the coming and going of travelers and peddlers, had hidden. The drunks around Kazan Station were difficult to see at first because they were as gray as the pavement. These were not casual drunks or men on a bender but dedicated alcoholics literally pickled in vodka. So many were bandaged or bloody they could have been a battlefield tableau. One held up a cardboard sign that said "Give Us Money or We'll Die."

Behind the station lay a dark alley of shuttered kiosks and homeless people wrapped in rags and newspaper. Those capable of standing staggered sideways. In the faint light a woman dressed in rags tied a bouquet of lavender. The one kiosk that was open sold vodka, of course. Shadows dashed by. Street kids. "These are free people," Sasha said.

"You mean homeless."

"No, there are shelters. They choose this. Free people."

We watched prostitutes in tight pants grind by. They have a reputation for breaking clonidine pills into soluble powder. Clonidine is a powerful blood pressure medication. One spiked vodka and the customer passes out, ready to be stripped. When the victim wakes in his under clothes, he probably won't run to the nearest militia officer. Drunk or not, he should know that at Three Stations the police are the pimps.

As we moved farther into the shadows behind the station, we came upon a scuffle between two gangs, Russian versus Tajik, about eight on each side, ages from 10 to 20. No knives were in sight, although a Tajik had a Russian down and was pounding his face into the concrete.

Sasha told me to stay where I was and waded alone into the melee. The Tajik paused, his fist cocked, trying to figure who this interloper was. The Russian on the ground lifted his battered head, trying to work out the same thing. I heard Sasha give them the Russian equivalent of "Break it up and go home." But the gangs were home, both sides claiming the same turf; that was the problem. About the only thing they hated more than each other was an outsider.

They weren't innocents. They dealt drugs, rolled drunks, and swarmed over anyone they caught alone and unarmed. The Tajik picked up his hat, a jaunty fedora, and immediately I thought of the Cat in the Hat. The Russian got to his feet. He looked like an ingrate to me. Suddenly we were in Dirty Harry territory. Did Sasha have a gun? Did the gang feel lucky? Well, did they?

Not tonight. Instead, they beat a sullen retreat. I may have been an easy target, but Sasha was definitely not to be messed with. The Cat in the Hat saluted him and called him "brother," as if they'd meet again.

As a matter of fact, tucked into his belt, Sasha had a pistol that he's proud of because it was given to him as an award for meritorious service. One side of the gun frame is inscribed like a trophy with his name. He hates to use it.

CARS

During the day the streets of Moscow are dominated by black Mercedes sedans with tinted windows so opaque they are against the law, which no one pays attention to. When Mercedes cluster at a ministry gate, I am reminded of a Roach Motel.

At night the BMWs and Porsches come out to play. Night traffic around the Kremlin has a centrifugal force that catapults them to speeds no police car can match, and even if a driver is caught, he simply bribes the police on the spot. It's not unlike American fishing: catch and release. Russia has an alarming accident record. Considering that a driver's license can be had for a bribe instead of a demonstrated ability to operate a vehicle, the numbers aren't so bad.

A special suicide feature of several Russian avenues and highways is a middle lane that runs in both directions. This lane is reserved for cars with blue roof lights so that high officials can hurry to affairs of state. Such a light is a desirable item for New Russians in a rush; the going price for a blue light and official license plates is $50,000. It is not unusual to see two motorcades speeding toward each other in a Russian version of chicken.

SOBRIETY

It was late in the afternoon, the sun dissolving into afterglow by the time I arrived for lunch at Alexei's apartment (not his real name). Alexei and Andrew were halfway through a second bottle of vodka, and the best I could do was try to catch up. I was outclassed. Thin as a drinking straw, Alexei was an art critic, scholar, and collector of fine porcelains, an intellectual who became more animated with each round. Andrew was British but did business in Russia and stayed in practice vodka-wise, so to speak.

Right off the bat Alexei swore he had seen a video that caught the President of the United States as he stuck a wad of chewing gum under a table of inlaid stones at the Hermitage Museum. Alexei was sure that George W. Bush had declared war on Russian culture. It turned out he had just gone through the humiliating experience of being denied an American visa. He said the State Department as good as accused him of trying to sneak into the United States when it was the other way around. The United States was invading Russia through gentrification. There was even a neighborhood in Moscow that had banned Russian cars, he'd heard. Only foreign cars were allowed!

Anyway, why would he want to be American, he asked? Moscow was safer at night than New York. He could walk around the center of Moscow at any hour, drunk or sober.

Alexei gave an example. A week ago he had visited an artist's studio. This artist had an interest in Nazi art, in its narcissism and banality. It was a deep discussion, and around two in the morning they ran out of vodka. They were nearly drunk, but Alexei knew a shop across town that was open. They walked blocks and blocks discussing Fascist paintings, sculpture, and architecture. At the shop they bought a few bottles, turned to leave, and found their way blocked by four skinheads tattooed with swastikas and portraits of Hitler. The biggest of the lot demanded to know why they were bad-mouthing the Führer. Alexei expected to suffer a beating, at least a little kicking and stomping, when the artist, although nearly drunk, opened a bottle, tossed aside the cap, and invited the skinheads to his studio. On the way they passed the bottle around while the artist held forth on modern art, starting with Cézanne. The lecture was so boring and the skinheads became so inebriated they couldn't walk unaided. So Alexei and the artist dumped them one by one in various courtyards, and that was the difference between being drunk and being nearly drunk.

What this had to do with the safety of Moscow's streets escaped me; but I was in no condition to give chase. Somehow it had gotten dark. Alexei opened a window to the background din of the city, which prompted me to ask if he'd ever heard about late-night racing of cars or motorcycles in Moscow. It was a stretch, but I asked.

"On the Garden Ring?" Alexei said.

That he knew even that much surprised me.

"Yes. The record time for a car to go completely around is six minutes."

"Five minutes," he corrected me.

"Have you . . . ?"

"Nine minutes." He sighed for the glory that might have been. "I stopped for red lights."

CASINO

Andrei Sychev looked out over the 220 slot machines, 30 gaming tables, sports bar, and VIP hall and confided that he felt like the captain of a sinking ship. As an employee of the Udarnik Casino he did not understand why City Hall wanted to shut it down and "kill a goose that lays nothing but golden eggs." Each slot, for example, generated a generous profit every month, and yet the government accused casinos of "moral damage," having closed some already and vowed to relocate others to "Las Vegas zones" on the far borders of the Russian Federation by the end of next year. To some, a Moscow night without the bright lights of casino marquees may seem like a year without spring, but officials have already closed hundreds of gaming sites large and small. Who would be next?

Some of Sychev's dealers had already jumped ship for employment with better security. This created a ripple effect because regular customers like to play with a favorite dealer.

Was the Udarnik Casino a criminal enterprise? Absolutely not, according to Sychev. That is, no more than any other enterprise. Maybe 10 percent. For their own protection everybody had a "roof." Don't think of it as the mafia, think of it as alternative police.

Alexei had told me that Americans would never understand Russia because Americans saw things as black or white, nothing in between, while Russians saw a gray area of perhaps 80 percent.

Which brings us to . . .

THE MAYOR

Not since Stalin has anyone left his stamp on Moscow as much as Mayor Yuri Luzhkov. A sawed-off colossus, he raises skyscrapers with one hand and flattens historic neighborhoods with the other. The floodlights that illuminate Moscow's classical palaces at night are under his command. He garnishes the city with statues that infuriate the critics, whom he ignores. He is what Russians call a *muzhik*, a man of the earth, and, although he and Vladimir Putin have been rivals in the past, they seem to agree that gaudy casinos are out of step with Moscow's new maturity and dignity, even if Putin reportedly complains that he never knows what the skyline of Moscow will look like when he gets out of bed in the morning.

The feeling in Moscow is that Luzhkov may be corrupt, but he gets things done. When construction funds ran short for the behemoth Cathedral of Christ the Savior, the story goes, he didn't hesitate to shake down businessmen and mafia alike to finish the job. According to one estimate, in 2005 Russians shelled out $316 billion in bribes. Why not a donation for a worthy cause?

It was a happy coincidence that a company owned by the mayor's wife, Yelena Baturina, landed so many construction contracts in the city. In fact, Baturina is the only woman among Moscow's billionaires.

THREE STATIONS—PART TWO

Sasha and I took the pedestrian underpass from Kazan Station because the more distance between us and the Cat in the Hat the better, and it was reassuring to find two uniformed security men sitting in the walkway, even if one was reading a comic book and the other was asleep. The shop stalls in the tunnel were shuttered except for one window displaying mobile phones.

We emerged in front of Yaroslavl Station. It was 3 a.m., and all the civilians had retreated to the waiting rooms and ceded the night to vodka zombies, prostitutes, and teenage gangs too spaced from huffing glue to notice us.

Incredibly, with one step into the waiting hall we reentered the normal world. There were cafés, a bookshop, a playpen, closed, to be sure, but evidence of normal life. Normal people were asleep in chairs. Healthy babies curled up on their mothers' laps. In some parts of the world people share a river with crocodiles. You just had to be careful.

But there was more. Returning through the underpass we came upon two men robbing a drunk. One lifted the victim by the neck while the second went through his pockets, although the way the drunk flopped back and forth made the task difficult. We had to get around them to pass. Sasha placed himself on the inside, between the action and me. The security men stayed seated and watched with mild curiosity; they were paid to protect the window of mobile phones, nothing else.

What happened took ten seconds. Essentially, the thieves took the money and ran. They wrested a roll of bills from the drunk's inside jacket pocket, let him drop, and vanished up the stairs to the street. The drunk spat blood and sighed. He rolled to a sitting position and waved off any help.

At night?

At Three Stations?

Nothing happened.

DIAGHILEV

Amid clouds of smoke, strobe lights, and the deafening beat of house music, the new lords of oil, nickel, and natural gas arrived at Diaghilev with women as mute and beautiful as cheetahs on a leash.

In this cacophony a millionaire could expand and relax. For one thing, no guns are allowed inside Diaghilev. The club had a 40-man security force, and any customer who felt in dire need of protection was assigned a personal bodyguard. A bomb dog had sniffed the chairs, and a security briefing had alerted the staff about special needs, such as guests from Iran who did not want to be photographed drinking champagne with scantily clad models. I had followed Yegor through a back door. How Yegor arranged my visit I did not know, but the chief of security was not pleased.

The club incorporated relentless sound, color, and motion. Psychedelic visions splashed across screens and vodka bars. A UFO and a crystal chandelier contested air space, and a contortionist added a touch of Cirque du Soleil. It was a simple system. Face control admitted more women than men and only enough guests to achieve critical mass. The more people who were turned away the more people who wanted to get in. The real Diaghilev was the fur-trimmed impresario who founded the Ballets Russes a hundred years ago. First of all, he was a showman. He would have loved this.

New Russians climbed to their VIP tables, waving to fellow New Russians and celebrities. Television personalities and Eurotrash leavened the mix, and soon the floor was so crowded people could only dance in place, something six-foot models in six-inch heels managed gracefully.

Yegor kept asking a question I finally understood over the din, "Are you happy? Did you get what you came for?"

I didn't know. Was this what millions of Russians died for in wars and prison camps? Had they faced down a KGB coup and dismantled an empire so a few gluttons could party through the night? Gogol had likened Russia to a troika of speeding horses, not a Bentley in a ditch.

Suddenly, the speakers went silent for a booming, "I love Moscow!"

On the runway an American singer had taken over the microphone. She was black—not many in Moscow—and she sang the blues. The boys on the VIP tier went on chatting at a shout and pouring each other cognac. Then the entire crowd joined in one refrain in English, "What are we supposed to do after all that we've been through?" I had no idea what song it was. They sang it over and over. "What are we supposed to do after all that we've been through?"

Soon after Diaghilev was, in a time-honored tradition of nightclubs, gutted by fire. Now it is better than hot, it is legend.

LIGHTS

On my last night in Moscow Yegor showed me the future.

We drove beyond the Garden Ring and followed the river to a dark industrial area, where we parked and walked along a chain-link fence. If this was the future, I wasn't impressed.

"Look up," Yegor said.

"I don't see anything."

"Look higher!"

Against the night stood a ladder of lights so high I couldn't be sure where it stopped, until a red beam crawled to the edge of an open floor somewhere near Mars.

"Moscow City," he said. "A city within a city."

It was a magic beanstalk, a complex of 14 buildings, including the Russia Tower, at 113 floors projected to be the tallest skyscraper in Europe. A giant crane performed a pirouette at the top of what will be the Moscow Tower, a mere 72 stories high. Work was going on day and night. A floodlight revealed figures in yellow vests clambering over the load the crane had delivered. From what seemed an incredible distance we heard the stutter of a rivet gun, the clap of metal plates, even voices, creating a curious intimacy.

Buildings were in every stage of construction. Those already completed resembled silver spaceships about to depart. The scale was enormous. The excavation alone could swallow the pyramids of Giza. The complex is planned to house City Hall, offices, and luxury apartments with views halfway to Finland.

This is the advantage of being in Moscow after dark.

In the daytime you see only architecture.

At night you see blazing ambition.

The Moscow Bombings Don't Matter[*]

By Julia Ioffe
Foreign Policy, March 30, 2010

After Monday's shock, Tuesday morning in Moscow dawned bright and tense. No one had yet claimed responsibility for the twin suicide blasts that killed 39 people and injured dozens more in the Moscow metro, and the headlines, especially in the Western press, teemed with preemptive analysis: Did the trail really lead, as the FSB alleged, to the restive Northern Caucasus? Would there be more attacks? And if so, would there be massive retaliation, or even war? Were the attacks bad for Prime Minister Vladimir Putin: a critical blow to his steely appeal, and a political contract based on trading liberties for security? Or were they good for him, a pretext to tighten the screws at home? What if Putin used the attack as proof that his dauphin President Dmitry Medvedev had lost control of the situation, necessitating Putin's triumphant return to the presidency in 2012?

These are, of course, important, rational questions. But they only matter if you view yesterday morning's subway bombing as a big deal—and many political observers in Russia, from Kremlin insiders to linchpins of the opposition, do not. Was it gruesome and tragic and of earth-shifting significance to all those who lost friends and relatives? Absolutely. Was it a game changer in the grander scheme of things? Probably not.

"Is it a big deal?" asks Yulia Latynina, a veteran opposition Russian journalist who has long reported on the Caucasus. "No, it's not. What was it that even happened? Russia has been exploding for 11 years, just not in Moscow."

In other words, when taken in the broader context of Russia and the slow-motion conflict in the Northern Caucasus—the 2004 explosion in the market in the southern Russian city of Samara (10 dead, 60 wounded), the two Russian passenger planes that simultaneously fell from the sky that same year (89 dead), the suicide bombing that nearly killed the Ingush president in June—the blasts in the Moscow subway by two female jihadis were just another parry, and not a very dam-

---

aging one at that. According to Irina Adrionova, the spokeswoman for the Russian Ministry of Emergency Situations, this blast was far less severe than Moscow's last subway double-bombing, back in 2004. "Yesterday's explosion took place when the train was already at the platform and had its doors open so the initial wave of the blast was more diffused than in 2004, when the train was in the tunnel," Adrionova explained. "And, in 2004, we also faced a fire of the highest magnitude."

Many observers—myself included—were struck by the orderliness of the emergency response. The Emergency Ministry instantly organized an information point for reporters and concerned relatives, posted frequently updated information on the victims' whereabouts on its website, and recorded announcements listing hotline numbers, including one for psychological help, to be played in the metro. Digital billboards across the city flashed the numbers, too. By 5 p.m., just nine hours after the first blast, the metro was fully operational, in time for the evening rush hour. Even Medvedev and the normally floridly thuggish Putin were relatively measured in their responses.

"The main thing was that there was no panic this time," Adrionova told me. And she's right. Riding the metro all day, I was struck by the fatalistic calm of the passengers. When I boarded a train just outside the Red Square early Monday afternoon, body bags were just starting to emerge from Lubyanka station. And yet the passenger next to me was explaining the unbelievable complexities of his hairdo to his girlfriend as if nothing had happened.

The psychological aspect of March 29 is important, of course, but it's mostly notable for its relative smallness. Much has been made of the fact that the first bomber set herself off just under Lubyanka, the KGB/FSB headquarters. But Russians have an ambivalent and uneasy relationship with the security forces, which means the message goes right over the heads of the masses. This attack, though it struck at the most mundane part of life, the morning commute, did not have the psychological force of Beslan or the 2002 Nord-Ost theater siege. "If you compare this to a [Shamil] Basayev attack, this did not have the same psychological trauma," says Gleb Pavlovsky, who heads a think tank with ties to Medvedev, referring to the Chechen warlord responsible for both the Beslan and Nord-Ost attacks.

"Unfortunately, in Russia, the attitude is that until it doesn't affect me personally, I can feel safe," says Masha Lipman, an analyst with Moscow's Carnegie Center. "And ultimately, it was just 39 people in a city of 10 million."

But will the March 29 Moscow subway attacks become a provocative dropping of the gauntlet? And how will the Kremlin respond? Only a day has passed and definitive forecasts would be foolhardy, but let's look at the proposed scenarios.

First: Bombings in the heart of Russia become a pattern, and Moscow retaliates with brute force, launching another war in the Caucasus.

"I don't think so," says Grigory Shvedov of the Caucasian Knot, an information web portal about the region. "There are already around 80,000 troops and 50,000 officers in the region. What can they start there that's new or supplementary? It's hard to imagine. A third Chechen War," he adds, "is not really likely."

Instead, observers from Pavlovsky to opposition figure and former parliament speaker Vladimir Ryzhkov think we are likely to see an increasing shift toward a softer, more political line in the Caucasus. The approach seemed to start with the January appointment of Alexander Khloponin as the Kremlin emissary responsible for restoring order there; his plan is more hearts-and-minds oriented than prior Kremlin strategies. "I'm a cautious optimist," the normally dour Ryzhkov says of the prospect of seeing more of a "strategy of political process and dialogue" in the region.

As for a stepped-up campaign from the Caucasus militants, Latynina cautions that it's important not to overestimate the abilities of this corps, who last attacked in November when they bombed the Nevsky Express train and whose Monday bombing was rather sloppy: One bomber got lost, they took too long to detonate their explosives, and one of the explosive belts didn't even go off. "All that stuff you see in the movies—the fancy hotels, the fake passports—our terrorists aren't capable of that," Latynina says. "Our terrorists sit in three-star hotels with their own passports, unless they're lucky and they can get the passport of a dead relative who was wanted for planting explosives. It's James Bond, Caucasus style."

Second: The attack is a big blow to Putin's credibility as someone who can maintain order.

Nope. There have been no attacks for six years, and Putin is still, by far, the most popular figure in the country. Russians don't trust their police, their parliament, or their judges, but they trust him—which is why, in the midst of flat-bottomed economic crisis, he still has an 80 percent approval rating.

The danger to Putin's rule—and it is still his—is going to come not from security threats, but from the erosion of his subjects' well-being. And let's not forget that on March 20, the so-called "Day of Wrath," organizers said they expected the number of protesters to double since the famous Kaliningrad protests that drew over 10,000 people in January. "Instead," say Lipman, "the number of people at the protests shrunk by half."

Third: Putin will use the bombing as a pretext to tighten the screws at home.

This is a reasonable expectation, given that this has been Putin's preferred response to external threats, real or imagined. In 1999, a string of apartment bombings that left nearly 300 people dead became a pretext to employ extra-harsh methods in Chechnya, and to consolidate power at home. After the attack in Beslan in 2004, Putin announced that security would be improved if only we got rid of direct elections of governors and let him appoint them instead.

But the situation is markedly different today. Putin, with the help of Vladislav Surkov, the chief architect of the current political model, long ago solidified the so-called power vertical, and it is in no real danger. In the early and mid-2000s, says Ryzhkov, "the state was going on the offensive." Today, it is secure—maybe even hubristic—which is why we didn't see a screw-tightening after the war in Georgia in August 2008, or during the worst of the financial crisis.

Of course, one can never underestimate Putin's predilection to screw-turning— he has already said he will seek out the suspected accomplices "at the bottom of the sewer"—but there just isn't a need this time, which is probably why he and Medvedev made sure to look calm as well as strong.

Fourth: Putin will use this as a way to make Medvedev look weak so he can take back the presidency in 2012.

"Look at any polls about who's more important, Medvedev or Putin," says Lipman. "The Russian people—and I'm talking about the Russian people here, not the elites—the Russian people say Putin is." (Forbes recently rated the most powerful people in the world: Putin was 3rd, Medvedev 43rd.)

"If they had open and free elections, and democratic observers came, Russian citizens would still elect Putin," says Shvedov. "He doesn't need to use the bombing [as a pretext] because he doesn't have to lift a finger to win."

On their own, then, and aside from the loss of life, the March 29 attacks are fairly meaningless. People avoided the metro for a day, maybe they'll avoid it for another week, but, as one Monday evening commuter told me, life goes on. "Even if I stay home today, I'd have to go tomorrow or the day after," he said. According to a recent poll, 62 percent of Russians said that they try to go on with their lives, avoiding contact with the government—which 85 percent of them know they can't influence—as much as possible. Life in Russia is about that: the mundane, the life in front of one's nose. So unless security once again becomes a daily issue, as it was in the first years of the Putin presidency, don't expect the occasional, messy attack to make Russians rally for change. Russians are used to the random, horrific event and have set their standards accordingly.

"What else can we do?" shrugged another Monday commuter. "I could be walking and an icicle will hit me in the head. We're all walking under God. When it's our time, he won't ask us."

Why Are Chechens So Angry?[*]

By Oliver Bullough
Transitions Online, April 6, 2010

Chechens and Russians are citizens of the same country, products of the same education system, holders of the same passports. And yet, two women could walk onto the Moscow metro and blow themselves up, along with 40 blameless commuters.

There could be no more graphic example of the giant gap in comprehension between the two nations than this, and it is a gap that has lasted since the first encounter between them back in the 18th century.

When these two peoples first met, it was the ultimate in culture clashes.

In 1721, Russian troops, servants of Peter the Great, emissaries of Europe's most autocratic state, rode west off their line of march and met Chechen horsemen. The Chechens came from an opposite culture. They had no government—every village ruled itself—with individuals moderating their behavior through the influence of custom, and the dangers of blood feud.

This first encounter set the tone for all that followed. The meeting turned into a fight. The Russian unit was wiped out.

A second invader was also, with more success, seeking to conquer the Chechen lands around this time, and that was Islam. Led by wandering adepts of the Naqshbandi Sufi groups, Chechens were believers by the end of the 18th century, and it was under the green or black banners of Islam, that resistance to Russia would be organized.

"On the opposite bank of the river Sunzha in the village of Aldy a prophet has appeared and started to preach. He has submitted superstitious and ignorant people to his will by claiming to have had a revelation," wrote a Russian major-general in a letter in 1785. This was unacceptable, and a mission was dispatched to Aldy to show the prophet who was calling himself Sheikh Mansur—who was boss.

---

* This article was first published in the on-line magazine openDemocracy.net. Republished by permission of openDemocracy and the author.

On arriving at Aldy, however, the Russians found it empty. They burned a few houses, and turned for home, only to discover their victory was far from complete. The villagers were waiting for them in the forests along the road and the punitive expedition turned into a humiliating rout. Half the force was destroyed and many of the rest drowned in the Sunzha.

The Naqshbandi brotherhood—of which Mansur may have been a part— spread deep into the mountains after his victory, as the highlanders enjoyed the breathing space given them by the Napoleonic Wars. Fresh from their victory over the French, however, the Russians did not plan to let this continue for long.

Alexander Yermolov, one of the greatest heroes of those wars against Napoleon, believed in controlling these turbulent people, and in writing his philosophy across the map.

Starting in 1817 he erected forts called Vnezapnaya ("Sudden"), Neotstupny Stan ("No Retreat"), Zlobny Okop ("Malicious") and Burnaya ("Storm"). At the heart of them all was a fort that would become a town, then a city. He gave it the same name as that used to describe Ivan "the Terrible": Grozny.

"The Caucasus may be likened to a mighty fortress, marvelously strong by nature, artificially protected by military works, and defended by a numerous garrison. Only thoughtless men would attempt to escalade such a stronghold. A wise commander would see the necessity of having recourse to military art; would lay his parallels; advance by sap and mine, and so master the place," said one of the Yermolov's generals, laying out a strategy that has been used ever since.

It was not a strategy calculated to win much support from civilians, however, as villagers found themselves treated as soldiers, resettled out of the mountains, or forced further into the high valleys if they refused to submit. Every summer the Russians destroyed Chechen villages, and every autumn the Chechens rebuilt.

In September 1819, the Russians came to Dadi-Yurt, where the inhabitants defied them. Encouraged by their women and children, the men fought to the last. The massacre was terrible. Only 14 men survived, and only 140 women and children were led into captivity. We do not have a Chechen voice to tell us how they felt after these horrors, but words written by Lev Tolstoy almost a century later ring true.

"The fountain had been fouled, evidently on purpose, so that water could not be taken from it. Similarly defiled was the mosque, and the mullah and his pupils were cleansing it," he wrote of a different massacre in his masterful book Hadji Murad.

"The elders of the village had gathered on the square and, squatting down, were discussing their position. Nobody even spoke of hatred of the Russians. The feeling that all Chechens, both young and old, experienced was stronger than hatred. It was not hatred, but the refusal to recognize these Russian dogs as people, and such revulsion, disgust and bewilderment before the ridiculous desire of these beings, that the desire for their destruction, like the desire for the destruction of rats, poisonous spiders and wolves, was just as natural a feeling as the feeling of self-preservation."

But Leo Tolstoy was a rare Russian, who could sympathize with the highlanders. Most Russians have forgotten these massacres, if they even knew about them in the first place, and their leaders even boasted at times of peace of the two nations' equality, as if the Chechens had willingly united with them to form a union state. The actions of their generals have been forgotten. In Soviet times, there was even a statue of Yermolov in the centre of Grozny and, seeing it, every Chechen would know what this supposed hero had done, but few Russians would.

Resistance to the Russians in the 19th century was largely led by Avars, neighbors of the Chechens from the high villages of Dagestan. The movement, which had been Naqshbandi in structure, collapsed in 1859 when Imam Shamil, its leader, was surrounded and surrendered. In captivity, he reminisced at length about his decades of war against the Russians. The Chechens had been some of his most ferocious warriors, but he had nothing good to say about them.

"There is nothing worse than this trash in the whole world. The Russians should say thank you to me that I corrected them a little. Without this you would have only one way to deal with them: shoot them to the last man, as is done with harmful animals," he told his Russian guardian.

"I did not fight them for their loyalty to the Russians. You know they never had that. I did it for their nasty character, and their inclination to theft and banditry. I am speaking the truth, and I am sure that you will now fight them, not for their loyalty to me, but for their same inclination to banditry, which they do not want to abandon."

It was a prophetic statement, and most of the Chechens did not take his surrender as a reason to stop fighting. They kept up sporadic resistance to the Russian Empire for the rest of its life, eventually taking advantage of the power vacuum after the revolution to re-establish an Islamic-based state taking in Chechnya and mountain Dagestan.

The Bolsheviks were sympathetic to the Chechens, and other repressed peoples of the Empire. They saw them as fellow-victims of the old regime, and thus natural allies in the task ahead.

"The old government, the landlords and the capitalists have left us as a heritage such browbeaten peoples as the Kirghiz, the Chechens and the Ossets, whose land served as an object of colonization by Cossacks and the kulak elements of Russia. These peoples were doomed to incredible suffering and extinction," said one Bolshevik official, himself a Georgian from the other side of the mountains, in 1921.

"The position of the Great-Russian nation, which was the dominant nation, has left its traces even on the Russian Communists, who are unable, or unwilling, to establish closer relations with the toiling native masses, to comprehend their needs, and to help them emerge from their backward and uncivilized state."

Hidden within his sympathy, there was a major and mistaken assumption, however, and that was the belief that the Chechens wanted to "emerge from their backward and civilized state". They did not. In fact, they rather liked it. United by the Sufi brotherhoods, they clung to their own traditions. Bandits haunted the mountains and, eventually, the patience of the sympathetic official—whose name, Joseph Stalin, was later known throughout the world—broke.

In the circumstances of World War Two, a war for the very existence of the Soviet state that he had built, Stalin could not tolerate lukewarm loyalty. So, on 23 February 1944, his security forces ripped the Chechens from their homes, shipped them by truck and railway, and dumped them in the wastes of Central Asia.

This is an event—one of several deportations that claimed between a quarter and half of the lives of the various deported nations—largely forgotten or ignored in Russia. Set against the suffering of their nation in World War Two, perhaps they consider it irrelevant. Among the Chechens, however, it has the status of a holocaust.

Survivors of the deportation live among the Chechens to this day. Researching my book, I tracked down many of them, recording their stories and trying to comprehend what had happened. Khozemat Khabilayeva, for example, was a girl when Stalin ordered the Chechens controlled forever, and had to walk—with her sister—for three days from their high village to the plains. Their mother had an infant to care for, so they were largely left to their own devices, and their lives were only saved by a faithful sheepdog called Khola, who curled up with them in the freezing nights, and kept them safe.

He could not be fitted into the trucks for deportation, however. The men's Islam refused to allow the proximity of a "filthy" animal, however faithful, and he was run over when they finally drove away. Khabilayeva cried when she told me of her dog, but her eyes were dry and hard when she talked of the horrors that awaited them in Kazakhstan.

"I saw how my cousin, my second cousin, died of hunger," she said. "This was a month after we arrived at our destination, he was 11 years old. We used to know the time from the sirens of the factories. He asked me when the siren would go off, and I said soon. He went to sleep and just died there, with all this green stuff coming out of his mouth."

Between 1926 and 1939, the nation grew by 26 percent. In the next 20 years, it grew by only 2.5 percent. That statistic hides a lot of death. And there was humiliation too. The nation was kept under police guard in the villages of Central Asia, and a generation grew up hardened by the experience, and surrounded by nostalgia for their lost homeland. Among those who were born at this time were Zelimkhan Yandarbiyev, Akhmed Zakayev, Apti Bisultanov, and others—men who would first lead a cultural renaissance, and then a political and military campaign.

When the nation returned from exile after Stalin's death, it was excluded from the best jobs and traumatized by its experiences, and Chechens became infamous as gangsters in the Soviet Union. The Chechen mafia became a brand to be conjured with, renowned for brutality and impenetrability.

Young men born in exile sought to restore their destroyed culture. Working in Grozny, where even speaking Chechen was enough to get a boy a slap in the 1960s and 1970s, they staged plays and wrote poems, discussing the Caucasus war, the deportations and everything else.

Names given to children reflected the focus on history. One boy, for example, was born in the mountain village of Vedeno in 1965. His father, Salman Basayev, called him Shamil after the 19th-century leader. He would go on to outdo even his famous namesake for mercilessness.

So, as the 1990s dawned, and the Soviet Union fell apart, Russians and Chechens were as divided as ever. Huge crowds of Chechens gathered in central Grozny, to discuss their past and their future, to publicly dance the zikr—the circular ritual of the Sufis—and to mingle. Russians, who still made up much of the population of the city, were confused and uncertain.

"In 1981, the Russians in Grozny would not even reply if I said hi to them on the street. Now, they would come up to me and ask how I was doing," remembered one of the nationalist activists of those times many years later.

In 1990, the Chechens organized a national congress, at which an Air Force General called Dzhokhar Dudayev made an electrifying speech. It was a call to arms, an appeal to Chechens to restore their lost independence, and it made a sensation. Dudayev was a handsome man, with a twinkling smile. He had commanded a nuclear bomber wing. He was a star.

When, a year later, Soviet hardliners tried to head off the liberalizing reforms coming out of the Kremlin, Dudayev spoke out. While communist officials waited to see who would win the coup, his supporters took over the streets, seized the Supreme Soviet and threw a Russian communist out of the window. That was the only casualty of the revolution in Chechnya, but it was a decisive one nonetheless.

On November 2, 1991, he declared Chechnya independent.

Under Soviet law, he had no right to do so. Only Union Republics—like Ukraine, Georgia, Kazakhstan, or Russia itself—had the right to secede. But, Chechens argued, the laws had been written without their input, they had never asked to [. . .] join the state, and the state had happily broken the laws against them.

For a couple of years, there was an uneasy coexistence. Russia had other things to worry about and could ignore the showman in charge of Chechnya. But, as the economy collapsed, both Dudayev and Boris Yeltsin in the Kremlin began to feel the need for an external enemy. Dudayev's anti-Russian rhetoric was unwise and non-productive, and Yeltsin was more direct. In November, he sent tanks, seeking, in the words of one of his aides "a short, victorious war to bolster his support."

For the Russians, it may have been a restoration of constitutional order. For the Chechens, it was a continuation of the same war that started in 1721. The nation united behind Dudayev, and the Russians were stunned by the ferocity of the resistance.

Frustrated and angry, the Russians poured shells into Grozny. One man who lived through the horrors of winter 1994 and spring 1995 said he counted 47 shells landing on the city in less than a minute, and he speculated on the chaos that had broken out after 1991.

"When the government in Chechnya became Chechen, it lost that aura that any government puts around itself. For a Chechen, it had ceased to be a government but was someone's son or brother who ended up in a good position when the Muscovites left. And, by what right? Why not me? How is his father better than mine," the man, Sultan Yashurkayev, asked.

The Russian savagery was not at that time matched on the Chechen side. Captured conscripts were at first treated well, and handed back to the mothers who came to look for them. But the atmosphere did not last. In June 1995, a group of Chechens led by Shamil Basayev—the young man who bore the Imam's name—seized a hospital in the town of Budyonnovsk north of Chechnya, and demanded a cease-fire.

One of Basayev's lieutenants later justified the raid, which resulted in more than 100 hostages dying, by comparing it to an attack on his home village.

"We analyzed the tactics of the Russian troops on Chechen territory and concluded that only diamond cuts diamond. Therefore, we concluded that the only way to stop the war was to retaliate in the same way," he said.

"We did not make these plans except as a last resort. Why was the world silent when Shali was bombed, when some 400 people were killed and wounded? In fact, the evil we did in Budyonnovsk was not even 30 percent of what they did in Shali."

Russia's humiliation appeared complete when Prime Minister Viktor Chernomyrdin was filmed negotiating with this bearded bandit, and finally agreeing to halt fire, and to let the group of kidnappers go. But actually, the disaster for Russia was only just beginning, the Chechens retook Grozny the next year, and Moscow was forced to admit defeat.

But tens of thousands of civilians had been killed, and the infrastructure ruined. Chechnya might have been free of Russian troops but, without outside assistance, it sunk into chaos, where money ruled and kidnapping was an industry. Western sympathizers were revolted by the murder of six sleeping Red Cross workers, and the decapitation of some telephone engineers. Chechnya was on its own.

When Russian troops returned in 1999 there was less sympathy for the highlanders. The plucky freedom fighters were now seen as terrorists following an unprovoked assault by Basayev on Dagestan, and a series of mysterious apartment bombings that new Prime Minister Vladimir Putin blamed on them. The shells poured into Grozny once more. All bonds of humanity appeared to have been severed. In Aldy—Sheikh Mansur's village two centuries previously, now a suburb of Grozny—at least 60 Chechen civilians, women and old men, were killed in a passport check operation, in February 2000. It was just one of many massacres.

In June, a Chechen truck bomb killed at least two—and possibly many more—Russian soldiers. It was the first suicide bombing and, tellingly, was detonated by a woman.

Further atrocities from the Chechens followed—the Moscow theatre siege and the Beslan school siege were just the two highest-profile—and always Russia stood firm in its refusal to agree to peace talks, or a ceasefire. It handed government over to Akhmad Kadyrov, a leader of Chechnya's Sufis who had been so revolted by the chaos younger men like Basayev had brought that he was prepared to foreswear the dream of independence.

He was killed, and his son Ramzan took over, ruling with a clenched fist.

Russian incomprehension remained, however. It was almost like a reverse of Tolstoy's question: how could these Chechens be so cruel? What could have been done to Chechen women who were prepared to go and blow themselves up outside a rock concert in Moscow? Or a hotel in Moscow? Or a metro station in Moscow?

A clue was offered by Zarema Muzhakhoyeva, a young woman who lost her nerve, and gave herself and her suicide bomb up to police in 2003. Abandoned by her parents, she had been pregnant with her first child when widowed in 2000. Her daughter Rashana was taken from her, as is traditional, by her husband's family, and the young woman had been unable to accustom herself to life without her. She stole money from her aunt, grabbed Rashana and tried to flee to Moscow.

Ostracized by everyone, she had the great idea of selling her life. She was not drugged, as some Russian officials claim of suicide bombers, or indoctrinated, she was in despair and wanted just $1,000 to pay her aunt back with.

"Of course, even if at the cost of my life I returned this money, then the disgrace would still remain, but I needed to take action. I always wanted to be good," she told a journalist later.

Eventually, she lacked the desire to murder, and surrendered. But, if she hoped for leniency, she was mistaken. She was handed a 20-year jail sentence, despite her argument that leniency might encourage women sent out to die to surrender to police in future.

Chechen leaders had become so hardened to suffering that they would exploit such a dreadfully sad tale as a weapon of war.

This hard line on both sides has erased any chances of sympathy. In 2008, Vladimir Zhirinovsky—a Russian nationalist politician and leader of the inaptly named Liberal Democratic Party of Russia—suggested that all non-Russians should be deported from the North Caucasus.

Granted, he likes to play the clown, but he is an intelligent man and, in any healthy political system, should surely have been condemned for such an offensive suggestion, considering 100,000s of Chechens, Karachais, Balkars, Ingush and others had died in precisely such an operation just two years before he was born. The suggestion caused not a stir.

In the circumstances, it is not uncommon for young Russians now—as Imam Shamil did, back in the 1860s—to speculate that the Chechens are like wild animals. A young Russian lady I spoke to once suggested a high wall should be built around Chechnya and that anyone coming out should be shot.

But, while researching my book, I came to a very different conclusion. I met Chechens from communities in Turkey and Jordan—products of 19th century emigration—in Poland, Austria and Belgium—products of an ongoing exodus of refugees—and in Kazakhstan, where some have stayed since the deportations of Stalin.

In the steppes east of Astana, Kazakhstan, there is a small settlement called Krasnaya Polyana, made up of three adjoining collective farms. Here, astonishingly, is a little Chechnya of 1,300 people or so, almost exclusively Chechen. Their community was founded in the horrors of 1944 by a noble man, a Sufi sheikh, called Vis Hadji.

His fame spread through the diaspora and, gradually, Chechens squeezed out non-Chechens until the current ethnically solid settlement was formed. Here are highlanders on what must be some of the flattest land on earth, but they are happy because they are left alone. They practice polygamy; they dance their circular prayer dances, with their soaring prayer chants; they raise crops; and they live in peace.

Alavdi Shakhgeriev is one of the men I spoke to in the village. Deported from Chechnya as a 14-year-old to the town of Karaganda, he had a sister to support. In a bleak example of Soviet jurisprudence, he was not allowed to work in a coalmine, the only work available, because that would have violated his rights as a child. Being deported, orphaned and abandoned did not, apparently, violate those rights at all.

He had found peace, however, in Krasnaya Polyana.

Since Vis Hadji died, the community has been led by an old man called Abubakar Utsiev, who was deported as a 19-year-old and left to fend for himself. Perhaps he would have despaired without the holy man, who taught him how to survive.

"This man did not look for anything, he ate just a little," remembered Utsiev, careful—as are all the Chechens there, not to say Vis Hadji's name. "I studied with him, and learned from him. I looked for no honors, I worked honestly. I have a garden, livestock, and this has been my life's work."

It is a poor village, but a peaceful one, something that is rare for Chechens. Most importantly, everyone else leaves it alone. Perhaps that is all that they ever needed.

Send Me to Siberia[*]

Oil Transforms a Russian Outpost

By Paul Starobin
National Geographic, June 2008

It's around midnight, and the couples on the dance floor at the Palace Restaurant are gently swaying to a slow one. "Za nas, za neft—To us, to oil," the singer croons,

> Wherever life sends us,
> To us, to oil . . .
> We fill our glasses to the brim.

It is Oilers' Day in the western Siberian province of Khanty-Mansi. This annual holiday, honoring the hard labor of the oil workers, the neftyaniki, falls early in September, after the worst of the summer mosquito season and before the first snowfall, in October. Hours earlier, as daylight faded, thousands crowded into a huge outdoor sports complex. A stage was framed by a deep-green backdrop of unbroken forest. Balloons were released, torches were lit, and a troupe belted out a song:

> There is only one joy for us,
> And this is all we need,
> To wash our faces in the new oil,
> Of the drilling rig.

Little wonder Russians are toasting oil: These are boom times. Global oil prices have increased tenfold since 1998, and Russia has pulled ahead of Saudi Arabia as the world's top crude oil producer. The Kremlin's budget now overflows with funds for new schools, roads, and national defense projects, and Moscow's nouveau riche are plunking down millions of dollars for mansion-scale "dachas."

The pumping heart of the boom is western Siberia's boggy oil fields, which produce around 70 percent of Russia's oil—some seven million barrels a day.

* Article by Paul Starobin from *National Geographic*, June 2008. Copyright © 2008 National Geographic Society. Reprinted with permission. (www.nationalgeographic.com).

For Khanty-Mansi, a territory nearly the size of France, the bonanza provides an unparalleled opportunity to create modern, even desirable living conditions in a region whose very name evokes a harsh, desolate place. Khanty-Mansi's regional capital, scene of the holiday revelries, is being rebuilt with oil-tax proceeds. The new structures include an airport terminal (once a wooden shack with an outhouse), an art museum featuring paintings by 19th-century Russian masters, and a pair of lavishly equipped boarding schools for children gifted in mathematics and the arts. Even the provincial town of Surgut, a backwater only a few decades ago, is laying out new suburbs and is plagued by traffic jams.

But the opportunity presented by oil could slip through the region's fingers. Despite the remarkable surge in oil prices, oil production in western Siberia has leveled off in recent years. Output barely rose from 2004 to 2007—a period when the rulers of the Kremlin, a cold-eyed and control-oriented crew, seized choice fields once held by private oil barons. The oligarchs, as they were known, were rapacious sorts who jousted among themselves for spoils. But they also heavily invested in the fields in order to maximize production and profits. The Kremlin, by contrast, aims to exploit oil not only as a source of national wealth, but also as a political tool for making Russia a great world power once again. Its heavy-handed tactics have made foreign investors wary and could undermine the boom—and with it Khanty-Mansi's chances for a brighter future.

Western Siberia's great oil deposits lie under lands that an exiled Marxist revolutionary, suffering in the gulag, once called the "waste places of the Earth." But to someone visiting by choice, oil country looks fetchingly wild and pristine. The terrain is dominated by taiga—dense forest of spindly birch, cedar, and pine—and boloto, peaty marsh that is frozen for most of the year and in spots bubbles with methane. There are no mountains and few hills, but there are numerous lakes, rivers, and streams.

Oil exploration began in earnest here in the mid-1960s. When geologists reported that large reserves of oil were waiting to be tapped, the Kremlin organized a frenzied military-style invasion of "pioneers" and bulldozers to ramp up production. Western Siberia, it turned out, had even more black gold than anyone had dreamed: More than 70 billion barrels have been pumped over the past 40 years.

In the early days "Siberia was all frontier," says Khanty-Mansi's governor, Alexander Filipenko. The governor appears older than his 58 years, with a shock of gray hair, watery eyes, and a mottled nose that has weathered its share of frost. Filipenko arrived in Khanty-Mansi in the early 1970s with orders to lay a bridge over the Ob River, which in the late 19th century was a route for squalid barges transporting prisoners to their final places of banishment. The bridge project took four years of toil under brutal conditions. Yet despite the hardships, the governor looks back at that time the way an old man might recall his first love for a beautiful young woman.

Filipenko is equally passionate about his latest project—the redevelopment of the provincial capital, Khanty-Mansiysk, a town of 60,000. He attends to every detail, and he has the funds to remake the capital to his liking. The province's oil industry generates 40 billion dollars in annual tax revenues, 4.5 billion dollars of which Khanty-Mansi gets to keep for its own use. The rest goes to Moscow.

His party background notwithstanding, Filipenko's vision is a distinctly non-Soviet one. The capital's leading architectural symbols include a shopping emporium topped by an enormous green dome in the shape of a chum, the traditional tent used by the region's indigenous people—the Khanty, Mansi, and others who herd reindeer, hunt, and fish. That symbolism would have been unthinkable in Soviet times, when the state, with its ideological cult of "the worker," denied the very idea of culturally derived identity.

When Siberia's oil lands came under development, native people were forcibly herded into villages and cut off from their hunting and fishing grounds. Following the breakup of the Soviet Union, the nomads won legal status as "aboriginal people," with the right to roam the oil fields. In spite of their new status and the architectural homage in the capital, their lot has hardly improved. Their numbers are small, about 30,000 in all; their languages are nearly extinct; and they are heavily afflicted by the scourges of contemporary Russia—AIDS, alcoholism, and tuberculosis. Some oil-tax money is being invested in medical ships that stop along the rivers to care for patients. But critics say these floating clinics diagnose disease, then leave patients with no means to get treatment.

Rural Russia is also being depopulated by the flight of young people to Moscow and other cities. To counter these trends, Filipenko has implemented ambitious plans to turn Khanty-Mansi into a place young people will choose to live in rather than leave. And this effort, he boasts, is working. He notes that Khanty-Mansi has the third highest birthrate among provinces in Russia, and unlike the country as a whole, whose population is in decline, Khanty-Mansi's has increased 18 percent since 1989, from a combination of births and immigration.

Oil composes 90 percent of the capital's economy, which is not surprising given the surge in oil prices. But it points to a problem shared by all resource-dependent economies: At some point the resource will be exhausted, and new sources of prosperity will have to be found. Recognizing the need to develop economic prospects beyond oil, Filipenko persuaded some 80 top researchers from Akademgorodok—a famed science and research town in southern Siberia created in Soviet times—to move to his regional capital to staff a new institute specializing in information technologies. The institute provides consulting services to oil companies, but it also takes on projects in unrelated fields such as nanotechnology.

It's the start of a "Silicon Taiga," says Alexander Sherbakov, a 60-year-old mathematician with a gray walrus mustache. As the era of easy oil comes to an end, he says, "we're going to grow our own scholars" by creating information-age jobs for the younger generation. Unlike investment in oil, investment in science, he says, can guarantee an everlasting bright future for the region's economy and its people.

That's undoubtedly an optimistic assessment. For one thing, the touted model, Silicon Valley, is located in temperate California. In Soviet times the Kremlin could simply order top scientists to move to remote research centers. In post-Soviet times Russia's top researchers can live and work wherever they choose, and most are choosing to live in prosperous cities such as Moscow and St. Petersburg.

While the oil boom has yet to make Siberia a magnet for Russia's knowledge class, it is attracting many other newcomers: impoverished immigrants from beyond Russia's borders. Early one morning, in a vacant lot just off the highway to Filipenko's showcase capital, a group of about 15 shabbily dressed men ranging in age from their 20s to their 40s are waiting for offers of work, however menial. A white Nissan pulls up, and several of the men walk over to talk to the driver, who is looking for a few hands to dig potatoes. But his offering price, just under ten dollars a day, isn't enough, and he drives away without any takers.

These men are what Russians, borrowing a German word, call gastarbeiters—guest workers. They are nearly everywhere in Khanty-Mansi. Most are Muslims from Tajikistan, the former Soviet republic in Central Asia whose economy was shattered by civil war in the mid-1990s. They come here in spring and return home before winter arrives. It's not every day they find a job, but when they do they can earn about $20 lugging bags of cement for a construction crew or doing household cleaning. They wire funds back to their families, and their employers avoid paying taxes on the wages.

The men balk at my request to see their living quarters. One says he is ashamed to show me how he lives. "I don't want you to get the wrong idea," he says. "We are not bandits; we are civilized people. We just need work."

The men are supposed to obtain registration papers certifying their place of residence, but, as they tell me, they have no authorized place to live, bunking instead in unheated garages illegally rented to them. A work boss—a kind of Mafia figure—obtains papers for them by bribing the registration office, but those documents, listing a false address, leave the gastarbeiters at the mercy of the police. When they are found out, they're sometimes forced to pay a spot "fine" (read "bribe"), and repeat offenders may face deportation. Russia's federal government recently put the burden on employers to register the workers and check their identifications, but such measures are unlikely to stem the tide so long as the oil boom continues.

A flood of Russians from economically depressed cities west of the Urals is also swelling the oil towns of western Siberia. Forty years ago Surgut was a collection of wooden hovels, in a place where temperatures can plunge to minus 60 degrees Fahrenheit and midwinter darkness lasts for all but a few hours a day. Today Surgut is one of western Siberia's largest cities, with 300,000 people. The new arrivals are voting with their feet, a sign that Russia's new market economy is actually working.

The polish and prosperity on view in Surgut were once unthinkable in Russia's hinterlands. A combined day care and preschool the city recently remodeled with 5.2 million dollars largely from oil revenue now has a heated indoor swimming pool and hydromassage whirlpool; an animal collection with rabbits, turtles, and parrots; and a room with a small wooden stage on which colorfully costumed children diligently perform fairy tales. When weather doesn't permit outdoor exercise, the children can ride around in toy cars in a large, glass-enclosed playroom kept at a moderately chilled temperature. And then the toddlers can be soothed by a hot drink from the herbal tea bar.

I understand that the "foreigner" is being shown the finest kindergarten in town, but only so much can be faked. Stuck in Surgut's traffic jams are as many Hondas, Toyotas, and Nissans as inexpensive Russian-made Ladas. Two-car families are becoming more common with the rise in living standard.

The housing stock of a typical Russian city consists of large (and ugly) multistoried concrete apartment blocks. Surgut boasts a suburban development of single-family town houses, aimed at a new upper middle class of oil company managers, bankers, and entrepreneurs. The redbrick houses, each with its own small plot of land, are being built along a tree-lined stretch of riverfront at an average cost of $400,000. Envious townspeople coined an ironic sobriquet for the elite community: *Dolina Nischikh*, Valley of the Beggars.

Surgut might have fallen apart, as did some other Russian cities, in the chaos following the collapse of the Soviet Union. That it didn't is a testament to the rootedness and stability of its political and business leadership.

"I was born in Surgut, my children were born here, and my grandchildren were born here," Alexander Sidorov, the city's longtime mayor, proudly declares. Surgut's economic anchor, the oil company Surgutneftegas, Russia's fourth largest producer, is majority owned by local managers. And unlike most Russian oil barons, who rule their western Siberian empires from Moscow, Surgutneftegas's general director, billionaire Vladimir Bogdanov, makes his home in town. Though now a towering figure in Surgut, Bogdanov started out as a common neftyanik.

Surgutneftegas is using the oil boom to finance an ambitious modernization program. At the oil field management center, computer engineers have custom designed an enormous digital map to monitor and adjust the field's performance. The map displays real-time information sent by coded radio signal from pump stations, active wells, and pipelines. From this display, managers can tell how much electric power is being consumed, whether a well needs repairs, and whether a pipeline is leaking.

Protection of the environment, barely a concern in Soviet times, is becoming part of the new ethos. It's not that the oil industry has suddenly become softhearted toward flora and fauna. Rather, high oil prices provide an incentive to minimize waste, as do license agreements that include big fines for spills. Moreover, as Russian oil firms have become global players, they've also become more sensitive to international concerns about the environment. "Maintaining a good reputation is very important," says Alexey Knizhnikov of the World Wildlife Fund in Moscow. "Otherwise, doing business becomes difficult."

Lubov Malyshkina, director of the environmental department at Surgutneftegas, is a chemical engineer with an advanced degree in the science of corrosion protection and geoecology. She also serves as an elected official in the regional parliament. In Soviet times, she says, the oil ministry in Moscow, oblivious to local conditions, would send chemicals that proved useless to treat oil spills and other hazards. Now Malyshkina's department, drawing on a nearly 500-million-dollar budget, makes its own purchases. She shows me one: a Swedish-made Truxor vehicle with tanklike treads that break up oil-saturated peat so that spills can be cleaned up. The company is also investing five million dollars in a new plant for recycling old tires into fibers that can be mixed into the asphalt used to pave company roads.

One aspect of the oil industry here hasn't changed: The neftyanik's job is still hazardous and grueling. At a rig about an hour's drive from Surgut, villagers gathering mushrooms are dwarfed by massive pumps, whose rhythmic motion suggests a giant bird dipping its beak to the soil. Metal stairs slick with oil lead to a platform where a drill is boring through rock with a diamond-coated bit nearly a foot in diameter. It's noisy and the air is foul, but this is a good spot to be in winter, I'm told, because the platform is bathed in steam. The men work eight-hour shifts for up to 30 straight days, sleeping on-site in trailer wagons, then rest off-site for up to 30 days. Alcohol is strictly forbidden. Drink all you want during your rest, the men are told, but return sober.

Yet the jobs are a route to a prosperity unimaginable a few years ago. The least experienced workers get a monthly salary of $1,000, the most senior hands as much as $4,000. And there are bonuses for exceeding daily quotas. A thrifty neftyanik can save enough to purchase a flat in Surgut's apartment complexes—if not a town house in the Valley of the Beggars.

All of this is impressive, of course. But the larger question for Surgutneftegas, and every oil firm in Khanty-Mansi, is whether they can rise to the myriad political, economic, and technical challenges on the horizon. While most analysts expect western Siberia to remain the dominant source of Russia's oil for at least the next 20 years, the region's oil fields are aging. Coaxing additional barrels of oil from the ground is becoming more difficult and expensive, and maintaining production will require infusions of capital and expertise from sources outside Russia. But burdensome taxes—all gross revenues above $25 a barrel go to the federal government—and Kremlin-backed power plays have chilled the investment climate like a Siberian blizzard. One need only visit Nefteyugansk, a city of 114,000 on the Ob River about an hour's drive from Surgut, to see why.

A black gusher of trouble is what the oil boom has been for Nefteyugansk, which has the look and feel of an unkempt industrial park. The central plaza is strewn with iron pipes, and down by the river a crumpled barrel of Shell oil floats next to a dilapidated dock. A few paces inside the gate of the town's cemetery lies the grave of Vladimir Petukhov, the burial ground's most famous resident. In 1996 the townspeople elected Petukhov as their mayor. Two years later, as he walked to work on a June morning, he was shot to death by a pair of gunmen. An etching on his black marble gravestone depicts him in a crewneck sweater and leather jacket.

For more than ten years oil has been at the center of a violent and chaotic power struggle in Nefteyugansk. The difficulties began in the mid-1990s, when a nouveau riche Moscow banker snagged one of Russia's prime oil producers—and the town's sole large employer—in a privatization auction. The banker, Mikhail

Khodorkovsky, made the Nefteyugansk unit the core subsidiary in his new oil company, known as Yukos. But he antagonized the city by delaying tax payments, causing city workers to go unpaid for months. Mayor Petukhov, a former neftya-nik, led public protests against the new Moscow owners, who, he said, "spit into our faces, the faces of oilers." The mayor's murder, at the age of 48, outraged the townspeople, many of whom connected the deed to his stand against Yukos. "This blood is on your hands," read anti-Yukos banners put up at city hall by Petukhov's mourners.

For five years no one was brought to justice. During this time the city was gov-erned by a corrupt official who eventually was sent to jail for swindling oil workers out of their promised retirement homes in Russia's balmy Black Sea region. Oil prices, meanwhile, went ever higher, inflating the value of Khodorkovsky's hold-ings. And then the hammer came down.

In June 2003, Moscow prosecutors arrested Yukos's security chief on charges of organizing the execution of Petukhov. Four months later they arrested Khodork-ovsky on charges of fraud and tax evasion. Tax authorities seized the Nefteyugan-sk subsidiary and handed it over to a Kremlin-controlled company called Rosneft. Khodorkovsky was convicted and carted off to jail in southeastern Siberia, where his face was slashed by an inmate. Meanwhile, the security chief was convicted in a trial heavily publicized on state television. In the latest development, prosecu-tors announced last February that Yukos co-owner Leonid Nevzlin also would be charged in Petukhov's murder.

Perhaps it did happen the way the government claimed, but ask folks in Neft-eyugansk about the murder, and they tend to shrug and say they don't know what to believe. The coordinated elements of the Yukos affair have the whiff of a Moscow plot hatched by the KGB types in control of the Kremlin. The result, in any case, is that a cash cow—and still the town's livelihood—has passed from the hands of a Moscow oligarch into the hands of the Kremlin.

When I show up in town, Sergey Burov has been mayor for four months. He was once a deputy director for Rosneft and before that a senior manager for Yu-kos. He, too, is no stranger to violence: In 2005, while walking to his car in the morning, he took a bullet to the stomach. It looked like another contract job, but prosecutors closed the case without finding a culprit.

Burov is a burly man whose wide shoulders stretch his suit. He is interested in talking about the town's future, not its bloody past. In partnership with Rosneft, he tells me, the city administration has ambitious plans to redevelop Nefteyugansk. Come back in two years, he says, and I will see an entirely different town, maybe even a yacht club. After the interview his press secretary shows off an indoor sports facility with an Olympic-size swimming pool. In the central plaza, the one littered with pipe just a few days earlier, workers are starting to install brick walk-ways and flower beds.

Are things finally looking up for Nefteyugansk? Residents seem skeptical. "Maybe Rosneft feels better being here," Vasily Voroshilov, a 52-year-old oil well repairman, says. "But we don't feel it."

That skepticism is shared by many observers outside Russia, who say it's one thing to seize control of an oil company and quite another to run it. Says one analyst of the Kremlin's takeover of Russian oil, "You can steal a Chevy, but that doesn't mean you know how to drive it."

For all the wealth that oil can produce, it is often as much a curse as a blessing for countries such as Russia. Early in the 1990s, before the oil boom, Boris Yeltsin encouraged local provinces to grab what autonomy they could. This was when Russia's potential for political pluralism and Western-style grassroots democracy looked greatest. When oil prices rose toward the end of the decade, the Kremlin realized that this source of wealth could be used to bring about a humiliated Russia's global resurgence. Salvation by oil has since become an article of national faith.

"Oil," said a 16-year-old student at Khanty-Mansiysk's school for math whizzes, "is the only way for our country to stand up, to survive." Actually, there are many ways that the Russians, a creative and educated people, can revive their country. But oil suggests national potency, and Russia's petroleum patrimony lends itself to patriotic incantations of an almost mystical kind. At the festivities on Oilers' Day one of the songs, a salute to the collective might of the neftyaniki, proclaimed, "We are the fingers pressed tightly into a fist."

"Russia's superpower status today comes from energy, not its military," says Julia Nanay, a senior director at PFC Energy, a global consultancy based in Washington, D.C. "The Kremlin determines what happens with oil in western Siberia. They want to control production and exports in order to maximize Russia's geopolitical relevance."

Just as the tsars of old exercised monopolies on valuable commodities such as fur and salt, the Kremlin wants direct control over oil—and over the oligarchs who produce it. Those who come to heel survive; those who don't risk suffering Khodorkovsky's fate, or worse.

One of the survivors is Vagit Alekperov, president of Russia's biggest private oil company, Lukoil. Starting out working on the rigs near his native Baku, Alekperov was sent to Siberia in the late 1970s to manage an oil-production team. A notoriously strict paternalist, he angered his men by banning the sale of alcohol in the village. Several of them grabbed hunting rifles and fired shots at his cabin, but Alekperov, ever the survivor, wasn't there at the time.

During the final days of the Soviet Union, Alekperov forged Lukoil from prime oil assets in western Siberia. Today the company is a global multinational with hydrocarbon reserves second only to ExxonMobil—and some 2,000 gas stations in the U.S. Though most of Lukoil's reserves are in western Siberia, Alekperov keeps his headquarters just two miles from the Kremlin. Like other survivors, he knows that he must be attentive to any change in political mood that could affect Lukoil's fortunes, for better or worse.

A distinguished-looking man with bronze skin and a crop of steel gray hair, Alekperov dresses in impeccably tailored suits. A tough guy, he can also charm. When pressed on whether oil consumers around the world should feel comfortable now that Russia has a large finger on the globe's petroleum tap, he leaned back in his chair, smiled expansively, and asked, "Do I look like a bear?" I couldn't help laughing. "We just want to make money."

Having gobbled up Yukos, might the Kremlin want to swallow Lukoil next? "I don't think either the government or the president of Russia will target such a company," Alekperov remonstrates. I decide not to mention that Khodorkovsky had told me the same thing not long before his arrest.

Lukoil's base of operations in Khanty-Mansi is the town of Kogalym. A roadside floral arrangement spells out the company's name not far from the golden domes of a Russian Orthodox cathedral and the green minaret of a mosque. At a refurbished maternity house—what Russians call a *roddom*—Dr. Galina Pustovit, director of the gynecology department, shows off new Western-standard medical equipment. In a country where many women deliver their babies in Soviet-era buildings reeking of sour cabbage and damp concrete, this gleaming facility rates four stars.

When I mention to Pustovit that Russia's oil industry is known for being corrupt, the doctor gives me a sharp look. "This is oil," she says, sweeping a hand around the gynecology ward. "Oilers built this hospital. All of the objects in this city have been built with oil money, including our beautiful boulevard." Don't judge us too harshly, her look says: Life in these parts has never been better.

Russia Fears Embrace of Giant Eastern Neighbour[*]

By Luke Harding
The Observer, August 2, 2009

It was an unashamed display of military force, involving tanks, fighter jets and more than 3,000 soldiers. Last week China and Russia held their biggest joint military exercises ever—their battalions streaking across the plateaus and shimmering plains of Shenyang province.

The exercises come as Moscow and Beijing prepare to celebrate an important moment in history: 60 years of diplomatic relations. After long periods of frigidity during the cold war, the two countries now claim to be enjoying an unprecedented strategic partnership.

But the military manoeuvres—named Peace Operation 2009—were not just about showing off, unleashing rockets at imaginary terrorist enemies or threatening the US. Instead their aim was to send an unambiguous message to the internal Muslim populations of China and Russia: no dissent will be tolerated.

Both countries are now facing simmering Muslim uprisings. In China's case, this comes from Uighurs whose revolt in the north-west province of Xinjiang this summer has been brutally suppressed. Russia, meanwhile, is facing an insurgency of its own in the north Caucasus republics of Ingushetia, Chechnya and Dagestan.

But while China and Russia have much in common, including a mutual fear of separatism and Islamic radicalism, there are also signal differences. Despite last week's exercises, and a visit to Russia by Hu Jintao, the Chinese president, in June, politicians in Moscow harbour a deep-seated fear of China—in particular, of Chinese encroachment.

Russian TV recently claimed that Beijing has drawn up a secret plan. According to this top-secret blueprint, China is determined to grab back Russia's remote, but vast, far east region. China's strategy includes persuading migrants to settle in Russia, marry local women and steal or co-opt local businesses.

Russia's far east has always been the most strategically vulnerable part of Moscow's fissiparous imperium, in what is the world's biggest country. Some 6,100km (3,800 miles) and an eight-hour flight from Moscow, the far east is home to just 6.5 million Russian citizens. Next door, across the Amur river in north-eastern China, there are 107 million Chinese. Given this demographic imbalance, there is a primordial fear in the Russian imagination that China will eventually try to steal back the Europe-sized far east of Russia—a region rich in mineral resources, trees, coal and fish. The salmon alone are an attractive target. A quarter of the world's Pacific salmon spawn in the volcanic Kamchatka peninsula. According to the Russian TV scenario, Beijing is furtively plotting to undo the Russian colonisation of the Pacific coastal region, started in the 18th century by tsarist-era adventurers. The area's original inhabitants were Chinese. These early nomads eked out a meagre living while dodging the tigers that still haunt the Sikhote-Alin mountains.

In reality, the relationship is far more fascinating than the baseless fears of Russia's nationalists. Over the past decade the number of Chinese migrants working in Russia's far east has actually fallen. In Moscow, the authorities have recently shut down the capital's enormous Cherkizovsky market, turfing thousands of Chinese out of a job. The huge bazaar was home to Chinese traders selling billions of dollars-worth of grey-sector goods. (According to China's Xinhua agency, losses from Wenzhou in Zhejiang province alone amount to more than $800m, after Russian police confiscated their stocks.) Some 150 Chinese workers have been deported since the market was closed on 29 June.

Most experts believe China's own strategic goals do not include Russia's far east, or primitive territorial expansion. Instead Beijing's priorities lie elsewhere. They include development, reunification with Taiwan and internal stability, which experts suggest is more of a priority than ever following last month's ethnic riots against Han Chinese in Xinjiang.

According to Dr Bobo Lo, a lecturer on Chinese-Russian relations at the Centre for European Reform, Beijing's real challenge to Moscow is rather different. He argues that the rise of China will lead to the "steady marginalisation of Russia from regional and global decision-making". The Chinese do not want to invade Russia militarily because, he points out, they would lose.

Any loss of influence would alarm the Kremlin, which still sees itself as a major global power. Over the past nine years, under president and then prime minister Vladimir Putin, Russia has worked hard to recover its superpower status. However, few outside Moscow doubt that the main challenge to the United States's increasingly wobbly global and economic hegemony comes not from Putin's Moscow but Hu's Beijing.

In the meantime, informal ties between China and Russia are blossoming. During the summer, after the ice encrusting the Amur river melts, Russian tourists are now travelling to China from the attractive Russian town of Khabarovsk. Their destination is the gleaming Chinese town of Fuyuan, reached by whizzy hydrofoil.

Yesterday, cruising down the Amur, Captain Alexander Udenka pointed out to the Observer the border between China and Russia. On the river's right bank is China and a series of low green mountains and Fuyuan's newly built high-rises. Out on the river, Chinese fishermen zip around in speedboats, looking for the giant but elusive Amur sturgeon.

Over on the left bank, meanwhile, is Russia. Here there is no sign of human activity. The sandy bays are empty. There are not even any watchtowers—merely a shimmering green embankment of dense willows and oaks, as well as Manchurian nut trees and Japanese cherries—all apparently further evidence of far eastern Russia's lack of people.

"In 1969 China and Russia fought a war over one of these river islands," Udenka explains, sitting in his captain's cabin and steering in the middle of the river. "It was a small war. Now there are good relations between Russia and China. We trust each other," he adds, in broken Chinese.

A decade ago Fuyuan was little more than a village with a few pigs. Now it is a brash town, offering goods at less than half the price in Russia. During the season several hundred Russian tourists visit every day, staying on cheap two-day packages, and haggling with Chinese locals who have rapidly mastered the Russian language.

Everything conceivable is on sale in Fuyuan—fur coats, computers, mobile telephones, socks and even sex toys. After trudging round the market for several hours, most Russians relax with a massage—£10 for a one-hour session—or get their hair highlighted. Others tuck into a tasty lunch of silver carp caught from the Amur, or pork dumplings.

"I still haven't managed to get the hang of chopsticks," Igor, a 23-year-old Russian tourist confessed to the Observer. Igor showed off his new purchases —a black cowboy hat, a fake Armani jacket, Gillette Mach 3 razors and a bottle of aftershave with an English logo, "Love Affairs". Asked why he had decided to buy a cowboy hat, Igor replied: "I got drunk last night." Local Russians can travel to Fuyuan without a visa. This suits Fuyuan's traders, many of whom have moved from elsewhere in China. "I like Russians. They are pretty indiscriminate. They just grab everything and run," said Li Wing, 42, who owns a sex shop in Fuyuan.

Fuyuan ends abruptly. Its shopping centre peters out at a decorative Chinese gate. From here, there is a stunning view of the Amur river and Russia. Up in the woods, among the pine trees, there is evidence of the environmental cost that new Chinese towns such as Fuyuan are wreaking: heaps of rubbish, plastic bags and a dead owl.

The problem of what to do with the far east has long exercised Moscow's leadership. The Soviet Union offered generous subsidies to cajole workers and young couples to start a new life here. They got higher salaries, career opportunities, and flats. There were also cheap air fares back to European Russia. The incentives were needed given the region's harsh climate—scorching summers and freezing winters, with January temperatures regularly falling below -30C.

However, after the demise of the Soviet Union this system collapsed. With a ticket to Moscow now costing £500 return, a new generation has grown up with weaker ties to the capital. Instead of visiting St Petersburg, local Russians are more likely to holiday in China—travelling by bus to the Chinese seaside resort of Dalian and other destinations in China's north east.

Gradually, Asiatic Russians are getting to know their neighbours better. Farther down the Amur in the border town of Blagoveshchensk, Russian pensioners have even started buying up apartments on the Chinese side of the river. Other young Russians head west: since the early 1990s the Russian far east's population has plunged by 1.6 million. This exodus is a source of increasing worry for the Kremlin. On Friday Putin travelled to Khabarovsk to unveil a new pipeline stretching from the Russian island of Sakhalin to Khabarovsk and the far eastern port of Vladivostok. The pipeline will take gas to China, Japan and South Korea—part of an attempt to stimulate the region's economy.

In June, during his trip to Russia, Hu attended a summit of the Shanghai Co-operation Organisation, and held talks in Moscow with Russia's president, Dmitry Medvedev, which led to the signing of a massive oil deal. He also had tea with Putin. The deal reinforced China's growing economic influence in the region, and its emergence as a competitor with Russia for Central Asia's energy reserves.

In Khabarovsk, meanwhile, few locals see much prospect of the far east breaking away from Moscow. Despite improved understanding between China and Russia, the cultures remain too different. (The Chinese see the Russians as western-centric.) In Khabarovsk, the last stop on the Trans-Siberian Railway before Vladivostok, nobody is talking about secessionism.

"I've had a few relationships with Russian girls. But I'll end up marrying a Chinese one," says Tsi Ke, 25, who has lived for the past decade in Khabarovsk. Tsi owns a thriving Chinese restaurant, where blonde Russian waitresses wear Chinese dresses. He adds: "In China we believe a wife should stay at home a lot and be like a daughter to your own parents. For us, marriage isn't just between two people but between two families."

A more pressing problem for the Kremlin is the growing estrangement between Russia's western and eastern halves. Resentment of Moscow and its far-away bureaucrats is rising. There have been grassroots protests in Khabarovsk and in Vladivostok after Moscow raised duties on second-hand Japanese cars late last year, killing off a major regional business. Anti-Kremlin protests are continuing.

In May, Medvedev dropped into Khabarovsk for an EU-Russia summit. (The venue—10 hours' flight from Brussels—was apparently chosen by Russia to punish the EU's pampered representatives, several of whom fell asleep during sessions).

Medvedev flatteringly described the far east as his "favourite part" of Russia, and expressed sympathy with students too broke to travel to Moscow. This summer the Kremlin has introduced a scheme offering some discounted tickets to the under-23s.

It remains to be seen whether the scheme will make much difference. In reality, though, successive governments in Moscow have done little to develop the far east—making the region susceptible to civic unrest and discontent. The region suffers from "long-term neglect by Moscow" and "appalling corruption and mis-government at regional level", Bobo Lo says.

Despite last week's show of unity during military manoeuvres, the relationship between Beijing and Moscow is no longer one of equals. Russia may see China as an important strategic counterweight to the US—with whom it is currently in conflict over a range of issues, including the planned US missile defence shield in central Europe.

But the Chinese know that it is they, and not Putin's Russia, who are destined to become the world's newest superpower. And according to Bobo Lo, China is not interested in allowing strategic accommodation with Moscow to disrupt Beijing's more important partnership with Washington. "Washington is still the world's only indispensable partner," he notes.

A HISTORY OF TENSION

- Throughout much of the cold war Beijing and Moscow were enemies. However, Stalin had encouraged and financed Mao Zedong's revolution, recognising his communist People's Republic in October 1949. The partnership survived Stalin's death and the early Khrushchev years.

- In 1959 the two countries squabbled over which should lead the world communist movement, an ideological quarrel replicated in communist parties across Asia and Africa. Khrushchev's decision to back down during the 1962 Cuban missile crisis also needled Mao.

- In March 1969 tensions exploded when Russia and China fought a brief war in Russia's far east over the disputed Damansky island (now known as Zhenbao), close to Khabarovsk.

- Tensions continued in the 1970s and 1980s, especially after the Soviet invasion of Afghanistan. Détente only became possible after the Soviet Union's demise.

- Over the past two decades relations between Beijing and the Russian Federation have improved, with booming trade, agreement on many international issues, and growing military co-operation. In 2004 Russia settled a long-running border dispute with China, handing over Tarabarov island in the Amur river, and half of another large island, Bolshoy Ussuriysky.

- China's rise, however, is likely to place increasing strain on the relationship. Experts believe that, as China becomes a world superpower, Russia's influence will diminish—a fate the Kremlin is unlikely to accept.

Restlessness in Russia's Western Outpost[*]

By Michael Schwirtz
The New York Times, March 26, 2010

Amid the sagging Soviet-era apartment blocks and hulking government buildings here [in Kaliningrad], it can be difficult to imagine that this was once a German city graced with gingerbread-style facades and Teutonic spires.

About all that remains of the 700-year-old city once called Konigsberg—which was bombed to oblivion in World War II, then taken over by the Soviet Union and renamed in 1946 after the death of a Bolshevik hero, Mikhail Kalinin—are some weathered houses and a few reconstructed cathedrals. But that does not mean residents of this island of Russian territory wedged between Poland and Lithuania do not entertain certain European expectations.

"I would like to bring Konigsberg back to Europe," Rustam Vasiliev, a local blogger and political activist, said, intentionally using the former German name of this city. "I've got no Kremlin in my head."

People like Mr. Vasiliev have become a headache for the Kremlin, as some of the largest antigovernment protests in Russia in recent years have broken out here, in part because of the failure of officials to bring the region more in line with the standards of Western Europe.

The Kremlin has had similar problems in other far-flung regions, notably in the Far Eastern city of Vladivostok, where the economy has been drawn into the orbit of local Asian powers.

Here in Russia's western extreme, people take pride in their European cars but complain about their city's pocked roads. Advertisements for concerts in Warsaw and Berlin hang on the crumbling facades of long-neglected apartment buildings. When local people talk of Russia, they often seem to mean not their own country, but some foreign land to the east.

"We are located outside of Russia's borders and within the borders of the European Union," said Vytautas V. Lopata, a cafe owner and local independent politician. "Here, people are freer. They see how people live in Europe; they have heightened demands."

When it comes to politics, Kaliningrad is by no means a thriving democracy. People here have nevertheless come to enjoy a level of openness not found elsewhere in Russia. There are independent television stations and real opposition politicians in the local Parliament (though their influence is minimal). Small street protests are not uncommon and are generally tolerated by the authorities.

By contrast, even the tiniest antigovernment demonstrations in Moscow are quashed by riot troops, sometimes violently. And when protests broke out in Vladivostok last year, the authorities sent those same Moscow riot troops to suppress them.

But officials both here and in Moscow were clearly caught off guard in January when as many as 10,000 people poured into a central Kaliningrad square to demand the resignation of the regional governor and other officials from Prime Minister Vladimir V. Putin's political party, United Russia.

Since then, the authorities have been scrambling to contain the damage lest the dissatisfaction in Kaliningrad spread to the rest of the country. They were able to head off another protest scheduled for last weekend, in part by making serious promises to opposition leaders to resolve their major complaints.

Still, it is unclear how long the tentative peace will hold, especially given that there has been no shortage of unfulfilled promises here.

Though Kaliningrad remained under Moscow's control after the Soviet collapse, its location outside contiguous Russia seemed to hold out the promise that the formerly sealed military zone would be opened to the prosperity of the West.

But membership in the European club has always been elusive, to the dismay of many here. The region remained relatively poor, even as its neighbors—until recently, at least—prospered. Like all Russians, Kaliningraders must submit to the lengthy process of applying for visas to visit cities a few hours' drive away.

"Here we are like fish in an aquarium," said Konstantin Doroshok, one of the leaders of the January protests. "And the water has not been changed in a while, and we are going extinct."

Things did not always feel this constricted, Mr. Doroshok, 40, said. Just a few years ago, he and many others were doing good business importing European cars into Kaliningrad to resell to Russians farther east, one of many similar professions that thrived here because import tariffs from European countries into Kaliningrad were cheaper than those for the rest of Russia.

A year ago, however, the Kremlin sharply increased customs duties on imported cars, which Mr. Doroshok said effectively killed his business. He was also slapped with what he said were fabricated charges of failing to pay customs duties and fined about $600,000.

"One fine day it seems that one of the oligarchs calculated how much he failed to earn as a result of the fact that citizens of Russia were importing automobiles independently," he said, "and decided to try to push us out of this business."

It was then that Mr. Doroshok and others angry over Kremlin interference in their way of life decided to push back.

A series of demonstrations culminating in the large January protests compelled Kaliningrad's Kremlin-appointed governor, Georgy V. Boos, for the first time to hold serious talks with opposition leaders, including Mr. Doroshok. Though protest leaders called off a planned demonstration last week, several hundred people gathered in central Kaliningrad, shouting "Down with Boos!"

"There was an underestimation by us and me personally of the need to devote more time to communicating with people," Mr. Boos said of the protests at a news conference here last week.

To deflect some of the ill will directed at the governing authorities here, some local United Russia leaders have even floated the idea of relinquishing some of the party's near monopoly on power—something that might be considered blasphemous elsewhere in the country.

"That would lower some of the political strain and allow for more democratic governance," said Konstantin I. Poliakov, the deputy head of United Russia's faction in the regional Parliament.

Many, like Mr. Lopata, the cafe owner, say that it makes little difference to the people of Kaliningrad who their leaders are as long as their region remains cut off from their real neighbors and under Moscow's thumb.

"We live within the European Union," Mr. Lopata said. "But it turns out that we live behind a fence."

Where the Salmon Rule[*]

By David Quammen
National Geographic, August 2009

The Kamchatka Peninsula, rugged and remote, is a vast blade of land stabbing southwestward through cold seas from the mainland of northeastern Russia. Its coastline is scalloped like the edges of an obsidian dagger. Its highlands rise to cone-shaped volcanic peaks, snow-streaked in summer, and to ridges of bare, gray rock. Its gentler slopes are upholstered in boreal greens. It's a wild place, in which brown bears and Steller's sea-eagles thrive on a diet rich in fatty fish. About 350,000 people inhabit Kamchatka Krai (its label as a governmental region), and they too are highly dependent on fish. In fact, you can't begin to understand Kamchatka without considering one extraordinary genus: Oncorhynchus, encompassing the six species of Pacific salmon.

Then again, it might also be said: You can't understand the status and prospects of Oncorhynchus on Earth without considering Kamchatka, the secret outback where at least 20 percent of all wild Pacific salmon go to spawn.

Although larger than California, the peninsula has less than 200 miles of paved roads. The capital is Petropavlovsk-Kamchatsky, on the southeastern coast, containing half the total population. Across a nicely protective bay sits the Rybachiy Nuclear Submarine Base, Russia's largest, in support of which the city grew during Soviet times, when the entire peninsula was a closed military region. Travel to most other parts of Kamchatka is still difficult for anyone who doesn't have access to an Mi-8 helicopter. But there is a modest network of gravel roads, and one of those winds upstream along a narrow waterway called the Bystraya River, amid the southern Central Range, to the Malki salmon hatchery, a complex of low buildings surrounded by trees.

Hatchery operations began in Kamchatka in 1914, during the twilight of the tsars, but this facility was established just three decades ago. In a lounge room off the entryway, someone hung a poster, declaring in Russian: "Kamchatka was created by nature as if for the very reproduction of salmon." That sounds almost like a myth of origins, but the poster listed some nonmythic contributing factors: Permafrost is largely absent, rain is abundant, drainage is good and steady, and because of Kamchatka's isolation from mainland river systems, its streams are relatively depauperate of other freshwater fish, leaving *Oncorhynchus* species to face few competitors and predators. The poster was right. Judged on physical and ecological grounds, it's salmon heaven.

Unfortunately, those aren't the only factors that apply. Kamchatka's tottering post-Soviet economy, fisheries-management decisions (and the politics behind them), and how those decisions are enforced will determine the fate of Kamchatka's salmon runs, driving them toward a future that lies somewhere between two extremes. Within a relatively short time, maybe ten years or twenty, the phrase "Kamchatka salmon" could represent a byword for good resource governance and a green brand, reflecting the greatest success story in the history of fisheries management. Or that phrase could memorialize the saddest and most unnecessarily squandered conservation opportunity of the early 21st century. Think: American alligator. Or think: passenger pigeon. At present, the situation is fluid.

Life is hard enough for a salmon, even without politics and economics. Consider the 1.2 million fry released each spring from the Malki hatchery. Roughly five inches long after their first months of growth, they face no easy path from infancy to adulthood. What they face, rather, is a high likelihood of early death. For starters, the hatchery lies about a hundred miles (as a fish swims) from the sea. Each little salmon must descend the Bystraya River to its confluence with a larger river, the Bolshaya. Eluding all manner of freshwater perils on the Bolshaya, it must gradually metamorphose into a different sort of fish, a smolt, capable of making the transition to life in salt water. From the mouth of the Bolshaya, on Kamchatka's west coast, it must enter the bigger world of the Sea of Okhotsk, a frigid but nourishing body of water between the peninsula and mainland Russia.

Then, for a period of two to five years (depending on the species), that fish must circulate through the Sea of Okhotsk or else southeastward around the peninsula's tip into the expanse of the Pacific. The fish might travel thousands of miles, finding its preferred food (mostly small squid and crustaceans) abundant but facing predation, competition, and other challenges of the marine environment. For instance, it might be caught in the open ocean by fishermen using enormous drift nets that trap everything in their path. If it survives these years of robust swimming and feeding, it will grow large, fat, and strong. That's the advantage of anadromy (a sea-run life history): The ocean years allow fast growth. Approaching sexual maturity, the fish will head homeward to spawn, using some combination of magnetic sensing and polarized light to find its way back to the Bolshaya River. From the estuary it will ascend upstream by smell, branching into the familiar Bystraya, and finally climbing through the same shallow riffles of the same smaller tributary that its parents ascended before it.

Thousands of eggs will be laid for every two adult fish that return. Unlike an Atlantic salmon or most other species of vertebrate, a Pacific salmon breeds once and then dies. Scientists call the phenomenon semelparity. For the rest of us: big-bang reproduction. After the adult has homed to its spawning stream, death follows sex as inexorably as digestion follows a meal. It's a life-history strategy, shaped by evolution over millions of years, that balances the costs of each spawning journey against the costs of reproductive effort, toward the goal of maximizing reproductive success. In plainer words: Since the likelihood of any fish surviving the whole journey not just once but twice is so slim, Pacific salmon exhaust themselves fatally—they breed themselves to death—at the first opportunity they get. Why hold back anything if you'll never have another chance?

So their lives enact a romantic but pitiless narrative. Their success rate is low, even under optimal circumstances. The miracle of salmon is that any of them manage to complete such an arduous cycle at all. And present circumstances on the Bolshaya River and its tributaries—though the wall poster at Malki didn't say so—are far from optimal.

Ludmila Sakharovskaya, director of the Malki hatchery, is a sweet-spirited woman with blond hair and silver glasses who has worked there since the early 1980s. She trained as a biologist in Irkutsk, a warmish city in south-central Siberia, before moving east to this severe outpost in search of a better livelihood. For almost three decades she has watched—she has lived, like a doting nanny—the cycles of salmon rearing, release, and return.

"Twenty years ago I remember lots of fish coming to this river," she told me, through a translator, on a crisp summer day, as we stood near her fish traps in a little tributary. Those traps were the end point for spawn-ready adults whose eggs and sperm would fuel the hatching and rearing operations of the hatchery. "A variety of species," Sakharovskaya said. "Now I don't see them."

The decline in the run of chinook, *Oncorhynchus tshawytscha*, has been especially severe, she said. These are deep-bodied and silvery creatures with purplish dorsal markings, largest of all salmon species, and therefore sometimes known as king salmon. Once they came in great, regal herds. Nowadays the Malki hatchery releases 850,000 chinook fry (as well as a lesser number of sockeye) annually, but not many adults return. What stops them? Two kinds of illegal harvest: overcatching (*perelov* is the Russian word) by licensed companies that have catch quotas but exceed them with impunity, and poaching by individuals or small crews, mostly for caviar, at concealed spots along the river. The poaching problem throughout Kamchatka is catastrophic in scale, totaling at least 120 million pounds of salmon annually, much of it controlled by criminal syndicates. A hatchery director can't fix that problem, Sakharovskaya noted, and the regulatory authorities evidently don't have the resources or the resolve to do it. So only the luckiest and most elusive of chinook reach their destiny here along the Bystraya. "We can almost count them on fingers," she said.

But the Bolshaya drainage is only one of many river systems on the peninsula, and its hatchery fish aren't representative of Kamchatka wild salmon. Circumstances elsewhere are different; threats, opportunities, regulations, and even bureaucratic structures all change year by year. The whole situation is as complicated as a nested set of *matryoshka* dolls—Putin containing Gorbachev containing Brezhnev containing Stalin. On the Kol River, for instance, which also drains to the west coast, there is no hatchery, no streamside road, and (so far) no tragedy of depleted runs. What the Kol represents is superb habitat, scarcely touched, and abundant runs of wild salmon, including all six species: chinook, sockeye, chum, coho, pink, and masu. Last year, over seven million fish returned to spawn, filling the Kol so fully that in some stretches salmon were packed side to side like paving bricks. The Kol also carries another distinction. By a 2006 decree of the Kamchatka government, that river (along with another nearby stream) became part of the Kol-Kekhta Regional Experimental Salmon Reserve, the world's first whole-basin refuge established for the conservation of Pacific salmon.

On the north bank now sits the Kol River Biostation, a cluster of simple wooden buildings that serves as base for a binational research effort, its field operations led by Kirill Kuzishchin of Moscow State University and his American colleague, Jack Stanford of the University of Montana. Kuzishchin, Stanford, and their team are studying the dynamics of the Kol ecosystem. They hope to address several big questions, including: How important are salmon to the health of the entire river ecosystem?

Kirill Kuzishchin is a burly man with a linebacker's neck, a sly smile, and a sharp scientific brain. He was raised on a farm near Moscow by his grandparents. At age four he caught his first fish and was evermore fascinated by things piscine; even now, as an associate professor in the ichthyology department at Moscow State, he loves to cast a line when collection of specimens is required. Among the chief lessons of his studies in freshwater ecology is that a river is more than its main channel. "The whole floodplain acts as one single organism," Kuzishchin told me during a late evening talk at the Kol station. Water flows not just downstream but from channel to channel, both on the surface and via the underground aquifer; leaves fall into the river from riparian trees and bushes, supplying food and mineral nutrients to aquatic insects and microbes; whole trees topple into the water, providing cover for fish. "Everything is connected," he said. "The faster the growth of the trees, the more of them falling down into the river, the more habitats we have."

But nutrients are continually lost from the upper reaches by the same gravitational pull that takes water, silt, and other material downstream. So why don't these rivers gradually lose productivity? The reason is upstream migration by millions of salmon, Kuzishchin explained. The fish themselves bring nutrients such as nitrogen and phosphorus, accumulated during the years at sea, and surrender those precious loads to the ecosystem as their bodies decay. One aspect of the fieldwork by his and Stanford's team is to gauge the amount of nutrients at the Kol headwaters that are delivered and redelivered by salmon.

The scientists do that by testing for a certain isotope of nitrogen, N-15, which is relatively rare compared with other forms of nitrogen but far more abundant in oceans than in rivers. High concentrations of N-15 in the Kol's water during the season after spawning and decay, and in the leaves of the willow and cottonwood trees lining the banks, reflect the fact that salmon are bringing nutrients upstream. It's a circular effect, Kuzishchin said. Take the salmon away (for instance, by over-harvesting or by poaching), and the very leaves of the trees will be deprived of nitrogen. So will the microbes and insects that eat the leaves. The entire ecosystem will lose nutrients, possibly to the point that it could no longer support large runs of salmon, even if they were reintroduced. He repeated his ecological maxim: "Everything is connected."

Jack Stanford made the same point more bluntly: "If you harvest all your fish, you cannot have a productive system."

During a fieldwork excursion upstream from the station, I saw the Kol River's fecundity for myself. We ascended the main channel in motorized johnboats, then proceeded by foot, bashing across the jungly floodplain through a dense thicket of green plants, ten feet high but as delicate as celery, toward a side channel where the team would gather data. Kuzishchin led, chopping a corridor through the vegetation. It was mostly annual growth, consisting of thistle, nettle, cow parsnip, a white-flowered thing called Kamchatka meadowsweet, along with some grasses and ferns, together constituting a fast-growing floodplain assemblage known in Kamchatka as *shelomainik*. Finally we reached the little spring-fed channel, and as Kuzishchin and the others prepared to collect stream insects, algae, tiny fish, depth and flow readings, and willow leaves for nitrogen testing, I asked Stanford: What allows all this herby growth to spring up here, within such a short growing season, every year?

"In a word," he said, "salmon."

The salmon support a human ecosystem too. Near the mouth of the Bolshaya in a town called Ust-Bolsheretsk, a local official, Sergei Pasmurov, received me in a sparsely furnished office behind leather-padded doors. Beneath a photo of Vladimir Putin glowering down from behind a fern, Pasmurov offered a candid sketch of local history, which had been difficult recently.

Throughout the Soviet era, Ust-Bolsheretsk was a sizable agricultural center, a base for several large state farms that kept dairy cattle and grew turnips, tomatoes, and other vegetables in hothouses. Fishing was important also, with two fish-processing plants operating here. Population stood at about 15,000 for the district, including Ukrainians, Belorussians, Irkutsk Siberians—people from all over the U.S.S.R.—as well as indigenous Kamchatkans of the Itelmen ethnic group. Then, so abruptly, so harshly, came the end of the Soviet Union, without which those government-supported agricultural collectives failed. Suddenly there was an unfamiliar phenomenon, unemployment, and the population fell markedly. Dairy production dropped; vegetables became scarce. Pasmurov described the whole cascade of changes concisely and bundled them into one freighted word—*razval-ilsya*—that my translator rendered as "the ruining." Fishing became, for lack of alternatives, the major economic activity of the district.

Fishing is seasonal, also cyclical, with up-and-down fluctuations from year to year. Even during a good year the river can't support everyone. Nonetheless, about 20 different companies or individuals are currently licensed to fish hereabouts, Pasmurov told me. The number of operators and the quota allotted to each are regulated—but not very stringently—by the Federal Agency of Fisheries. "It results in reducing fish," he said. Year to year, the runs are becoming smaller. Poaching also plays a role. The Bolshaya is a large river, easily accessible by road, therefore hard to protect. Access will become easier still, he added, now that a pipeline is being built to carry natural gas from the west coast to Petropavlovsk, crossing the Bystraya and a dozen other rivers (including the Kol, notwithstanding its protected-area status). The pipeline itself might be clean and leakproof, Pasmurov said, but the road built alongside it will invite more poaching, especially for caviar.

And caviar—valuable, preservable, portable—is what most poachers are after. "It's more convenient, easier to hide," he said. "You just salt it, put it in tanks, hide it in the forest." Later a truck, or even a helicopter, comes to collect the stash. Netting the salmon as they near their spawning streams, slitting them open, stripping out the eggs, tossing the carcasses aside as waste, a gang of poachers can do huge damage in a very short time. Their wholesale customers might even include some of the big fish-processing plants: laundering caviar for the open market.

I heard the same thing about caviar from other sources, including an ex-poacher on the Kol, who recalled that in the days before protection a small team could harvest five tons in a season. There might be 15 such teams on the river, each man making ten times the money he could in a legal fishing job. Do the arithmetic, and you find that at least 75 metric tons of illegally taken salmon eggs (each mass of eggs accounting for 20 percent of the female's body weight) amounts to more than three-quarters of a million pounds of illegally killed fish. The carcasses of those salmon are left for bears and other scavengers—a short-term benefit to the ecosystem, yes—but every salmon thus intercepted leaves no offspring to perpetuate the run.

On the lower Bolshaya I saw the business of salmon fishing as practiced legally. It was a chilly July morning. A dozen men stood ready in waders, wool caps, and rubber gloves as a net was stretched far out across the river's channel by motorboat, then swung gradually downstream and drawn closed against the same bank, trapping hundreds of sockeye and coho in a watery corral. The men began walking the net back upstream, drawing it tighter toward the shallows, herding salmon onto a gravel beach. The fish, big and silvery (not yet flushed red, as they would be if they reached their spawning grounds), flopped robustly until there was nowhere to go. The men lifted them by their tails, one by one, and tossed them into a cargo boat. When that boat was full, it departed upstream to a landing, for unloading onto a truck, and another took its place. Within half an hour, from one set of the net, the crew took what looked like at least a thousand pounds of fish.

At one point a man lifted a nice-looking fish by the tail and tossed it back into the river. It was a female, heading upstream to spawn, I was told, so they didn't want to kill it. One fish, at least, might fulfill her reproductive potential. But whether this operation would abide by its legal quota was another issue, impossible for me to judge as a casual observer.

Long before the Russian residents of Kamchatka (who are immigrants and descendants of immigrants) came to depend on salmon fishing as a pillar of the economy, the Itelmen people and other indigenous Kamchatkans had developed cultural, religious, and subsistence practices centered on salmon. The Itelmen, in particular, made their settlements along the banks of rivers, mostly in the southern two-thirds of the peninsula, where they harvested salmon using fish traps and weirs. They dried the pink flesh, they smoked it, they fermented fish heads in barrels. "Those fermented heads had a great deal of vitamins," one Itelmen elder told me. "They cleaned out your stomach and all the bad things in your body." The Itelmen even venerated a god, known as Khantai, whose iconic representation was half fish and half human. In autumn the people set up a tall, wooden Khantai idol facing the river, offered it oblations, then celebrated a harvest festival of thanksgiving for the fish that had come and supplication for more to follow.

A revived form of that ancient festival is held each year in Kovran, on the west coast, which now constitutes the capital of Itelmen life. Kovran villagers still fish by the traditional methods. But starting in the Soviet era, other things changed, threatening Itelmen traditions while bringing little relief to their hard lives.

Irena Kvasova, an Itelmen activist I met at a small office in a backstreet of Petropavlovsk, told me that Soviet policy had required country people, including her mother, to abandon their remote hamlets and aggregate in centers such as Kovran. There they became laborers on collective farms or fishing collectives, a very different existence for people accustomed to independence and living off the land. The Itelmen received tax exemptions, true, and the government bought the ferns and berries they gathered and the game they hunted, at fair prices.

But during the more fevered decades of Stalinism, Soviet authorities felt a need to find "enemies of the state." People anonymously denounced their neighbors, sometimes just to settle a grudge. Kvasova's own great-grandfather had been one victim. A proud Itelmen, a hunter and fisherman, leader of the collective council, he was targeted in a poison letter, arrested, and sent to the camps beyond Magadan—that is, the Kolyma River region, grimmest of all islands in the Gulag Archipelago—where he died. In the aftermath, her family stopped communicating, even with one another, so as to avoid attracting suspicion.

In the 1970s, as the Soviet regime became relatively less sinister but more stolidly bureaucratic, outsiders, arriving from the south, received positions and enjoyed benefits while the Itelmen people were marginalized in their own communities. Gorbachev's perestroika, followed by the collapse of the state, followed by orgiastic privatization, completed the process of dispossessing the native people of lands, waters, and living resources they had husbanded for millennia.

One sign of that progressive dispossession is that the Itelmen must compete with commercial Russian fishing companies for limited salmon-fishing quotas. The Itelmen number only about 3,500 people, one percent of Kamchatka's total. Power resides in Petropavlovsk, not in Kovran, and power influences the granting of quotas and fishing sites from river to river. The bureaucrats who grant those quotas and sites on the Kovran River have been generous to outsider-owned commercial companies, an Itelmen leader named Oleg Zaporotsky told me, while restricting the local people to quotas that are marginal, even for subsistence. The companies employ a few Itelmen, but generally not in the better-paying jobs. And beyond the issue of subsistence fishing, Zaporotsky explained, some Itelmen want to establish their own fishing-and-processing cooperatives, which would bring income to the community, support schools and other institutions, and provide good jobs that would keep people from drifting away.

Zaporotsky himself has partnered with others to buy a diesel generator for freezing fish, the first step toward claiming a market share. "If we don't create some small enterprises," he told me, "these settlements won't survive." So far the bureaucrats have refused to grant commercial-scale quotas to Zaporotsky's local group or any other.

On the opposite side of the Pacific, the wild salmon runs of North America (south of Alaska), once great, have been devastated—and in some cases obliterated—by dambuilding, dewatering for irrigation, overfishing, agricultural pollution, and other forms of habitat degradation, and they've been genetically diminished by reliance on hatcheries. The people of Kamchatka have a chance to be wise and provident where Americans and Canadians have been stupid and careless. For Kamchatka to become the world's foremost wild salmon refuge, the runs in its rivers don't need to be restored; they need only to be protected from poaching, overcatching, oil and gas spills, disruptive and poisonous mining, and other forms of shortsighted mistake. The region could also become one of the richest export producers of fresh salmon, frozen salmon, and caviar. Those two prospects aren't incompatible; they're interlocked.

This is why the Wild Fishes and Biodiversity Foundation (WFBF), of Kamchatka, and its American partner, the Wild Salmon Center (WSC), supplied help and encouragement when the Kamchatka government created the Kol-Kekhta Regional Experimental Salmon Reserve, and why they support current efforts toward designating another protected area for salmon, on the Utkholok River up north. WFBF and WSC have also backed an ambitious vision of adding five more such protected areas—on the Oblukovina, Krutogorova, Kolpakova, and Opala Rivers (all draining to the west coast), and the Zhupanova River (draining east), each to encompass not just the river itself but its full drainage basin, including the headwater streams in which the salmon spawn and all the terrestrial habitat. Those five areas, together with the Kol and the Utkholok, would make Kamchatka the planet's greatest, boldest experiment in nurturing wild salmon species for their own sakes and for the measured use of humankind. And it could actually happen—if long-term management perspectives informed by scientific research, along with honest governance backed by strict enforcement, are allowed to triumph over the scramble for short-term gain by insiders.

Of course, some people prefer the old way, whether that represents Soviet-flavored enterprises (the V. I. Lenin Fishing Collective still operates from a large building near the Petropavlovsk waterfront) or heedless private resource extraction in the spirit of Standard Oil, Anaconda (copper), and Peabody (coal). History and human need lie heavily on Kamchatka. A huge bronze statue of Lenin himself, thick-limbed and implacable, still stands in the plaza outside the main government offices. Moscow still sets the course. People without jobs still need to eat, and fish are there for the taking.

It's a long journey from idealistic plans to concrete, well-enforced protections, just as it's a long journey from the deep Pacific to the gravelly shallows of the Bystraya River. I can't forget what Ludmila Sakharovskaya said as we stood stream-side at the Malki hatchery. Twenty-five years of hatching and nurturing fish, releasing them, seeing ever fewer return, had made her cynical. She was tired too, eager to take her pension and go to Irkutsk. Yes, we have reforms now, she said—or anyway, there's talk of reforms. But that's just talk, just formalities. Poaching is easy to do and hard to prevent. She knows of whole settlements, in the mountains, filled with people who could seek a legal job but don't, who live out the winter waiting for summer, when they can poach salmon.

Were things better during the Soviet era?

She considers that for a second or two, and answers carefully: "Better for fish."

Appendix

CZARS OF RUSSIA AND THEIR REIGNS (1547–1721)

RURIK DYNASTY

Ivan IV (the Terrible), b. 1547–1584

Feodor I (the Bellringer), 1584–1598

GODUNOV DYNASTY

Boris Godunov, 1598–1605

Feodor II, 605

Dmitriy I (False Dmitriy), 1605–1606

SHUISKY DYNASTY

Basil IV, 1606–1610

Dmitriy II (False Dmitriy II), 1610

THE HOUSE OF ROMANOV

Mikhail I, 1613–1645

Alexis I, 1645–1676

Feodor III, 1676–1682

Ivan V, 1682–1696

CZARS OF RUSSIA AND THEIR REIGNS (1547–1917)

THE HOUSE OF ROMANOV, CONT.

 Peter I (the Great), 1682–1725

Catherine I, 1725–1727

 Peter II, 1727–1730

Anna Ivanovna, 1730–1740

 Ivan VI, 1740–1741

Elizabeta Petrovna, 1741–1762

 Peter III, 1762

Catherine II (the Great), 1762–1796

Paul I, 1796–1801

Alexander I, 1801–1825

Nicholas I, 1825–1855

Alexander II, 1855–1881

Alexander III, 1881–1894

Nicholas II, 1894–1917

Courtesy of the Russian Museum

A painting of Vladimir I and Rogneda, 1770, by an unknown artist. Vladimir was the first ruler of Kievan Rus', which was the precursor to the country of Russia.

Courtesy of the Tretyakov Gallery

A painting of Czar Ivan IV (the Terrible) by Viktor Vasnetsov, 1897. Ivan IV was the first Russian czar.

Courtesy of Kensington Palace, England

Portrait of Czar Peter I (the Great) by Godfrey Kneller, 1698.

Courtesy of Beinecke Rare Book and Manuscript Library, Yale University

Czar Nicholas II and his family. Nicholas II was the last of the Romanov czars, who ruled Russia for more than 300 years. He was executed—along with his wife, four daughters, and son—after the Revolution of 1917.

Photo by Karl Bulla

Grigori Rasputin (1869–1916) was a controversial Russian mystic who influenced Czar Nicholas II and his family, becoming especially close to Nicholas's wife, Alexandra. While some looked upon him as a religious prophet, others called him the "Mad Monk" and saw him as a corrupting influence on Russian government.

Courtesy of the Russian Federation

Joseph Stalin (left) and Vladimir Lenin in 1919, two years after the October Revolution which gave power to the Bolsheviks. Lenin became leader of what would become the Soviet Union in 1922. After his death, Stalin would take over.

Courtesy of the Russian Federation

During the Soviet era, millions of citizens were sent to labor camps, or gulags, for crimes that ranged from ownership of land to simply criticizing the government. Many died from the harsh conditions. Others were executed. This picture shows the Perm 36 camp, one of the most notorious.

Winston Churchill (left), Franklin D. Roosevelt (center), and Joseph Stalin, known as the "Big Three," at the Yalta Conference in February 1945, in the waning days of World War II. In Russia, the conflict is called "The Great Patriotic War."

John F. Kennedy Presidential Library and Museum

Soviet security general Nikita Khrushchev (left) and U.S. president John Kennedy, during a summit in Vienna, Austria, in 1961. By the 1960s, the Cold War rivalry between the United States and Soviet Union had intensified. The Soviet satellite Sputnik was launched in 1957, starting a "space race" between the two countries. Although the sides never fought directly, they came close on several occasions and engaged in a series of proxy wars. Throughout this time, both superpowers stockpiled arms, fueling fears of nuclear war.

President Ronald Reagan and Soviet General Secretary Mikhail Gorbachev at the Hofdi House in Reykjavik, Iceland, during the Reyjavik Summit in 1986, just a few short years before the Soviet Union collapsed.

Boris Yeltsin (1991–1999), Russia's first popularly elected president, took office shortly before the collapse of the Soviet Union. In the post-Soviet era, Yelstin led the Russian Federation. Economic crises caused Yeltsin's popularity to wane, though he won reelection in 1996. He resigned in 1999 and passed away in April 2007.

Vladimir Putin (2000–2008) was appointed president of the Russian Federation after Boris Yeltsin's resignation and was elected in his own right in 2000. Voters overwhelmingly awarded him a second term in 2004. Under his presidency, Russia's economy rebounded and the country enjoyed a period of relative stability. In 2008, with Putin constitutionally unable to seek a third term, his protégé Dmitry Medvedev was elected president. Medvedev subsequently named Putin his prime minister.

Dmitry Medvedev (2008–), the current Russian president, succeeded Vladimir Putin in 2008. His term has been dominated by global recession, war with Georgia in the Southern Caucusus, terrorist threats, and corruption. Seen as more liberal than his predecessor, the 44-year-old Medvedev is the youngest Russian leader in more than 100 years.

Images courtesy of the Russian Federation

Bibliography

Books

Applebaum, Anne. *Gulag: A History*. New York: Doubleday, 2003.

Badcock, Sarah. *Politics and the People in Revolutionary Russia: A Provincial History*. New York: Cambridge University Press, 2007.

Beavor, Antony. *The Fall of Berlin 1945*. New York: Viking, 2002.

Bodin, Per-Arne. *Eternity and Time: Studies in Russian Literature and the Orthodox Tradition*. Sodertalke, Sweden: Almqvist & Wiksell International, 2007.

Bucher, Greta. *Daily Life in Imperial Russia*. Westport, Conn.: Greenwood Press, 2008.

Butler, Francis. *Enlightener of Rus': The Image of Vladimir Sviatoslavich across the Centuries*. Bloomington, Ind.: Slavica, 2002.

Carruthers, Susan L. *Cold War Captives: Imprisonment, Escape, and Brainwashing*. Berkeley, Calif.: University of California Press, 2009.

Catherine the Great. *The Memoirs of Catherine the Great*. New York: Modern Library, 2006.

Chamberlain, Lesley. *Lenin's Private War: The Voyage of the Philosophy Steamer and the Exile of the Intelligentsia*. New York: St. Martin's Press, 2007.

Christian, David. *A History of Russia, Mongolia and Central Asia*. New York: John Wiley & Sons, 1999.

Colton, Timothy J. *Yeltsin: A Life*. New York: Basic Books, 2008.

Cracraft, James and Daniel Rowland, eds. *Architectures of Russian Identity: 1500 to the Present*. Ithaca, N.Y.: Cornell University Press, 2003.

Dimnik, Martin. *The Dynasty of Chernigov, 1146–1246*. New York: Cambridge University Press, 2003.

Evangelista, Matthew. *Chechen Wars: Will Russia Go the Way of the Soviet Union?* Washington, D.C.: Brookings Institution Press, 2003.

Figes, Orlando. *A People's Tragedy: The Russian Revolution, 1891–1924*. New York: Penguin, 1996.

———. *Natasha's Dance: A Cultural History of Russia*. New York: Picador, 2003.

———. *The Whisperers: Private Life in Stalin's Russia*, New York: Picador, 2007.

Frankel, Max. *High Noon in the Cold War: Kennedy, Khrushchev, and the Cuban Missile Crisis*. New York: Ballantine, 2004.

Franklin, Simon. *Writing Society and Culture in Early Rus, c.950–1300*. New York: Cambridge University Press, 2002.

Franklin, Simon and Emma Widdis, eds. *National Identity in Russian Culture: An Introduction*. New York: Cambridge University Press, 2004.

Goldman, Marshall I. *Petrostate: Putin, Power, and the New Russia*. New York: Oxford University Press, 2008.

Jagielski, Wojciech. *Towers of Stone: The Battle of Wills in Chechnya*. New York: Seven Stories Press, 2009.

Kagarlitsky, Boris. *Back in the USSR*. London, U.K.: Seagull Books, 2009.

Hosking, Geoffrey. *Russia and the Russians: A History*. Cambridge, Mass.: Belknap Press, 2001.

Lohr, Eric and Marshall Poe, eds. *The Military and Society in Russia, 1450–1917*. Cambridge, Mass.: Brill Academic Publishers, 2002.

Mankoff, Jeffrey. *Russian Foreign Policy: The Return of Great Power Politics*. Lanham, Md.: Rowman & Littlefield, 2009.

Massie, Robert K. *Peter the Great : His Life and World*. New York: Ballantine Books, 1981.

———. *The Romanovs: The Final Chapter*. New York: Ballantine Books, 1996.

Merridale, Catherine. *Night of Stone: Death and Memory in Twentieth-Century Russia*. New York: Penguin, 2002.

———. *Ivan's War: Life and Death in the Red Army, 1939–1945*. New York: Metropolitan Books, 2006.

Millar, James R., ed. *Encyclopedia of Russia History*. New York: MacMillan Reference, 2004.

Montaigne, Fen. *Reeling in Russia: An American Angler in Russia*. New York: St. Martin's Press, 1998.

Pipes, Richard. *The Russian Revolution*. New York: Knopf, 1990.

Priestland, David. *Red Flag: A History of Communism*. New York: Grove Press, 2009.

Rappaport, Helen. *Conspirator: Lenin in Exile*. New York: Basic Books, 2010.

Rawicz, Slavomir. *The Long Walk: The True Story of a Trek to Freedom*. Guilford, Conn.: Lyons Press, 1956.

Reed, John. *Ten Days That Shook the World*. New York: Boni and Liveright, 1919.

Remnick, David. *Lenin's Tomb: The Last Days of the Soviet Empire*. New York: Random House, 1993.

Schwartz, Richard Alan. *The Cold War Reference Guide*. Jefferson, N.C.: McFarland & Company, 1996.

Service, Robert. *Lenin: A Biography*. New York: Macmillan, 2000.

———. *Russia: Experiment with a People*. Cambridge, Mass.: Harvard University Press, 2003.

———. *History of Modern Russia: From Tsarism to the Twenty-First Century*. Cambridge, Mass.: Harvard University Press, 2009.

———. *Trotsky: A Biography*. Cambridge, Mass.: Harvard University Press, 2009.

———. *Stalin: A Biography*. Cambridge, Mass.: Belknap Press 2009.

Solzhenitsyn, Alexander. *August 1914*. New York: Farrar, Straus and Giroux, 1972.

———. *Gulag Archipalego 1918–1956: An Experiment in Literary Investigation*. New York: Harper & Row, 1974.

———. *November 1916*. New York: Farrar, Straus and Giroux, 1999.

Sulzberger C. L., *The Fall of Eagles*. New York: Crown Publishers, 1977.

Szporluk, Roman. *Russia, Ukraine, and the Breakup of the Soviet Union*. Stanford, Calif.: Hoover Institution Press, 2000.

Tayler, Jeffrey. *River of No Reprieve: Descending Siberia's Waterway of Exile, Death, and Destiny*. New York: Houghton Mifflin Harcourt, 2006.

Thomson, Peter. *Sacred Sea: A Journey to Lake Baikal*. New York: Oxford University Press, 2007.

Thubron, Colin. *Among the Russians*. New York: HarperCollins, 1984.

————. *In Siberia.* New York: HarperCollins, 1999.

Tolstoy, Leo. *War and Peace.* Maude, Louise and Aylmar (trans). Chicago: Encyclopaedia Brittanica, 1955.

Trotsky, Leon. *Marxism and Terrorism.* New York: Pathfinder Press, 1995.

————. *My Life: An Attempt at an Autobiography.* Mineola, N.Y.: Dover, 2007.

Volkov, Solomon. *St. Petersburg: A Cultural History.* New York: Free Press, 1995.

Wettlin, Margaret. *Fifty Russian Winters: An American Woman's Life in the Soviet Union.* New York: John Wiley & Sons, Inc., 1992.

Wirtschafter, Elise Kimerling. *Russia's Age of Serfdom 1649–1861.* Blackwell History of Russia Series. Malden, Mass.: Wiley-Blackwell, 2008.

Ziegler, Charles E. *The History of Russia.* Westport, Conn.: Greenwood, 2009.

Web Sites

Readers seeking additional information on Russia and related topics may wish to consult the following Web sites, all of which were operational as of this writing.

Cold War Museum

http://www.coldwar.org

The Cold War between the United States and Soviet Union. lasted from the 1940s until the dissolution of the USSR in 1991. It was called a "cold war" because there was no direct military confrontation between the two superpowers. The historic rivalry now has its own museum, the Web site for which is filled with information, including on-line exhibits, a Cold War timeline, gallery, and other resources.

C.R.E.E.S.: Center for Russian, East European, and Eurasian Studies

http://www.ii.umich.edu/crees

C.R.E.E.S. is a department of the University of Michigan at Ann Arbor. The Web site contains numerous links to resources about Russia and Eastern Europe—including audio and video lectures, workshops, and other academic programs.

GULAG: Soviet Labor Camps and the Struggle for Freedom

http://gulaghistory.org/nps/onlineexhibit/dissidents/movement.php

This Web site is a combined effort of the Gulag Museum of Perm-36 (Russia), the U.S. National Park Service, George Mason University, and Harvard University. It is the on-line companion to a traveling exhibit created to educate people about the Gulags, or Soviet-era labor camps. Included are personal accounts, photographs, teachers resources, and much more.

The Harriman Institute at Columbia University

http://www.harrimaninstitute.org

The Harriman Institute is the Russian, Eurasian, and Eastern European department of Columbia University. Its Web site features links to events at the Institute, programs of study offered, and access to the the journal *The Harriman Review*.

Russia Profile

http://www.russiaprofile.org

This Web site aims to provide "the most comprehensive and concise view of business, economic, political and cultural trends and processes underway in Russia." It features a wealth of news articles and commentary, a calendar of events, and a list of outside links for further research.

Russian and East European Institute at University of Indiana

http://www.indiana.edu/~reeiweb

The Web site of the Russian and East European Institute at the University of Indiana provides details about programs of study, news, events, a list of materials at their library, and much more.

Russian Embassy in Washington

http://www.russianembassy.org

The Web site of the Russian Embassy in Washington, D.C., features news articles and pictures as well as links to officials in the embassy and other agencies and material concerning U.S.-Russian relations.

St. Petersburg Times (Florida): Romanov Timeline

http://www2.sptimes.com/Treasures/TC.2.3.html

This timeline from Florida's *St. Petersburg Times* charts the Romanov Dynasty from 1600 to 1917, when the Russian Revolution ended the monarchy. There are links material on each czar, including pictures and short biographies.

The State Hermitage Museum

http://www.hermitagemuseum.org

The State Hermitage Museum, located in St. Petersburg, Russia, is one of the largest art museums in the world. Similar to the Louvre, in Paris, France, it is housed in a complex of state buildings and has a collection of more than 3 million artifacts. It was founded by Catherine the Great in 1764. The museum's Web site features on-line exhibits and a digital collection.

TravelAllRussia.com

http://www.travelallrussia.com

This is a Web site dedicated to traveling in Russia, whether by boat, tour bus, or other means. One can book trips, research particular regions, peruse travel tips, and read stories by people that have visited the country.

The Washington Post: Country Guide

http://www.washingtonpost.com/wp-srv/world/countries/russia.html

The Washington Post Country Guide entry on Russia includes the following chapters: "Land and People," "Economy," "Government," and "History." The information is extensive and easy to follow.

World Bank: Russian Federation

http://web.worldbank.org/WBSITE/EXTERNAL/COUNTRIES/ECAEXT/RUSSI ANFEDERATIONEXTN/0,,menuPK:305605~pagePK:141159~piPK:141110~theSiteP K:305600,00.html

The World Bank, an international financial institution, provides data on its Web site for a number of countries. This site focuses on the Russian Federation and contains a great deal of information on the country's financial situation. It includes news articles, discussion forums, grant programs, Webcasts, statistics, educational opportunities, and more.

Additional Periodical Articles with Abstracts

More information about Russia can be found in the following articles. Readers interested in additional material may consult the *Readers' Guide to Periodical Literature* and other H.W. Wilson publications.

Russia Backs Choice of Religion Class in Schools. *The Christian Century* v. 126 p19 August 25, 2009.

Russian president Dmitry Medvedev has supported attempts by religious leaders to introduce religion into schools, the author reports. At a recent meeting with religious leaders, he described the introduction of religion at the school level as helping to strengthen the moral and spiritual foundations of society, as well as bolstering the unity of a multiethnic and multireligious Russia. Medvedev was responding to an appeal by Russia's Muslim, Jewish, Buddhist, and Orthodox leaders.

Orthodox Resurgence. John P. Burgess. *The Christian Century* v. 126 pp25–28 June 16, 2009.

The massive persecution of the Russian Orthodox Church under communism has been followed by what appears to many Orthodox to be a miracle of rebirth, Burgess observes. In the 20 years since the fall of the Soviet regime, the number of monasteries has increased from 22 to 804, and the percentage of Russians identifying themselves as Orthodox rose from 20 percent to perhaps as much as 80 percent. Nonetheless, although there is a renewal of Orthodox life in certain ways, at the same time Russia is becoming religiously pluralistic while remaining highly secular.

Starlight in Hell. Algis Valiunas. *First Things* pp31–35 June/July 2009.

Humanity in the face of inhumanity is perhaps the great theme of Russian literature, Valiunas contends. War, political devastation, and the savage perversities of the Russian character are nearly always present as a backdrop for individual courage, kindness, generosity, and nobility. Russian literature is read because it reveals the full range of the soul, from the bestial to the holy. Interestingly, however, Russian literature most frequently depicts the sacred soul in contrast to the souls of those who live by something other than the sacred, who create themselves in accordance with a master idea, generally a revolutionary political idea, that allows any manner of violence and barbarism to be used to achieve their intentions. A survey of the work of a number of Russian writers, including Leo Tolstoy, Fyodor Dostoyevsky, and Alexander Solzhenitsyn, illustrates the theme.

Failing the Stalin Test: Russians and Their Dictator. Theodore P. Gerber and Sarah E. Mendelson. *Foreign Affairs* v. 85 pp2–8 January/February 2006.

The writers discuss the results of three surveys they have conducted in Russia since 2003, which indicate that Stalin is not stigmatized in the country today. In fact, one-quarter or more of Russian adults claim they would definitely or probably vote for Stalin if he were a presidential candidate, and fewer than 40 percent claim they certainly would not. Furthermore, most young Russians are not revolted by the man, who was responsible for millions of deaths and enormous suffering. Russian youth can be persuaded to view Stalin as neither a neutral nor a positive figure in their country's history, the article contends, but only if a widespread campaign endorsed by international donors is launched. Left to their own devices, young Russians share the tendency of young people everywhere not to challenge their attitudes.

Samizdat in the 21st Century. Leon Aron. *Foreign Policy* pp131–33 July/August 2009.

According to Aron, Russia's economic failure, and Vladimir Putin's part in it, is the subject of an increasingly loud, surprisingly heated debate playing out on the Russian-language Internet, where several opposition Web sites publish untouched by heavy-handed Putin-era rules on mass media, and in the pages of the struggling but still influential Moscow liberal media. Taken together, these writings comprise a new literature of crisis, an intellectual debate that is not only about who is to blame but also what is to be done.

A Diplomatic Mystery. Bill Bradley. *Foreign Policy* p30 September/October 2009.

The writer considers the mystery of how exactly the United States ended up expanding NATO into Eastern Europe after the cold war, when NATO's ostensible aim would seem to have expired along with the Soviet Union itself. The Russians insist that the expansion of NATO violated an explicit vow made by the first Bush administration. The Americans have not just denied it but appear quite unaware of how much this dispute has affected U.S. dealings with Russia.

Haunted by Stalin's Ghost. Catherine Merridale. *History Today* v. 59 September 2009 pp32–38.

Although Russia experienced a renaissance in the study of history after the Cold War, myths about the country's past have also flourished, Merridale writes. From 1986 onward, the past seemed to come to life, breaking through a tissue of political illusion to reclaim its position at the center of Russia's national imagination. Today, however, public hunger for historical facts, revelations, and confessions has evaporated. Resurgent Russia's national identity depends almost entirely on a reading of the past, a tale of progress and triumph shaped largely by direct government intervention. Heroes and horseback chases are elements of the new popular history, as are unicorns and mythic spirituality, but reputable historical research is generally missing.

Trotsky Exiled to Siberia: November 2nd, 1906. Richard Cavendish. *History Today* v. 56 p62 November 2006.

This article centers on the exile of Leon Trotsky to Siberia in 1906 and his subsequent escape. Trotsky, the Soviet's chairman and principal spokesman, and 14 others were exiled for life to Siberia on November 2, 1906, after a trial on charges arising out of the failed Russian Revolution of 1905. The prisoners were bound for Obdorsk, but at Berezov in Ostyak territory, close to the Arctic Circle, Trotsky organized his escape with the aid of a local surveyor named Rokoshovsky. Coached by a fellow prisoner who was a doctor, he mimicked the symptoms of sciatica and was left behind for treatment in a local hospital. He subsequently escaped hidden in frozen hay on a sleigh driven by an intoxicated Zyryan tribesman. After seven days of sleighing, Trotsky reached the Urals and at Rudniki caught a train to St. Petersburg before joining his wife, Natalia, in Finland. He based himself in Vienna for the next decade until the Bolsheviks at last succeeded in Russia in 1917.

Watching Stalin Win. Paul R. Gregory. *Hoover Digest* pp153–66 Fall 2007.

Verbatim transcripts of power struggles in the Soviet Politburo, unseen for more than 70 years, are due to be published, Gregory notes. The transcripts reveal frank discussions by the USSR's ultimate decision-making body as it developed a political, economic, and social system and battled over who would lead the country. The transcripts, which chart a crucial 15-year period during which the last opposition to Josef Stalin was eliminated, have surfaced thanks to the Hoover Archives' pioneering efforts to microfilm important Soviet state and party documents, and with a key clue from visiting Russian archivists. Excerpts from the transcripts are reproduced and discussed.

Common Ground in the Caucasus. Henry A. Kissinger and George P. Shultz. *Hoover Digest* pp121–26 Winter 2009.

Reprinted from the *International Herald Tribune*, September 30, 2008, this article suggests the controversy over Georgia stands comparison with an issue from history: In 1914, an essentially local problem was viewed by so many countries through the lens of established fears and frustrations that it resulted in World War I. A general war will not happen now, but there is a danger that a conflict derived from ancestral passions in the Caucasus could be used as an excuse for a wider conflict, which would undermine the effort to establish a new international order in a world of globalization, nuclear proliferation, ethnic conflicts, and technological revolution. The writers explain why America, Europe, and Russia must not allow the conflict in Georgia to blind them to their shared interests.

Georgia Didn't Pick That Fight. John B. Dunlo. *Hoover Digest* pp131–36 Winter 2009.

Georgian president Mikheil Saakashvili made a serious mistake when he had his military confront invading Russian forces, Dublo observes, but the reality is that the five days of conflict in South Ossetia and Georgia were initiated by Russia, Dunlo writes. The Russian leadership and state-controlled media have relentlessly claimed that Georgia started the conflict, but such assertions do not tally with the findings of Andrei Illarionov, Russian president Vladimir Putin's chief economic adviser between 2000 and 2005 and later a prominent opposition figure. Illarionov conducted his own research mission to both South Ossetia and Georgia and used his vast number of contacts in the region to obtain vital information. The writer discusses the evidence that proves Russia had positioned tanks and troops for an invasion of Georgia long before it was "provoked."

The Ship of Philosophers: How the Early USSR Dealt with Dissident Intellectuals. Paul R. Gregory. *Independent Review* v. 13 pp485–92 Spring 2009

When the German steamer *Oberbuergermeister Hacken* set sail from Petrograd on September 28, 1922, many of its passengers knew they were leaving the Soviet Union forever, Gregory writes. These passengers represented the cream of Russian intellectual life, and they had been banished by the Bolsheviks as part of Soviet Union's repression of intellectuals. This process, begun in May 1922, was one of the last major programs carried out by Vladimir Lenin before he was incapacitated by his first stroke. The initiative resulted in imprisonment, internal exile, or banishment for hundreds of leading thinkers. The policy continued under Stalin, but was expanded in the late 1920s and became even more broad during the Great Purge of 1937–1938.

Signs of Recovery Abound in Russia. Paul Sweeney. *Institutional Investor International edition* v. 34 pp84–88 June 2009.

Investors are returning to Russian equities, but they want reassurance that the current rally is sustainable and are seeking direction on which sectors of the economy are likely to enjoy the strongest growth, Sweeney observes. Analysts who can guide investors through the economic recovery can be found in the 2009 All-Russia Research Team, *Institutional Investor*'s sixth annual ranking of Russia's leading securities researchers. Russia's best analysts in 2009 are presented, and their work is discussed.

A Vision for U.S.-Russian Cooperation on Nuclear Security. Linton F. Brooks. *Issues in Science and Technology* v. 26 pp25–28 Fall 2009.

The writer argues that Russia and the United States are in an ideal position to develop a real partnership to pursue enhanced global nuclear security with an emphasis on other countries. One way to start taking steps toward building partnership, Brooks writes, is to outline a vision of the world of 2015 that might be achieved if the United States and Russian leaders are committed to the task. In this vision, the two nations will understand each other's perceptions of nuclear threats, although they may not completely agree on these, and will view each other's strategic forces with reduced concern. The probability that political strains will remain in 2015 would be unrealistic to ignore, the author writes.

Putin on a Show. Michael Petrou. *Maclean's* v. 122 pp24–26 August 24, 2009.

Although it is easy to forget, Petrou writes, Vladimir Putin is no longer Russia's president and head of state. Officially, Putin should be subordinate to his one-time protege, Dmitry Medvedev, who succeeded Putin as president in May 2008. Russia's 1993 constitution precluded Putin from running for a third consecutive term as president, so he endorsed Medvedev, his one-time chief of staff who had never before held elected office. Nonetheless, the former president is still the most powerful man in Russia, and he does not intend to let go of the reins, the author writes.

Russia's Faux Reformist. Nancy Macdonald. *Maclean's* v. 122 pp30–31 December 14–21, 2009.

Although Russian president Dmitry Medvedev preaches transparency, he has made scant progress, Macdonald writes. Medvedev's tenure has not seen greater freedom for media, free speech has been increasingly blocked, and the number of murders and assaults on journalists and human-rights activists has actually risen. For Medvedev, the new embezzlement trial for Mikhail Khodorkovsky—the founder of the Yukos oil company and a rival to Vladimir Putin—who has said he does not understand the charges against him and could face 22 more years in prison, embodies the "legal nihilism" the president is pledging to combat, the author writes.

Potemkin Prisons: Inside the Museum of the Gulag. Jonathan Brent. *The New Criterion* v. 27 pp18–23 May 2009.

The writer discusses the State Museum of the History of the GULAG in Moscow. Opened on May 18, 2004, this museum was established by the personal directive of Yuri Luzhkov, the Mayor of Moscow. It is obvious that those who run the museum are well-intentioned and committed to memorializing the suffering of people who passed through the GULAG system, the author writes, but they lack both funds and facilities. Furthermore, Brent adds, they lack a perspective. Recently, President Medvedev announced that it is time for Russia to face its tortured past, but the effort to do so in the form of this museum is just another evasion disguised as disclosure, Brent concludes.

King & the Commissars. Andrew Stuttaford. *The New Criterion* v.28 pp58–60 March 2010.

Stuttaford reviews the book *Red Star over Russia: A Visual History of the Soviet Union from the Revolution to the Death of Stalin*, by David King. Compared with the narrower focus of some of King's earlier books, *Red Star over Russia*, described as "a fast-forward visual history of the Soviet Union" from 1917 until just after the death of Stalin, is an unruly sprawling epic, Stuttaford writes. It is also marked by the suspicion that King, drawing on his own archive, has pursued the aesthetically and commercially effective to the potential detriment of other, higher, concerns, the reviewer adds. Nevertheless, Stuttaford writes, it remains an extraordinary creation, presenting an expanse of material that is broad enough to sustain more than one interpretation of the Soviet revolution and its consequences.

Finally, Russia Sees America as It Really Is. Garry Kasparov. *New Perspectives Quarterly* v. 26 p37 Winter 2009.

The writer discusses Russia's attitude to the election of President Barack Obama. As Kasparov sees it, Obama has a small window of opportunity to capitalize on the world's curiosity and goodwill toward him. Although Obama already enjoys the advantage of not being George W. Bush, who Kasparov says symbolized every problem anyone has ever had with America, the world's raft of grievances with Bush will rapidly be shifted to Obama if he fails to support his inspiring rhetoric with concrete action. Kasparov writes that Obama could make a promising start by pointing out that he does not consider the people of Russia to be adversaries of the United States.

Putin's Shock Forces. Owen Matthews and Anna Nemtsova. *Newsweek* v. 149 p38 May 28, 2007.

The Kremlin is funding a shadowy youth movement called Nashi, its latest weapon in the drive to reclaim Russia's bygone regional dominance, the authors report. Extremely disciplined and generously bankrolled by the Kremlin, these militant young nationalists have created a formidable organization to oppose alleged enemies at home and abroad and to glorify imperial Russia and the Soviet Union. When Estonia decided to remove a statue of a World War II–era soldier from Tallinn on April 27, Russia did not try to conceal its rage. A Nashi-led mob closed down the highway from Russia into Estonia. In Moscow, Nashi protesters stormed a press conference by the Estonian ambassador, fleeing only when her bodyguards sprayed them with pepper gas.

Cleaning Up Dirty Police in Russia. Owen Matthews. *Newsweek* v. 155 p7 April 12, 2010.

The recent suicide bombings in Moscow seem to be increasing pressure for reform of the political system, Matthews writes. There has been a backlash against Russian police incompetence, although criticism of the police was brewing before the deadly attacks. Popular anger had been building for at least a year, following a series of scandals, including a supermarket shooting spree by a drunk officer, a YouTube appeal by a police major complaining of "pure banditry" among his colleagues, and press revelations concerning the blackmailing, terrorizing, and kidnapping of businessmen for profit by paramilitary cops. President Dmitry Medvedev and his liberal supporters have been calling for an overhaul of Russia's notoriously corrupt Interior Ministry for a year, but the reform program has not delivered many results to date. The terror attacks should accelerate the pace of change, Matthews writes.

Obama's Bad Cop. Michael Hirsh. *Newsweek* v. 155 pp31–35 May 3, 2010.

As secretary of state, Hillary Clinton has taken a hard line with Iran, Russia, and even Israel, and her sometimes hawkish views are finding favor with President Obama, Hirsh reports. The marked differences between Obama and Clinton over foreign policy on the campaign trail were, as many on both sides now acknowledge, largely political theater. The metamorphosis of bitter combatants into bona fide partners is not 100 percent complete, but it is far along, Hirsh writes.

Turkmenistan Keeps Russia at Bay. *Petroleum Economist* v. 76 pp29–30 October 2009.

The European Union (EU)'s influence over Central Asian gas supplies appears to have strengthened, but Russia's control over Turkmenistani exports seems to be shaky, the writer observes. A recent meeting between Presidents Dmitry Medvedev of Russia and Gurbanguly Berdymukhamedov of Turkmenistan failed to produce an agreement on when Turkmenistan would resume exports to Russia, halted since the spring. Both the EU and China will hope to take advantage of the situation, and Turkmenistan is seeking to connect to the EU-backed Nabucco pipeline project.

How China Won and Russia Lost. Paul Gregory and Kate Zhou. *Policy Review* pp35–50 December 2009/January 2010.

China and Russia in the 1980s provide a unique case study in why certain reforms succeed and others do not, Gregory and Zhou write. The contrast contradicts the idea that a strong, perhaps totalitarian state is required for effective reform. In the Russian situation, a one-party state failed in its efforts to impose reform from above, whereas, in China, a one-party state opened the economy but opposed grassroots reforms, which it reluctantly accepted when their success could no longer be denied. Both nations, the authors write, appear to have learned the wrong lesson from the other: China that political reform will wipe out the Communist Party, and Russia that only a powerful authoritarian leader can introduce effective reforms.

Ike and his Spies in the Sky. David Haight. *Prologue* v. 41 pp14–22 Winter 2009.

As U.S. president, Dwight D. Eisenhower was concerned about surprise attacks on the United States by a nuclear-armed Soviet Union and sought the best available intelligence, Haight observes. He understood that knowledge based on reliable intelligence is power, but information about the Soviets' military capability was proving elusive to the techniques of traditional espionage. To counter the Soviet military threat, the Eisenhower administration developed a strategic posture policy, the "New Look," which included an expansion of U.S. intelligence collection and analysis. The president authorized aerial intelligence-gathering programs to better assess the military capability of the Soviet Union, China, and other communist nations to launch a surprise attack, and he approved over-flights of the Soviet Union by military aircraft in a highly compartmentalized intelligence program called SENSINT, or Sensitive Intelligence.

Russian Youth Policy: Shaping the Nation-State's Future. Douglas W. Blum. *The SAIS Review of International Affairs* v. 26 pp95–108 Summer/Fall 2006.

The collapse of the USSR and the resulting devastation of Russia's economy created a multitude of acute social problems, Blum writes. At the same time, the sudden, massive exposure to globalization constituted a double-edged sword: while opening up a world of possibilities, it also exacerbated cultural fragmentation and diminished social cohesion. As a result, since 1991 Russia—like all of the other post-Soviet states—has been embroiled in the process of nation-building, which involves the creation of new institutions of governance as well as new systems of meaning and order. Increasingly, the focus of such efforts has been on the socialization of youth, reflecting a recognition that successful nation-building depends on enlisting the loyalty and participation of young people. Youth policy thus represents part of a larger attempt to anchor state and society within a sound institutional framework—one which, under Putin, is marked by a telltale mixture of delegation and centralization. This article reviews the pattern of current youth policymaking in Russia, outlining the contours of the relevant legislation as well as the nature of the political process involved.

Someplace Else. Kristina Gorcheva-Newberry. *The Southern Review* (Baton Rouge, La.) v. 45 pp268–74 Spring 2009.

Kristina Gorcheva-Newberry remembers her childhood male best friend in Russia, recounting incidents from their childhood, teenage, and young adult years. Gorcheva-Newberry explains that he was the friend she went to in the middle of the night when she left her husband and he was the friend who saw her off at the airport when she left Russia to go to America. She reveals that he has since been killed execution style, shot twice in the heart and once in the head.

The Remaking of Russia. Harold E. Rogers. *USA Today Periodical* v. 137 pp31–33 March 2009.

It seems Russian prime minister Vladimir Putin is keen to be viewed on the international stage not as a dictator, but as a lawful and popular representative of the Russian people, Rogers writes. Under Putin, the author adds, Russia has certainly shown no real enthusiasm for Western-style democracy, but after the chaos of the post-Communist era, the people want a strong leader. Putin is forthright in public about how outdated Russia is and has firm ideas about how to achieve his objectives, and he plans to tidy up what he regards as the disorder of the democratic experiment. The writer discusses whether a modern state can be established without liberty or based on a government of specialists with very little involvement of the people, and whether the government can rule with contained feedback from society.

Building on an Empire. Nick Holdsworth. *Variety* v. 412 ppA16–17 October 27–November 2, 2008.

Yuri Sapronov is currently overseeing a major expansion of Russian World Studios (RWS), Holdsworth observes. The first $100 million stage of a new $250 million studio in St. Petersburg—Russia's first purpose-built moviemaking complex in 60 years—has already opened for business. RWS is hoping to attract foreign producers to its new studios with traditional offers of excellent crews, equipment, facilities, and competitive prices plus the possibility of co-financing projects as coproductions. Sapronov says that the current financial crisis should also contribute to lowering film industry prices in Russia.

Film, TV: Comrades in Creativity. Ali Jaafar. *Variety* v. 409 pp1 December 17–23, 2007.

According to Jaafar, Russian TV networks are closely tied to Russian films, with several domestic box office winners having received significant funding from networks and other networks having played significant roles as film buyers and occasional investors. The Russian TV business's role in the film industry dates back to the mid-1990s, when Russian film production slumped, leading a generation of aspiring film talent to migrate to the TV sector. According to CTC-Media chief Alexander Rodnyansky, Russia has no major studios and no place for filmmakers to pitch their products and seek financial support.

Russia. *Variety* v. 397 ppA1+ January 31–February 6, 2005.

Constituting a special section on the Russian entertainment industry, the articles in this issue discuss copyright theft, Hollywood's interest in the Russian film market, the interest Russian film producers are taking in Hollywood's marketing techniques, the work of

Kazakh film director Timour Bekmambetov, the declining interest in western television in Russia, and state interference in Russian television news. Profiles of Russia's top film producers are also presented.

Index

About the Editor

RICHARD JOSEPH STEIN was born in Findlay, a small town in Northwest Ohio. He holds a Bachelor of Arts degree in English from Siena Heights University in Adrian, Michigan. After graduating from college, Richard decided to follow pursuits away from home. He gathered some clothes and a handful of money, said a heartfelt farewell to his family, and set out on a midnight train to New York City. He was hired by the H. W. Wilson Company in 2001. Richard enjoys travel in his spare time, as well as numerous volunteer projects throughout the city. He lives with his girlfriend in Washington Heights, in northern Manhattan.